# MY COMPLETE SPANISH LEARNING JOURNAL

Printed and Bound in The United States of America.

ISBN 13: 979-8601501460

First Edition, First Printing (d)

Cover Photo: Hospital de Santiago, Úbeda, UNESCO World Heritage Site, Jaén province, Andalusia. Spain by ABBPhoto (Licensed)

*Looking for an amazing online Spanish course? Go to page 514!*

*Need the best online Spanish tutor? Go to page 514!*

*Start journaling your Spanish language learning experience now? Go to page 98!*

# THIS JOURNAL
# IS THE
# PROPERTY OF:

‒ ‒ ‒ ‒ ‒ ‒ ‒ ‒ ‒ ‒ ‒ ‒ ‒ ‒ ‒ ‒ ‒ ‒ ‒ ‒ ‒ ‒

EMAIL: _____

DATE STARTED: _17_ / _5_ / _2020_

DATE ENDED: _____ / _____ / _____

# TABLE OF CONTENTS

## A "HOW TO USE THIS BOOK" VIDEO IS AVAILABLE!

Before starting to use this book, please watch the YouTube video specially created to teach users how to use each feature of this marvelous journal.

Visit www.dailylanguagejournal.com to watch the video.

*This book Is dedicated to you, the reader – the student of Spanish. May it be a useful and valuable tool to you as you journey toward conversational fluency.*

*- Dan Hall*

# REASONS, RESOURCES, OBSTACLES, AND PEOPLE

Complete this section before you begin. You will need to refer to it as you proceed to journal.

| WHY I WANT TO BECOME FLUENT IN SPANISH | DATE ACHIEVED |
|---|---|
| 1 | |
| 2 | |
| 3 | |

| RESOURCES I NEED TO BECOME FLUENT IN SPANISH | DATE OBTAINED |
|---|---|
| 1 | |
| 2 | |
| 3 | |

| THINGS THAT COULD INTERFERE WITH MY GOALS | PLANS TO AVOID THESE |
|---|---|
| 1 | |
| 2 | |
| 3 | |

| PEOPLE WHO CAN HELP ME ACHIEVE FLUENCY | HOW THEY HELP |
|---|---|
| 1 | |
| 2 | |
| 3 | |

# SPANISH COGNATES

Or, how to build your vocabulary with words you already know

## 40%
### OF ALL WORDS

**You know more than you think you do!** At least, you know more Spanish words than you think you do. This fact is because many Spanish and English words share a common origin in another language, which makes them "cognates." Approximately 40% of all English words have a Spanish word with similar spelling and meaning!

Build your Spanish vocabulary fast by learning how to recognize English word endings that can be converted into Spanish words by simply changing those endings.

For example, English words that end in "ence" have similar words in Spanish which end in "encia." So, the English word *audi**ence*** becomes the Spanish word *audi**encia*** when this rule is applied! Compet**ence** becomes *compet**encia*** and *consequ**ence*** becomes *consecu**encia**.*

## 890
### COGNATE WORDS

**My Complete Spanish Language Learning Journal** will help you add 890 words to your language vocabulary by merely applying some basic cognate recognition rules. These are words you already know in English and can immediately start using in your quest to become fluent in Spanish.

This journal will also help you put your learning into immediate action. In the following pages, you will learn the basic cognate recognition rules and 890 example words. Next to each cognate pair, this journal will provide you with writing space to create a practice sentence. As you examine each new cognate pair, cement that new word into your memory by writing a sentence using that word *en español*.

## 29
### COGNATE RULES

**My Complete Spanish Language Learning Journal** will provide you 29 simple rules that will help you identify cognates as you study Spanish. Of course, please remember, some cognates are false cognates (also known as false friends). They don't mean the same in Spanish as they do in English. But, they are the exception.

# COGNATES ENDING WITH -AL
## AL = AL

English words ending in "al" are *usually* identical to their Spanish equivalent

| ENGLISH | ESPAÑOL | CREATE SENTENCE WITH COGNATED WORD |
|---|---|---|
| Abdominal | Abdominal | |
| Abnormal | Anormal | |
| Abysmal | Abismal | |
| Accidental | Accidental | |
| Actual | Actual | |
| Additional | Adicional | |
| Anal | Anal | |
| Bacterial | Bacterial | |
| Cabal | Cabal | |
| Casual | Casual | |
| Cathedral | Catedral | |
| Colonial | Colonial | |
| Computational | Computacional | |
| Conditional | Condicional | |
| Contextual | Contextual | |
| Conventional | Convencional | |
| Cultural | Cultural | |
| Departmental | Departamental | |
| Differential | Diferencial | |
| Digital | Digital | |
| Electoral | Electoral | |
| Essential | Esencial | |

| | |
|---|---|
| Exceptional | Excepcional |
| Exponential | Exponencial |
| Foundational | Fundacional |
| Functional | Funcional |
| Gravitational | Gravitacional |
| Ideal | Ideal |
| Immortal | Inmortal |
| Impartial | Imparcial |
| Institutional | Institucional |
| Intestinal | Intestinal |
| Mental | Mental |
| Moral | Moral |
| Mural | Mural˙ |
| National | Nacional |
| Observational | Observacional |
| Occasional | Ocasional |
| Plural | Plural |
| Professional | Profesional |
| Reputational | Reputacional |
| Rural | Rural |
| Special | Especial |
| Territorial | Territorial |
| Thermal | Termal |
| Traditional | Tradicional` |
| Tropical | Tropical |
| Vital | Vital |

# COGNATES ENDING WITH -ANT
## ANT = ANTE

English words ending in "ant" end with "ante" in Spanish

| ENGLISH | ESPAÑOL | CREATE SENTENCE WITH COGNATED WORD |
|---|---|---|
| Abundant | Abundante | |
| Antioxidant | Antioxidante | |
| Arrogant | Arrogante | |
| Aspirant | Aspirante | |
| Brilliant | Brillante | |
| Distant | Distante | |
| Elegant | Elegante | |
| Elephant | Elefante | |
| Emigrant | Emigrante | |
| Fragrant | Fragante | |
| Giant | Gigante | |
| Implant | Implante | |
| Important | Importante | |
| Insignificant | Insignificante | |
| Instant | Instante | |
| Lubricant | Lubricante | |
| Migrant | Migrante | |
| Observant | Observante | |
| Redundant | Redundante | |
| Restaurant | Restaurante | |
| Tolerant | Tolerante | |
| Vacant | Vacante | |

# COGNATES ENDING WITH -AR
## AR = AR

English words that end in "ar" are usually the same in English and Spanish

| ENGLISH | ESPAÑOL | CREATE SENTENCE WITH COGNATED WORD |
|--------:|---------|------------------------------------|
| Altar | Altar | |
| Bar | Bar | |
| Cellular | Celular | |
| Circular | Circular | |
| Familiar | Familiar | |
| Lunar | Lunar | |
| Muscular | Muscular | |
| Nuclear | Nuclear | |
| Particular | Particular | |
| Peculiar | Peculiar | |
| Polar | Polar | |
| Popular | Popular | |
| Radar | Radar | |
| Rectangular | Rectangular | |
| Registrar | Registrar | |
| Regular | Regular | |
| Secular | Secular | |
| Similar | Similar | |
| Singular | Singular | |
| Solar | Solar | |
| Stellar | Estelar | |
| Vulgar | Vulgar | |

# COGNATES BY ADDING AN "AR" OR "IR"

To the following words in English, "ar" or "ir" is added for Spanish

| ENGLISH | ESPAÑOL | CREATE SENTENCE WITH COGNATED WORD |
|---:|---|---|
| Abandon | Abandonar | |
| Adapt | Adaptar | |
| Adjust | Ajustar | |
| Admit | Admitir | |
| Adopt | Adoptar | |
| Affect | Afectar | |
| Affirm | Afirmar | |
| Aggregate | Agregar | |
| Assign | Asignar | |
| Augment | Aumentar | |
| Calculate | Calcular | |
| Calm | Calmar | |
| Cancel | Cancelar | |
| Comfort | Confortar | |
| Comment | Comentar | |
| Complement | Complementar | |
| Comport | Comportar | |
| Confirm | Confirmar | |
| Consider | Considerar | |
| Consult | Consultar | |
| Control | Controlar | |
| Create | Crear | |
| Debilitate | Debilitar | |

| | |
|---|---|
| Deform | Deformar |
| Demonstrate | Demostrar |
| Dilate | Dilatar |
| Elevate | Elevar |
| Exalt | Exaltar |
| Exist | Existir |
| Experiment | Experimentar |
| Export | Exportar |
| Fabricate | Fabricar |
| Ferment | Fermentar |
| Import | Importar |
| Insist | Insistir |
| Integrate | Integrar |
| Invent | Inventar |
| Invest | Invertir |
| Labor | Laborar |
| Limit | Limitar |
| Liquidate | Liquidar |
| Locate | Localizar |
| March | Marchar |
| Operate | Operar |
| Present | Presentar |
| Publish | Publicar |
| Support | Soportar |
| Prohibit | Prohibir |
| Represent | Representar |

# COGNATES ENDING WITH -ATE
## ATE = AR
English words that end in "ate" end in "ar" for Spanish

| ENGLISH | ESPAÑOL | CREATE SENTENCE WITH COGNATED WORD |
|---:|---|---|
| Abbreviate | Abreviar | |
| Abdicate | Abdicar | |
| Accelerate | Acelerar | |
| Accentuate | Acentuar | |
| Activate | Activar | |
| Administrate | Administrar | |
| Aggregate | Agregar | |
| Associate | Asociar | |
| Calculate | Calcular | |
| Celebrate | Celebrar | |
| Collaborate | Colaborar | |
| Communicate | Comunicar | |
| Complicate | Complicar | |
| Consolidate | Consolidar | |
| Cooperate | Cooperar | |
| Coordinate | Coordinar | |
| Create | Crear | |
| Decorate | Decorar | |
| Dedicate | Dedicar | |
| Demonstrate | Demostrar | |
| Depreciate | Depreciar | |
| Designate | Designar | |

| | | |
|---:|:---|:---|
| Dilate | Dilatar | |
| Elevate | Elevar | |
| Eliminate | Eliminar | |
| Enumerate | Enumerar | |
| Estimate | Estimar | |
| Evacuate | Evacuar | |
| Evaluate | Evaluar | |
| Exaggerate | Exagerar | |
| Fabricate | Fabricar | |
| Facilitate | Facilitar | |
| Fascinate | Fascinar | |
| Fluctuate | Fluctuar | |
| Formulate | Formular | |
| Illuminate | Iluminar | |
| Illustrate | Ilustrar | |
| Integrate | Integrar | |
| Investigate | Investigar | |
| Locate | Localizar | |
| Mediate | Mediar | |
| Narrate | Narrar | |
| Necessitate | Necesitar | |
| Negotiate | Negociar | |
| Operate | Operar | |
| Participate | Participar | |
| Navigate | Navegar | |
| Terminate | Terminar | |

# COGNATES ENDING WITH -ARY
## ARY=ARIO

English words that end in "ary" in Spanish end in "ario"

| ENGLISH | ESPAÑOL | CREATE SENTENCE WITH COGNATED WORD |
|---|---|---|
| Actuary | Actuario | |
| Adversary | Adversario | |
| Arbitrary | Arbitrario | |
| Calvary | Calvario | |
| Canary | Canario | |
| Commentary | Comentario | |
| Complementary | Complementario | |
| Diary | Diario | |
| Estuary | Estuario | |
| Extraordinary | Extraordinario | |
| Glossary | Glosario | |
| Hereditary | Hereditario | |
| Imaginary | Imaginario | |
| Judiciary | Judiciario | |
| Necessary | Necesario | |
| Ordinary | Ordinario | |
| Primary | Primario | |
| Salary | Salario | |
| Secretary | Secretario | |
| Solitary | Solitario | |
| Temporary | Temporal | |
| Vocabulary | Vocabulario | |

# COGNATES ENDING WITH -BLE
## BLE = BLE

English words that end in "ble" in Spanish end in "ble"

| ENGLISH | ESPAÑOL | CREATE SENTENCE WITH COGNATED WORD |
|---|---|---|
| Abominable | Abominable | |
| Adjustable | Ajustable | |
| Admirable | Admirable | |
| Adorable | Adorable | |
| Cable | Cable | |
| Combustible | Combustible | |
| Double | Doble | |
| Eligible | Eligible | |
| Favorable | Favorable | |
| Honorable | Honorable | |
| Horrible | Horrible | |
| Impossible | Imposible | |
| Improbable | Improbable | |
| Incredible | Increíble | |
| Memorable | Memorable | |
| Possible | Posible | |
| Questionable | Cuestionable | |
| Reasonable | Razonable | |
| Sensible | Sensible | |
| Tolerable | Tolerable | |
| Unstable | Inestable | |
| Visible | Visible | |

# COGNATES ENDING WITH -CT
## CT=CTO

English words that end in "ct" in Spanish end in "cto"

| ENGLISH | ESPAÑOL | CREATE SENTENCE WITH COGNATED WORD |
|--:|---|---|
| Abstract | Abstracto | |
| Act | Acto | |
| Compact | Compacto | |
| Conflict | Conflicto | |
| Contact | Contacto | |
| Contract | Contrato | |
| Correct | Correcto | |
| Defect | Defecto | |
| Derelict | Derrelicto | |
| Dialect | Dialecto | |
| Direct | Directo | |
| Effect | Efecto | |
| Exact | Exacto | |
| Impact | Impacto | |
| Imperfect | Imperfecto | |
| Inexact | Inexacto | |
| Insect | Insecto | |
| Intellect | Intelecto | |
| Pact | Pacto | |
| Perfect | Perfecto | |
| Product | Producto | |
| Select | Selecto | |

# COGNATES ENDING WITH -IFY
## IFY = IFICAR

English words ending in "ify", remove "ify" and add "ificar" (in some infinitive verbs)

| ENGLISH | ESPAÑOL | CREATE SENTENCE WITH COGNATED WORD |
|--------:|---------|------------------------------------|
| Certify | Certificar | |
| Clarify | Clarificar | |
| Classify | Clasificar | |
| Crucify | Crucificar | |
| Dignify | Dignificar | |
| Diversify | Diversificar | |
| Electrify | Electrificar | |
| Falsify | Falsificar | |
| Glorify | Glorificar | |
| Gratify | Gratificar | |
| Identify | Identificar | |
| Intensify | Intensificar | |
| Justify | Justificar | |
| Modify | Modificar | |
| Notify | Notificar | |
| Pacify | Pacificar | |
| Quantify | Cuantificar | |
| Simplify | Simplificar | |
| Solidify | Solidificar | |
| Unify | Unificar | |
| Specify | Especificar | |
| Verify | Verificar | |

# COGNATES BY REPLACING "E" WITH AN "AR"

English words ending with "e" remove the "e" and add "ar"

| ENGLISH | ESPAÑOL | CREATE SENTENCE WITH COGNATED WORD |
|---|---|---|
| Accuse | Acusar | |
| Admire | Admirar | |
| Adore | Adorar | |
| Analyze | Analizar | |
| Announce | Anunciar | |
| Authorize | Autorizar | |
| Balance | Balancear | |
| Base | Basar | |
| Capture | Capturar | |
| Cause | Causar | |
| Circle | Circular | |
| Civilize | Civilizar | |
| Combine | Combinar | |
| Commute | Conmutar | |
| Compare | Comparar | |
| Compensate | Compensar | |
| Compute | Computar | |
| Concentrate | Concentrar | |
| Conceptualize | Conceptualizar | |
| Conserve | Conservar | |
| Continue | Continuar | |
| Converge | Converger | |
| Converse | Conversar | |

| | | |
|---|---|---|
| Cure | Curar | |
| Declare | Declarar | |
| Decline | Declinar | |
| Denote | Denotar | |
| Determine | Determinar | |
| Escape | Escapar | |
| Estimate | Estimar | |
| Examine | Examinar | |
| Excuse | Excusar | |
| Explore | Explorar | |
| Fascinate | Fascinar | |
| Galvanize | Galvanizar | |
| Ignore | Ignorar | |
| Imagine | Imaginar | |
| Implore | Implorar | |
| Observe | Observar | |
| Organize | Organizar | |
| Paralyze | Paralizar | |
| Practice | Practicar | |
| Prepare | Preparar | |
| Recite | Recitar | |
| Retire | Retirar | |
| Standardize | Estandarizar | |
| Type | Tipificar | |
| Use | Usar | |
| Utilize | Utilizar | |

# COGNATES BY REPLACING "E" WITH AN "IR"

English words ending with "e" remove the "e" and add "ir" (for some infinitive verbs)

| ENGLISH | ESPAÑOL | CREATE SENTENCE WITH COGNATED WORD |
|---|---|---|
| Acquire | Adquirir | |
| Assume | Asumir | |
| Attribute | Atribuir | |
| Compete | Competir | |
| Debate | Debatir | |
| Decide | Decidir | |
| Deduce | Deducir | |
| Define | Definir | |
| Describe | Describir | |
| Distribute | Distribuir | |
| Divide | Dividir | |
| Evade | Evadir | |
| Exclude | Excluir | |
| Interfere | Interferir | |
| Introduce | Introducir | |
| Invade | Invadir | |
| Invite | Invitar | |
| Narrate | Narrar | |
| Perceive | Percibir | |
| Persuade | Persuadir | |
| Receive | Recibir | |
| Transcribe | Transcribir | |
| Write | Escribir | |

# COGNATES ENDING WITH -ENCE
## ENCE = ENCIA

English words that end in "ence" in Spanish end in "encia"

| ENGLISH | ESPAÑOL | CREATE SENTENCE WITH COGNATED WORD |
|---|---|---|
| Adolescence | Adolescencia | |
| Appearance | Comparecencia | |
| Audience | Audiencia | |
| Benevolence | Benevolencia | |
| Coincidence | Coincidencia | |
| Competence | Competencia | |
| Consequence | Consecuencia | |
| Convalescence | Convalecencia | |
| Decadence | Decadencia | |
| Difference | Diferencia | |
| Equivalence | Equivalencia | |
| Essence | Esencia | |
| Existence | Existencia | |
| Independence | Independencia | |
| Intelligence | Inteligencia | |
| Interference | Interferencia | |
| Obedience | Obediencia | |
| Patience | Paciencia | |
| Presence | Presencia | |
| Reference | Referencia | |
| Science | Ciencia | |
| Violence | Violencia | |

# COGNATES ENDING WITH -IC
## IC = ICO
English words that end in "ic" in Spanish end in "ico"

| ENGLISH | ESPAÑOL | CREATE SENTENCE WITH COGNATED WORD |
|---|---|---|
| Academic | Académico | |
| Acrobatic | Acrobático | |
| Alcoholic | Alcohólico | |
| Allergic | Alérgico | |
| Artistic | Artístico | |
| Athletic | Atlético | |
| Atomic | Atómico | |
| Authentic | Auténtico | |
| Automatic | Automático | |
| Basic | Básico | |
| Chaotic | Caótico | |
| Chronologic | Cronológico | |
| Concentric | Concéntrico | |
| Cubic | Cúbico | |
| Dynamic | Dinámico | |
| Eccentric | Excéntrico | |
| Electric | Eléctrico | |
| Erratic | Errático | |
| Esoteric | Esotérico | |
| Ethnic | Étnico | |
| Exotic | Exótico | |
| Fantastic | Fantástico | |

| | |
|---|---|
| Gastric | Gástrico |
| Generic | Genérico |
| Harmonic | Armónico |
| Ironic | Irónico |
| Lunatic | Lunático |
| Lyric | Lírico |
| Magnetic | Magnético |
| Medic | Médico |
| Narcotic | Narcótico |
| Organic | Orgánico |
| Panic | Pánico |
| Panoramic | Panorámico |
| Patriotic | Patriótico |
| Platonic | Platónico |
| Rhapsodic | Rapsódico |
| Romantic | Romántico |
| Scientific | Científico |
| Specific | Específico |
| Symbolic | Simbólico |
| Systemic | Sistémico |
| Topographic | Tipográfico |
| Toxic | Tóxico |
| Traffic | Tráfico |
| Aerobic | Aeróbico |
| Sporadic | Esporádico |
| Tropic | Trópico |

# COGNATES ENDING WITH -ID
## ID = IDO

English words that end in "id" in Spanish end in "ido"

| ENGLISH | ESPAÑOL | CREATE SENTENCE WITH COGNATED WORD |
|---:|---|---|
| Acid | Ácido | |
| Arid | Árido | |
| Avid | Ávido | |
| Fluid | Fluido | |
| Insipid | Insípido | |
| Intrepid | Intrépido | |
| Invalid | Inválido | |
| Liquid | Líquido | |
| Livid | Lívido | |
| Lucid | Lúcido | |
| Morbid | Mórbido | |
| Placid | Plácido | |
| Putrid | Pútrido | |
| Rapid | Rápido | |
| Rigid | Rígido | |
| Solid | Sólido | |
| Sorid | Sórdido | |
| Splendid | Espléndido | |
| Stupid | Estúpido | |
| Timid | Tímido | |
| Valid | Válido | |
| Vidid | Vívido | |

# COGNATES ENDING WITH -ILE
## ILE = IL

English words that end in "ile" in Spanish end in "il"

| ENGLISH | ESPAÑOL | CREATE SENTENCE WITH COGNATED WORD |
|---:|---|---|
| Agile | Ágil | |
| Automobile | Automóvil | |
| Docile | Dócil | |
| Erectile | Eréctil | |
| Facsimile | Facsímil | |
| Fertile | Fértil | |
| Fragile | Frágil | |
| Futile | Fútil | |
| Gentile | Gentil | |
| Hostile | Hostil | |
| Imbecile | Imbécil | |
| Juvenile | Juvenil | |
| Mercantile | Mercantil | |
| Mobile | Móvil | |
| Percentile | Percentil | |
| Profile | Perfil | |
| Quartile | Cuartil | |
| Senile | Senil | |
| Simile | Símil | |
| Tactile | Táctil | |
| Textile | Textil | |
| Virile | Viril | |

# COGNATES ENDING WITH -ISM
## ISM = ISMO
English words that end in "ism" in Spanish end in "ismo"

| ENGLISH | ESPAÑOL | CREATE SENTENCE WITH COGNATED WORD |
|---|---|---|
| Abolitionism | Abolicionismo | |
| Astigmatism | Astigmatismo | |
| Capitalism | Capitalismo | |
| Communism | Comunismo | |
| Despotism | Despotismo | |
| Skepticism | Escepticismo | |
| Expressionism | Expresionismo | |
| Extremism | Extremismo | |
| Fatalism | Fatalismo | |
| Feminism | Feminismo | |
| Idealism | Idealismo | |
| Mechanism | Mecanismo | |
| Narcissism | Narcisismo | |
| Nationalism | Nacionalismo | |
| Optimism | Optimismo | |
| Organism | Organismo | |
| Patriotism | Patriotismo | |
| Perfectionism | Perfeccionismo | |
| Pessimism | Pesimismo | |
| Professionalism | Profesionalismo | |
| Socialism | Socialismo | |
| Tourism | Turismo | |

# COGNATES ENDING WITH -IST
## IST = ISTA
English words that end in "ist" in Spanish end in "ista"

| ENGLISH | ESPAÑOL | CREATE SENTENCE WITH COGNATED WORD |
|---|---|---|
| Alarmist | Alarmista | |
| Analyst | Analista | |
| Artist | Artista | |
| Dentist | Dentista | |
| Extremist | Extremista | |
| Genealogist | Genealogista | |
| Idealist | Idealista | |
| Imperialist | Imperialista | |
| List | Lista | |
| Materialist | Materialista | |
| Nationalist | Nacionalista | |
| Novelist | Novelista | |
| Pragmatist | Pragmatista | |
| Protectionist | Proteccionista | |
| Publcist | Publicista | |
| Purist | Purista | |
| Realist | Realista | |
| Reformist | Reformista | |
| Socialist | Socialista | |
| Soloist | Solista | |
| Terrorist | Terrorista | |
| Tourist | Turista | |

# COGNATES ENDING WITH -LY
## LY = MENTE

English words that end in "ly", usually adverbs, in Spanish end in "mente"

| ENGLISH | ESPAÑOL | CREATE SENTENCE WITH COGNATED WORD |
|---|---|---|
| Absolutely | Absolutamente | |
| Abundantly | Abundantemente | |
| Additionally | Adicionalmente | |
| Attentively | Atentamente | |
| Completely | Completamente | |
| Correctly | Correctamente | |
| Directly | Directamente | |
| Especially | Especialmente | |
| Eventually | Eventualmente | |
| Evidently | Evidentemente | |
| Exactly | Exactamente | |
| Finally | Finalmente | |
| Fortunately | Afortunadamente | |
| Horizontally | Horizontalmente | |
| Immediately | Inmediatamente | |
| Naturally | Naturalmente | |
| Normally | Normalmente | |
| Perfectly | Perfectamente | |
| Really | Realmente | |
| Recently | Recientemente | |
| Secretly | Secretamente | |
| Totally | Totalmente | |

# COGNATES ENDING WITH -MENT
## MENT = MENTO

English words that end in "ment" in Spanish end in "mento"

| ENGLISH | ESPAÑOL | CREATE SENTENCE WITH COGNATED WORD |
|---|---|---|
| Apartment | Apartamento | |
| Argument | Argumento | |
| Armament | Armamento | |
| Cement | Cemento | |
| Department | Departamento | |
| Document | Documento | |
| Element | Elemento | |
| Experiment | Experimento | |
| Fragment | Fragmento | |
| Impediment | Impedimento | |
| Implement | Implemento | |
| Instrument | Instrumento | |
| Moment | Momento | |
| Monument | Monumento | |
| Ornament | Ornamento | |
| Pavement | Pavimento | |
| Pigment | Pigmento | |
| Sacrament | Sacramento | |
| Sediment | Sedimento | |
| Supplement | Suplemento | |
| Temperament | Temperamento | |
| Testament | Testamento | |

# COGNATES ENDING WITH -NT
## NT = NTE
English words that end in "nt" in Spanish end in "nte"

| ENGLISH | ESPAÑOL | CREATE SENTENCE WITH COGNATED WORD |
|---|---|---|
| Abundant | Abundante | |
| Accident | Accidente | |
| Adjacent | Adyacente | |
| Agent | Agente | |
| Appellant | Apelante | |
| Arrogant | Arrogante | |
| Aspirant | Aspirante | |
| Assistant | Asistente | |
| Brilliant | Brillante | |
| Coherent | Coherente | |
| Coincident | Coincidente | |
| Competent | Competente | |
| Component | Componente | |
| Congruent | Congruente | |
| Consistent | Consistente | |
| Constant | Constante | |
| Continent | Continente | |
| Decent | Decente | |
| Deficient | Deficiente | |
| Discriminant | Discriminante | |
| Distant | Distante | |
| Divergent | Divergente | |

| English | Spanish | |
|---|---|---|
| Efficient | Eficiente | |
| Elegant | Elegante | |
| Emigrant | Emigrante | |
| Equivalent | Equivalente | |
| Evident | Evidente | |
| Excellent | Excelente | |
| Exponent | Exponente | |
| Gallant | Galante | |
| Giant | Gigante | |
| Ignorant | Ignorante | |
| Immigrant | Inmigrante | |
| Implant | Implante | |
| Important | Importante | |
| Instant | Instante | |
| Intelligent | Inteligente | |
| Obedient | Obediente | |
| Permanent | Permanente | |
| President | Presidente | |
| Radiant | Radiante | |
| Restaurant | Restaurante | |
| Significant | Significante | |
| Tint | Tinte | |
| Tolerant | Tolerante | |
| Triumphant | Triunfante | |
| Urgent | Urgente | |
| Vacant | Vacante | |

# COGNATES ENDING WITH -OR
## OR = OR

English words that end in "or" in Spanish also end in "or

| ENGLISH | ESPAÑOL | CREATE SENTENCE WITH COGNATED WORD |
|---|---|---|
| Accelerator | Acelerador | |
| Accumulator | Acumulador | |
| Actor | Actor | |
| Author | Autor | |
| Collaborator | Colaborador | |
| Commentator | Comentador | |
| Competitor | Competidor | |
| Conservator | Conservador | |
| Coprocessor | Coprocesador | |
| Denominator | Denominador | |
| Dictator | Dictador | |
| Distributor | Distribuidor | |
| Elevator | Elevador | |
| Illuminator | Iluminador | |
| Incinerator | Incinerador | |
| Interceptor | Interceptor | |
| Legislator | Legislador | |
| Liquor | Licor | |
| Numerator | Numerador | |
| Orator | Orador | |
| Predecessor | Predecesor | |
| Radiator | Radiador | |

# COGNATES ENDING WITH -OUS
## OUS = OSO
English words that end in "ous" in Spanish end in "oso"

| ENGLISH | ESPAÑOL | CREATE SENTENCE WITH COGNATED WORD |
|---|---|---|
| Ambitious | Ambicioso | |
| Capricious | Caprichoso | |
| Contagious | Contagioso | |
| Curious | Curioso | |
| Delicious | Delicioso | |
| Fabulous | Fabuloso | |
| Famous | Famoso | |
| Furious | Furioso | |
| Generous | Generoso | |
| Glorious | Glorioso | |
| Gracious | Gracioso | |
| Harmonious | Armonioso | |
| Laborious | Laborioso | |
| Marvelous | Maravilloso | |
| Meticulous | Meticuloso | |
| Mysterious | Misterioso | |
| Nervous | Nervioso | |
| Numerous | Numeroso | |
| Odious | Odioso | |
| Precious | Precioso | |
| Religious | Religioso | |
| Vicious | Vicioso | |

# COGNATES ENDING WITH -SION
## SION = SION
English words that end in "sion" in Spanish end in "sion"

| ENGLISH | ESPAÑOL | CREATE SENTENCE WITH COGNATED WORD |
|---|---|---|
| Abrasion | Abrasión | |
| Accession | Accesión | |
| Admission | Admisión | |
| Aggression | Agresión | |
| Cohesion | Cohesión | |
| Commission | Comisión | |
| Compassion | Compasión | |
| Comprehension | Comprensión | |
| Compression | Compresión | |
| Concession | Concesión | |
| Conclusion | Conclusión | |
| Confession | Confesión | |
| Concession | Concesión | |
| Conversion | Conversión | |
| Decision | Decisión | |
| Dimension | Dimensión | |
| Discussion | Discusión | |
| Diversion | Diversión | |
| Division | División | |
| Emission | Emisión | |
| Evasion | Evasión | |
| Exclusion | Exclusión | |

| | | |
|---|---|---|
| Excursion | Excursión | |
| Expansion | Expansión | |
| Explosion | Explosión | |
| Expression | Expresión | |
| Illusion | Ilusión | |
| Immersion | Inmersión | |
| Incision | Incisión | |
| Intercession | Intercesión | |
| Intermission | Intermisión | |
| Invasion | Invasión | |
| Mission | Misión | |
| Obsession | Obsesión | |
| Occasion | Ocasión | |
| Omission | Omisión | |
| Oppression | Opresión | |
| Passion | Pasión | |
| Pension | Pensión | |
| Percussion | Percusión | |
| Perversion | Perversión | |
| Possession | Posesión | |
| Precision | Precisión | |
| Propulsion | Propulsión | |
| Recession | Recesión | |
| Revision | Revisión | |
| Session | Sesión | |
| Succession | Sucesión | |

# COGNATES ENDING WITH -TION
## TION = CIÓN

English words that end in "tion" in Spanish end in "ción"

| ENGLISH | ESPAÑOL | CREATE SENTENCE WITH COGNATED WORD |
|---|---|---|
| Abbreviation | Abreviación | |
| Acceleration | Aceleración | |
| Accumulation | Acumulación | |
| Action | Acción | |
| Addition | Adición | |
| Admiration | Admiración | |
| Adoption | Adopción | |
| Affirmation | Afirmación | |
| Anticipation | Anticipación | |
| Association | Asociación | |
| Attention | Atención | |
| Attraction | Atracción | |
| Authorization | Autorización | |
| Cancellation | Cancelación | |
| Celebration | Celebración | |
| Circulation | Circulación | |
| Civilization | Civilización | |
| Classification | Clasificación | |
| Collaboration | Colaboración | |
| Collection | Colección | |
| Combination | Combinación | |
| Compensation | Compensación | |

| | | |
|---|---|---|
| Complication | Complicación | |
| Composition | Composición | |
| Conservation | Conservación | |
| Constitution | Constitución | |
| Construction | Construcción | |
| Continuation | Continuación | |
| Contribution | Contribución | |
| Convention | Convención | |
| Cooperation | Cooperación | |
| Declaration | Declaración | |
| Decoration | Decoración | |
| Deduction | Deducción | |
| Definition | Definición | |
| Description | Descripción | |
| Direction | Dirección | |
| Discrimination | Discriminación | |
| Distinction | Distinción | |
| Distribution | Distribución | |
| Election | Elección | |
| Elevation | Elevación | |
| Elimination | Eliminación | |
| Enumeration | Enumeración | |
| Estimation | Estimación | |
| Evaluation | Evaluación | |
| Exaggeration | Exageración | |
| Examination | Examinación | |

# COGNATES ENDING WITH -TION (Part 2)
## TION = CIÓN
English words that end in "tion" in Spanish end in "ción"

| ENGLISH | ESPAÑOL | CREATE SENTENCE WITH COGNATED WORD |
| --- | --- | --- |
| Exception | Excepción | |
| Exemption | Exempción | |
| Exhalation | Exhalación | |
| Expedition | Expedición | |
| Exploitation | Explotación | |
| Exposition | Exposición | |
| Fabrication | Fabricación | |
| Fraction | Fracción | |
| Function | Función | |
| Generation | Generación | |
| Homogenization | Homogenización | |
| Identification | Identificación | |
| Illumination | Iluminación | |
| Indication | Indicación | |
| Information | Información | |
| Inspection | Inspección | |
| Institution | Institución | |
| Instruction | Instrucción | |
| Introduction | Introducción | |
| Investigation | Investigación | |
| Invitation | Invitación | |
| Lamentation | Lamentación | |

| | | |
|---|---|---|
| Nation | Nación | |
| Notion | Noción | |
| Operation | Operación | |
| Position | Posición | |
| Preparation | Preparación | |
| Production | Producción | |
| Pronunciation | Pronunciación | |
| Punctuation | Puntuación | |
| Ration | Ración | |
| Reaction | Reacción | |
| Reproduction | Reproducción | |
| Resolution | Resolución | |
| Revelation | Revelación | |
| Saturation | Saturación | |
| Section | Sección | |
| Segregation | Segregación | |
| Simplification | Simplificación | |
| Stabilization | Estabilización | |
| Standardization | Estandarización | |
| Subscription | Subscripción | |
| Traction | Tracción | |
| Tradition | Tradición | |
| Transformation | Transformación | |
| Vacation | Vacación | |
| Veneration | Veneración | |
| | | |

# COGNATES ENDING WITH -TY
## TY = IDAD

English words that end in "ty" in Spanish end in "idad"

| ENGLISH | ESPAÑOL | CREATE SENTENCE WITH COGNATED WORD |
|---:|---|---|
| Ability | Habilidad | |
| Activity | Actividad | |
| Adversity | Adversidad | |
| Atrocity | Atrocidad | |
| Austerity | Austeridad | |
| Authority | Autoridad | |
| Brutality | Brutalidad | |
| Calamity | Calamidad | |
| Capacity | Capacidad | |
| Charity | Caridad | |
| City | Ciudad | |
| Continuity | Continuidad | |
| Curiosity | Curiosidad | |
| Density | Densidad | |
| Dignity | Dignidad | |
| Eccentricity | Excentricidad | |
| Electricity | Electricidad | |
| Entity | Entidad | |
| Eternity | Eternidad | |
| Ethnicity | Etnicidad | |
| Facility | Facilidad | |
| Generosity | Generosidad | |

| | | |
|---|---|---|
| Hospitality | Hospitalidad | |
| Humanity | Humanidad | |
| Identity | Identidad | |
| Locality | Localidad | |
| Mortality | Mortalidad | |
| Multiplicity | Multiplicidad | |
| Nationality | Nacionalidad | |
| Necessity | Necesidad | |
| Novelty | Novedad | |
| Periodicity | Periodicidad | |
| Popularity | Popularidad | |
| Possibility | Posibilidad | |
| Proximity | Proximidad | |
| Publicity | Publicidad | |
| Reality | Realidad | |
| Security | Seguridad | |
| Serenity | Serenidad | |
| Severity | Severidad | |
| Tenacity | Tenacidad | |
| Unity | Unidad | |
| University | Universidad | |
| Utility | Utilidad | |
| Vanity | Vanidad | |
| Variety | Variedad | |
| Velocity | Velocidad | |
| Visibility | Visibilidad | |

# COGNATES ENDING WITH -Y (IA/ÍA)
## Y = IA or ÍA
English words that end in "y" in Spanish end in "ia" or "ía"

| ENGLISH | ESPAÑOL | CREATE SENTENCE WITH COGNATED WORD |
|---:|---|---|
| Academy | Academia | |
| Agency | Agencia | |
| Agony | Agonía | |
| Anatomy | Anatomía | |
| Archaeology | Arqueología | |
| Astronomy | Astronomía | |
| Audacity | Audacia | |
| Autonomy | Autonomía | |
| Battery | Batería | |
| Biography | Biografía | |
| Biology | Biología | |
| Calligraphy | Caligrafía | |
| Ceremony | Ceremonia | |
| Colony | Colonia | |
| Company | Compañía | |
| Competency | Competencia | |
| Copy | Copia | |
| Day | Día | |
| Democracy | Democracia | |
| Efficiency | Eficiencia | |
| Energy | Energía | |
| Envy | Envidia | |

| | | |
|---|---|---|
| Fallacy | Falacia | |
| Family | Familia | |
| Frequency | Frecuencia | |
| Galaxy | Galaxia | |
| Geography | Geografía | |
| Geometry | Geometría | |
| Glory | Gloria | |
| Guarantee | Garantía | |
| Harmony | Armonía | |
| History | Historia | |
| Irony | Ironía | |
| Melody | Melodía | |
| Memory | Memoria | |
| Pharmacy | Farmacia | |
| Philosophy | Filosofía | |
| Photography | Fotografía | |
| Psychology | Psicología | |
| Secretary (f.) | Secretaria | |
| Sociology | Sociología | |
| Spy | Espía | |
| Symphony | Sinfonía | |
| Technology | Tecnología | |
| Toxicology | Toxicología | |
| Tragedy | Tragedia | |
| Urgency | Urgencia | |
| Victory | Victoria | |

# COGNATES ENDING WITH -Y (IO)
## Y = IO

English words that end in "y" in Spanish end in "io"

| ENGLISH | ESPAÑOL | CREATE SENTENCE WITH COGNATED WORD |
|---|---|---|
| Accessory | Accesorio | |
| Anniversary | Aniversario | |
| Binary | Binario | |
| Complementary | Complementario | |
| Contradictory | Contradictorio | |
| Diary | Diario | |
| Dictionary | Diccionario | |
| Emissary | Emisario | |
| Fragmentary | Fragmentario | |
| Laboratory | Laboratorio | |
| Matrimony | Matrimonio | |
| Observatory | Observatorio | |
| Ordinary | Ordinario | |
| Reactionary | Reaccionario | |
| Remedy | Remedio | |
| Salary | Salario | |
| Summary | Sumario | |
| Temporary | Temporario | |
| Testimony | Testimonio | |
| Visionary | Visionario | |
| Voluntary | Voluntario | |
| Subsidy | Subsidio | |

# COGNATES ENDING WITH -TAR OR -TIR
## VOWEL + CONSONANT + T = TAR OR TIR

English words that end in "vowel + consonant + T" in Spanish end in "tar" or "tir"

| ENGLISH | ESPAÑOL | CREATE SENTENCE WITH COGNATED WORD |
|--------:|---------|------------------------------------|
| Accept | Aceptar | |
| Collect | Colectar | |
| Combat | Combatir | |
| Connect | Conectar | |
| Consist | Consistir | |
| Contrast | Contrastar | |
| Cost | Costar | |
| Deport | Deportar | |
| Experiment | Experimentar | |
| Ferment | Fermentar | |
| Infest | Infestar | |
| Insult | Insultar | |
| Orient | Orientar | |
| Preexist | Preexistir | |
| Prospect | Prospectar | |
| Protest | Protestar | |
| Repeat | Repetir | |
| Result | Resultar | |
| Retract | Retractar | |
| Subject | Subjectar | |
| Subvert | Subvertir | |
| Transport | Transportar | |

# SPANISH CONJUGATION QUICK GLANCE

Master your Spanish conjugation skills with these quick glance guides

## PRESENT TENSE (I eat, I do eat) — Present Indicative

| AR | | ER/*IR | |
|---|---|---|---|
| Yo | -o | Yo | -o |
| Tú | -as | Tú | -es |
| Él, Ella, Usted | -a | Él, Ella, Usted | -e |
| Nosotros, Nosotras | -amos | Nosotros/tras | -emos/*-imos |
| Vosotros | -áis | Vosotros | -éis/-ís |
| Ellos, Ellas | -an | Ellos, Ellas | -en |

## REGULAR PAST TENSE (I ate) — Preterite

| AR | | | | ER/*IR | | | |
|---|---|---|---|---|---|---|---|
| Yo | | + | -é | Yo | | + | -í |
| Tú | | + | -aste | Tú | | + | -iste |
| Él, Ella, Usted | stem | + | -ó | Él, Ella, Usted | stem | + | -ió |
| Nosotros/tras | | + | -amos | Nosotros/tras | | + | -imos |
| Vosotros | | + | -asteis | Vosotros | | + | -isteis |
| Ellos, Ellas | | + | -aron | Ellos, Ellas | | + | -ieron |

## IRREGULAR PAST SPINE VERBS — Preterite

| Infinitive Stem | | | | Add Stem To Ending | | | |
|---|---|---|---|---|---|---|---|
| Hacer | Hic- | Hiz-[3rd] | Saber | Sup- | Yo | | + | -e |
| Estar | Estuv- | | Querer | Quis- | Tú | | + | -iste |
| Poder | Pud- | | *Traducir | *Traduj- | Él, Ella, Usted | | + | -o |
| Poner | Pus- | | *Traer | *Traj- | Nosotros/tras | stem | + | -imos |
| Tener | Tuv- | | *Decir | *Dij- | Vosotros | | + | -isteis |
| Venir | Vin- | | *Conducir | *Conduj- | Ellos, Ellas | | + | -ieron/*-eron |

# SPANISH CONJUGATION QUICK GLANCE

Master your Spanish conjugation skills with these quick glance guides

## IR & SER — IR

| Preterite | | Imperfect | |
|---|---|---|---|
| Yo | Fui | Yo | Iba |
| Tú | Fuiste | Tú | Ibas |
| Él, Ella, Usted | Fue | Él, Ella, Usted | Iba |
| Nosotros, Nosotras | Fuimos | Nosotros, Nosotras | Íbamos |
| Vosotros | Fuisteis | Vosotros | Ibais |
| Ellos, Ellas | Fueron | Ellos, Ellas | Iban |

## IMPERFECT PAST TENSE (I was eating, I ate, I used to eat) — Preterite

| AR | | | | ER/*IR | | | |
|---|---|---|---|---|---|---|---|
| Yo | | + | -aba | Yo | | + | -ía |
| Tú | | + | -abas | Tú | | + | -ías |
| Él, Ella, Usted | | + | -aba | Él, Ella, Usted | | + | -ía |
| Nosotros, Nosotras | stem | + | -ábamos | Nosotros, Nosotras | stem | + | -ímos |
| Vosotros | | + | -abais | Vosotros | | + | -íais |
| Ellos, Ellas | | + | -aban | Ellos, Ellas | | + | -ían |

## DOING VERBS (I am eating) — Present Participle

| Use appropriate present form of Estar | | Add verb stem + ending |
|---|---|---|
| Yo | Estoy | AR verb stem + -ando |
| Tú | Estás | AR verb stem + -ando |
| Él, Ella, Usted | Está | AR verb stem + -ando |
| Nosotros, Nosotras | Estamos | ER verb stem + -iendo |
| Vosotros | Estáis | ER verb stem + -iendo |
| Ellos, Ellas | Están | ER verb stem + -iendo |

# SPANISH CONJUGATION QUICK GLANCE

Master your Spanish conjugation skills with these quick glance guides

| IMPERFECT PAST TENSE DOING VERBS (I was eating) | | Continuous Imperfect |
|---|---|---|
| **Use appropriate imperfect form of ESTAR** | | **Add verb stem + ending** |
| Yo | Estaba | |
| Tú | Estabas | **AR** verb stem + **-ando** |
| Él, Ella, Usted | Estaba | |
| Nosotros/tras | Estábamos | |
| Vosotros | Estabais | **ER** verb stem + **-iendo** |
| Ellos, Ellas | Estaban | |

| HAVE VERBS (I've eaten) | | Past Participle – Present Perfect |
|---|---|---|
| **Use appropriate present form of HABER** | | **Add verb stem + ending** |
| Yo | He | |
| Tú | Has | **AR** verb stem + **-ado** |
| Él, Ella, Usted | Ha | |
| Nosotros, Nosotras | Hemos | |
| Vosotros | Habéis | **ER** verb stem + **-ido** |
| Ellos, Ellas | Han | |

| WOULD VERBS (I would eat) | | WILL VERBS (I will eat) | |
|---|---|---|---|
| **Add infinitive verb + ending** | | **Add infinitive verb + ending** | |
| Yo | -ría | Yo | -ré |
| Tú | -rías | Tú | -rás |
| Él, Ella, Usted | -ría | Él, Ella, Usted | -rá |
| Nosotros, Nosotras | -ríamos | Nosotros, Nosotras | -remos |
| Vosotros | -ríais | Vosotros | -réis |
| Ellos, Ellas | -rían | Ellos, Ellas | -rán |

# SPANISH CONJUGATION QUICK GLANCE

Master your Spanish conjugation skills with these quick glance guides

| IRREGULAR "WOULD" AND "WILL" VERBS STEMS | | | | | |
|---|---|---|---|---|---|
| **VERB** | **IR. STEM** | **VERB** | **IR. STEM** | **VERB** | **IR. STEM** |
| **Haber** | Habr- | **Poner** | Pondr- | **Hacer** | Har- |
| **Poder** | Podr- | **Tener** | Tendr- | **Venir** | Vendr- |
| **Querer** | Querr- | **Valer** | Valdr- | **Decir** | Dir- |
| **Saber** | Sabr- | **Salir** | Saldr- | | |

| COMMANDS (Speak!) (Eat!) | | | | | Imperative |
|---|---|---|---|---|---|
| **AR** | | | **ER/IR** | | |
| Tú | Usted | Ustedes | Tú | Usted | Ustedes |
| Habla | Hable | Hablen | Come | Coma | Coman |
| No hables | No hable | No hanben | No comas | No coma | No coman |

# SPANISH CONJUGATION QUICK GLANCE

Master your Spanish conjugation skills with these quick glance guides

| IRREGULAR "TÚ" COMMANDS STEMS | | | | | Imperative |
|---|---|---|---|---|---|
| VERB | Tú Command | VERB | Tú Command | VERB | Tú Command |
| Ir | Ve | Poner | Pon | Salir | Sal |
| Hacer | Haz | Tener | Ten | Ser | Sé |
| Venir | Ven | Decir | Di | | |

| IRREGULAR "USTED" & "USTEDES" COMMANDS and SUBJUNCTIVE | | | | | |
|---|---|---|---|---|---|
| VERB | Ud./Uds. | VERB | Ud./Uds. | VERB | Ud./Uds. |
| Ir | Vaya | Venir | Venga | Decir | Diga |
| Hacer | Haga | Tener | Tenga | Ser | Sea |
| Poner | Ponga | Salir | Salga | Ver | Vea |
| Traducir | Traduzca | Traer | Traiga | Oir | Oiga |
| Conducir | Conduzca | Saber | Sepa | Valer | Vaiga |

# SPANISH CONJUGATION QUICK GLANCE

Master your Spanish conjugation skills with these quick glance guides

| PAST TENSE SUBJUNCTIVE VERBS (stem changes apply) | | | | Imperfect |
|---|---|---|---|---|
| **AR** | | **ER/*IR** | | |
| Yo | -ara | Yo | -iera | |
| Tú | -aras | Tú | -ieras | |
| Él, Ella, Usted | -ara | Él, Ella, Usted | -iera | |
| Nosotros, Nosotras | -áramos | Nosotros, Nosotras | -iéramos | |
| Vosotros | -arais | Vosotros | -ierais | |
| Ellos, Ellas | -aran | Ellos, Ellas | -ieran | |

| PRESENT TENSE SUBJUNCTIVE VERBS (stem changes apply) | | | | Present |
|---|---|---|---|---|
| **AR** | | **ER/*IR** | | |
| Yo | -e | Yo | -a | |
| Tú | -es | Tú | -as | |
| Él, Ella, Usted | -e | Él, Ella, Usted | -a | |
| Nosotros, Nosotras | -emos | Nosotros, Nosotras | -amos | |
| Vosotros | -éis | Vosotros | -áis | |
| Ellos, Ellas | -en | Ellos, Ellas | -an | |

# 100 Most Frequently Used Regular Verbs

| Frequency | Verb | Definition | Acquired |
|---|---|---|---|
| 1 | Pasar | To pass, to spend (time), to happen | ✓ |
| 2 | Deber | To owe, must, should, ought to | ✓ |
| 3 | Quedar | To stay, remain | ✓ |
| 4 | Hablar | To speak | ✓ |
| 5 | Llevar | To carry, bring | |
| 6 | Dejar | To leave, abandon, to let, allow | |
| 7 | Llamar | To call, to name | ✓ |
| 8 | Tomar | To take, drink | ✓ |
| 9 | Vivir | To live | ✓ |
| 10 | Tratar | To treat, handle | ✓ |
| 11 | Mirar | To watch, look at | ✓ |
| 12 | Esperar | To wait for, to hope | ✓ |
| 13 | Existir | To exist | |
| 14 | Entrar | To enter, go in, come in | ✓ |
| 15 | Trabajar | To work | ✓ |
| 16 | Ocurrir | To occur, happen | |
| 17 | Recibir | To receive, to welcome, greet | |
| 18 | Terminar | To finish, end | ✓ |
| 19 | Permitir | To permit, allow | ✓ |
| 20 | Necesitar | To need, require | ✓ |
| 21 | Resultar | To turn out (to be) | |
| 22 | Cambiar | To change | ✓ |
| 23 | Presentar | To introduce | |
| 24 | Crear | To create, to make | |
| 25 | Considerar | To consider | ✓ |
| 26 | Acabar | To finish, end | |
| 27 | Ganar | To win, gain, earn, get, acquire | ✓ |
| 28 | Formar | To form, shape, fashion, make | |
| 29 | Partir | To divide, to leave | |
| 30 | Aceptar | To accept, approve, to agree to | |
| 31 | Comprender | To understand, comprehend | ✓ |
| 32 | Lograr | To get, obtain, to achieve, attain | |
| 33 | Preguntar | To ask, inquire | ✓ |

| Frequency | Verb | Definition | Acquired |
|---|---|---|---|
| 34 | Estudiar | To study | ✓ |
| 35 | Correr | To run | ✓ |
| 36 | Ayudar | To help | ✓ |
| 37 | Gustar | To please, be pleasing | ✓ |
| 38 | Escuchar | To listen, hear | ✓ |
| 39 | Cumplir | To fulfil, carry out | |
| 40 | Levantar | To raise, to lift | ✓ |
| 41 | Intentar | To try, attempt | ✓ |
| 42 | Usar | To use | ✓ |
| 43 | Decidir | To decide, settle, resolve | ✓ |
| 44 | Olvidar | To forget | ✓ |
| 45 | Comer | To eat | ✓ |
| 46 | Ocupar | To occupy | ✓ |
| 47 | Suceder | To happen, to succeed, follow | |
| 48 | Fijar | To fix, fasten, secure | |
| 49 | Aprender | To learn | ✓ |
| 50 | Comprar | To buy, purchase | ✓ |
| 51 | Subir | To go up, rise, move up, climb, raise up | |
| 52 | Evitar | To avoid, to prevent | |
| 53 | Interesar | To interest, be of interest (to) | ✓ |
| 54 | Echar | To throw, cast, fling | |
| 55 | Responder | To respond, answer, reply to | |
| 56 | Sufrir | To suffer, to undergo, experience | |
| 57 | Importar | To import, to be important | ✓ |
| 58 | Observar | To observe | |
| 59 | Imaginar | To imagine | |
| 60 | Desarrollar | To develop, expand, to unroll, unwind, to unfold | |
| 61 | Señalar | To point out, indicate, to signal | |
| 62 | Preparar | To prepare, get (something) ready | ✓ |
| 63 | Faltar | To lack, be lacking, be missing | |
| 64 | Acompañar | To accompany | |
| 65 | Desear | To desire, want, wish | |
| 66 | Enseñar | To teach, instruct, train, educate | ✓ |

| Frequency | Verb | Definition | Acquired |
|---|---|---|---|
| 67 | Vender | To sell | ✓ |
| 68 | Representar | To represent | |
| 69 | Mandar | To order (give an order), to send | |
| 70 | Asegurar | To assure, secure, insure | |
| 71 | Matar | To kill, slaughter | ✓ |
| 72 | Guardar | To guard, protect, to keep | |
| 73 | Iniciar | To initiate, begin, start | |
| 74 | Bajar | To lower, go down, descend, download | ✓ |
| 75 | Notar | To note, notice, observe | |
| 76 | Meter | To put (in), place, insert | ✓ |
| 77 | Pretender | To attempt | |
| 78 | Cortar | To cut | ✓ |
| 79 | Corresponder | To correspond with | |
| 80 | Aprovechar | To take advantage of | ✓ |
| 81 | Apoyar | To support, hold up, to back | |
| 82 | Aumentar | To increase, add to, rise | |
| 83 | Abandonar | To abandon, leave behind, to quit, give up | |
| 84 | Quitar | To remove, take away | |
| 85 | Conservar | To preserve, conserve, to keep, retain | |
| 86 | Depender | To depend | |
| 87 | Compartir | To share, to divide (up) | ✓ |
| 88 | Consistir | To consist | |
| 89 | Funcionar | To function, to run | ✓ |
| 90 | Insistir | To insist | |
| 91 | Anunciar | To announce | ✓ |
| 92 | Comentar | To comment on | ✓ |
| 93 | Participar | To participate, to share in, to inform | |
| 94 | Escapar | To escape | |
| 95 | Tirar | To throw, to shoot, to throw away, to pull | |
| 96 | Contestar | To answer | |
| 97 | Preocupar | To worry | ✓ |
| 98 | Prestar | To lend | |
| 99 | Pesar | To weigh, to weigh down | ✓ |
| 100 | Viajar | To travel, journey | ✓ |

# 33 Most Frequently Used Irregular Verbs

| Frequency | Verb | Definition | Acquired |
|---|---|---|---|
| 1 | ser | to be (essential/permanent quality) | |
| 2 | haber | to have (to do something, auxiliary verb) | |
| 3 | estar | to be (health, location, state) | |
| 4 | tener | to have | |
| 5 | hacer | to do, make | |
| 6 | poder | to be able, can | |
| 7 | decir | to say, tell | |
| 8 | ir | to go | |
| 9 | ver | to see | |
| 10 | dar | to give | |
| 11 | saber | to know (information) | |
| 12 | querer | to want, love | |
| 13 | llegar | to arrive, come, reach | |
| 14 | poner | to put, place, set | |
| 15 | parecer | to seem, appear | |
| 16 | oír | to hear, listen to | |
| 17 | seguir | to follow, continue | |
| 18 | encontrar | to find, encounter | |
| 19 | venir | to come | |
| 20 | pensar | to think | |
| 21 | salir | to leave, go out | |
| 22 | volver | to return, go back | |
| 23 | conocer | to know (people, places) | |
| 24 | sentir | to feel, regret | |
| 25 | contar | to count, relate, tell | |
| 26 | empezar | to begin, start | |
| 27 | valer | to be worth, cost | |
| 28 | rehacer | to redo, rework, rebuild | |
| 29 | perder | to lose | |
| 30 | producir | to produce | |
| 31 | entender | to understand | |
| 32 | pedir | to request, ask for | |
| 33 | recordar | to remember, remind | |

# 500 Most Frequently Used Words

| # | Spanish | English | Acquired | # | Spanish | English | Acquired |
|---|---------|---------|----------|---|---------|---------|----------|
| 1 | como | as | ✓ | 34 | en | in | ✓ |
| 2 | yo | I | ✓ | 35 | nos | we | ✓ |
| 3 | su | his | ✓ | 36 | lata | can | |
| 4 | que | that | ✓ | 37 | fuera | out | ✓ |
| 5 | él | he | ✓ | 38 | otros | other | ✓ |
| 6 | era | was | ✓ | 39 | eran | were | ✓ |
| 7 | para | for | ✓ | 40 | que | which | ✓ |
| 8 | en | on | ✓ | 41 | hacer | do | ✓ |
| 9 | son | are | ✓ | 42 | su | their | ✓ |
| 10 | con | with | ✓ | 43 | tiempo | time | ✓ |
| 11 | ellos | they | ✓ | 44 | si | if | ✓ |
| 12 | ser | be | ✓ | 45 | lo hará | will | |
| 13 | en | at | ✓ | 46 | cómo | how | ✓ |
| 14 | uno | one | ✓ | 47 | dicho | said | |
| 15 | tener | have | ✓ | 48 | un | an | ✓ |
| 16 | este | this | ✓ | 49 | cada | each | ✓ |
| 17 | desde | from | ✓ | 50 | decir | tell | ✓ |
| 18 | por | by | ✓ | 51 | hace | does | ✓ |
| 19 | caliente | hot | ✓ | 52 | conjunto | set | |
| 20 | palabra | word | ✓ | 53 | tres | three | ✓ |
| 21 | pero | but | ✓ | 54 | querer | want | ✓ |
| 22 | qué | what | ✓ | 55 | aire | air | ✓ |
| 23 | algunos | some | ✓ | 56 | así | well | |
| 24 | es | is | ✓ | 57 | también | also | ✓ |
| 25 | lo | it | ✓ | 58 | jugar | play | ✓ |
| 26 | usted | you | ✓ | 59 | pequeño | small | ✓ |
| 27 | o | or | ✓ | 60 | fin | end | |
| 28 | tenido | had | | 61 | poner | put | ✓ |
| 29 | la | the | ✓ | 62 | casa | home | ✓ |
| 30 | de | of | ✓ | 63 | leer | read | ✓ |
| 31 | a | to | ✓ | 64 | mano | hand | ✓ |
| 32 | y | and | ✓ | 65 | puerto | port | ✓ |
| 33 | un | a | ✓ | 66 | grande | large | ✓ |

| # | Spanish | English | Acquired | # | Spanish | English | Acquired |
|---|---------|---------|----------|---|---------|---------|----------|
| 67 | deletrear | spell | | 101 | cualquier | any | |
| 68 | añadir | add | | 102 | nuevo | new | ✓ |
| 69 | incluso | even | | 103 | trabajo | work | ✓ |
| 70 | tierra | land | | 104 | parte | part | ✓ |
| 71 | aquí | here | ✓ | 105 | tomar | take | ✓ |
| 72 | debe | must | | 106 | conseguir | get | |
| 73 | grande | big | ✓ | 107 | lugar | place | ✓ |
| 74 | alto | high | ✓ | 108 | hecho | made | ✓ |
| 75 | tal | such | | 109 | vivir | live | ✓ |
| 76 | siga | follow | | 110 | donde | where | ✓ |
| 77 | acto | act | | 111 | después | after | ✓ |
| 78 | por qué | why | ✓ | 112 | espalda | back | ✓ |
| 79 | preguntar | ask | ✓ | 113 | poco | little | ✓ |
| 80 | hombres | men | ✓ | 114 | sólo | only | . |
| 81 | cambio | change | ✓ | 115 | ronda | round | |
| 82 | se fue | went | | 116 | hombre | man | ✓ |
| 83 | luz | light | ✓ | 117 | años | year | ✓ |
| 84 | tipo | kind | ✓ | 118 | vino | came | ✓ |
| 85 | fuera | off | | 119 | show | show | |
| 86 | necesitará | need | ✓ | 120 | cada | every | ✓ |
| 87 | casa | house | ✓ | 121 | buena | good | ✓ |
| 88 | imagen | picture | | 122 | me | me | ✓ |
| 89 | tratar | try | ✓ | 123 | dar | give | ✓ |
| 90 | nosotros | us | ✓ | 124 | nuestro | our | ✓ |
| 91 | de nuevo | again | ✓ | 125 | bajo | under | |
| 92 | animal | animal | ✓ | 126 | nombre | name | ✓ |
| 93 | punto | point | | 127 | muy | very | ✓ |
| 94 | madre | mother | ✓ | 128 | a través de | through | |
| 95 | mundo | world | ✓ | 129 | sólo | just | |
| 96 | cerca | near | ✓ | 130 | forma | form | ✓ |
| 97 | construir | build | | 131 | frase | sentence | ✓ |
| 98 | auto | self | | 132 | gran | great | ✓ |
| 99 | tierra | earth | | 133 | pensar | think | ✓ |
| 100 | padre | father | ✓ | 134 | decir | say | ✓ |

# 500 Most Frequently Used Words

| # | Spanish | English | Acquired | # | Spanish | English | Acquired |
|---|---------|---------|----------|---|---------|---------|----------|
| 135 | ayudar | help | ✓ | 168 | largo | long | ✓ |
| 136 | bajo | low |  | 169 | hacer | make | ✓ |
| 137 | línea | line | ✓ | 170 | cosa | thing | ✓ |
| 138 | ser distinto | differ |  | 171 | ver | see | ✓ |
| 139 | a su vez, | turn |  | 172 | él | him | ✓ |
| 140 | causa | cause | ✓ | 173 | dos | two | ✓ |
| 141 | mucho | much | ✓ | 174 | tiene | has | ✓ |
| 142 | significará | mean | ✓ | 175 | buscar | look | ✓ |
| 143 | antes | before | ✓ | 176 | más | more | ✓ |
| 144 | movimiento | move |  | 177 | día | day | ✓ |
| 145 | derecho | right | ✓ | 178 | podía | could | ✓ |
| 146 | niño | boy | ✓ | 179 | ir | go | ✓ |
| 147 | viejo | old | ✓ | 180 | venir | come | ✓ |
| 148 | demasiado | too | ✓ | 181 | hizo | did | ✓ |
| 149 | misma | same | ✓ | 182 | número | number | ✓ |
| 150 | ella | she | ✓ | 183 | sonar | sound |  |
| 151 | todo | all | ✓ | 184 | no | no | ✓ |
| 152 | hay | there | ✓ | 185 | más | most | ✓ |
| 153 | cuando | when | ✓ | 186 | personas | people | ✓ |
| 154 | hasta | up |  | 187 | mi | my | ✓ |
| 155 | uso | use | ✓ | 188 | sobre | over | ✓ |
| 156 | su | your | ✓ | 189 | saber | know | ✓ |
| 157 | camino | way |  | 190 | agua | water | ✓ |
| 158 | acerca | about |  | 191 | que | than | ✓ |
| 159 | muchos | many | ✓ | 192 | llamada | call | ✓ |
| 160 | entonces | then | ✓ | 193 | primero | first | ✓ |
| 161 | ellos | them | ✓ | 194 | que | who | ✓ |
| 162 | escribir | write | ✓ | 195 | puede | may | ✓ |
| 163 | haría | would |  | 196 | abajo | down |  |
| 164 | como | like | ✓ | 197 | lado | side | ✓ |
| 165 | así | so | ✓ | 198 | estado | been |  |
| 166 | estos | these | ✓ | 199 | ahora | now | ✓ |
| 167 | su | her | ✓ | 200 | encontrar | find | ✓ |

| # | Spanish | English | Acquired | # | Spanish | English | Acquired |
|---|---------|---------|----------|---|---------|---------|----------|
| 201 | cabeza | head | ✓ | 235 | sierra | saw | |
| 202 | de pie | stand | | 236 | lejano | far | |
| 203 | propio | own | ✓ | 237 | mar | sea | ✓ |
| 204 | página | page | | 238 | dibujar | draw | |
| 205 | debería | should | ✓ | 239 | izquierda | left | ✓ |
| 206 | país | country | ✓ | 240 | tarde | late | ✓ |
| 207 | encontrado | found | ✓ | 241 | ejecutar | run | |
| 208 | respuesta | answer | | 242 | no | don't | ✓ |
| 209 | escuela | school | ✓ | 243 | mientras | while | ✓ |
| 210 | crecer | grow | | 244 | prensa | press | |
| 211 | estudio | study | ✓ | 245 | Cerrar | close | ✓ |
| 212 | todavía | still | ✓ | 246 | noche | night | ✓ |
| 213 | aprender | learn | ✓ | 247 | reales | real | |
| 214 | planta | plant | ✓ | 248 | vida | life | ✓ |
| 215 | cubierta | cover | | 249 | pocos | few | ✓ |
| 216 | alimentos | food | | 250 | norte | north | ✓ |
| 217 | sol | sun | ✓ | 251 | libro | book | ✓ |
| 218 | cuatro | four | ✓ | 252 | llevar | carry | ✓ |
| 219 | entre | between | ✓ | 253 | tomó | took | ✓ |
| 220 | estado | state | | 254 | ciencia | science | ✓ |
| 221 | mantener | keep | | 255 | comer | eat | ✓ |
| 222 | ojo | eye | ✓ | 256 | habitación | room | ✓ |
| 223 | nunca | never | ✓ | 257 | amigo | friend | ✓ |
| 224 | último | last | ✓ | 258 | comenzó | began | |
| 225 | dejar | let | | 259 | gusta | idea | |
| 226 | pensado | thought | | 260 | peces | fish | |
| 227 | ciudad | city | ✓ | 261 | montaña | mountain | ✓ |
| 228 | árbol | tree | | 262 | Deténgase | stop | |
| 229 | cruzar | cross | | 264 | base de | grassroots | |
| 230 | granja | farm | ✓ | 265 | escuchar | hear | ✓ |
| 231 | duro | hard | ✓ | 266 | caballo | horse | ✓ |
| 232 | inicio | start | | 267 | cortada | cut | |
| 233 | podría | might | | 268 | seguro | sure | ✓ |
| 234 | historia | story | ✓ | 269 | ver | watch | ✓ |

# 500 Most Frequently Used Words

| # | Spanish | English | Acquired | # | Spanish | English | Acquired |
|---|---------|---------|----------|---|---------|---------|----------|
| 270 | colores | color | ✓ | 303 | chica | girl | ✓ |
| 271 | cara | face | | 304 | habitual | usual | |
| 272 | madera | wood | ✓ | 305 | joven | young | ✓ |
| 273 | principal | main | | 306 | listo | ready | ✓ |
| 274 | abierta | open | ✓ | 307 | por encima de | above | |
| 275 | parecer | seem | ✓ | 308 | nunca | never | |
| 276 | juntos | together | ✓ | 309 | rojo | red | ✓ |
| 277 | próximo | next | ✓ | 310 | lista | list | ✓ |
| 278 | blanco | white | ✓ | 311 | aunque | though | |
| 279 | niños | children | ✓ | 312 | sentir | feel | ✓ |
| 280 | comenzar | begin | ✓ | 313 | charla | talk | |
| 281 | conseguido | got | | 314 | pájaro | bird | |
| 282 | caminar | walk | ✓ | 315 | pronto | soon | ✓ |
| 283 | ejemplo | example | ✓ | 316 | cuerpo | body | ✓ |
| 284 | aliviar | ease | | 317 | perro | dog | ✓ |
| 285 | papel | paper | ✓ | 318 | familia | family | ✓ |
| 286 | grupo | group | ✓ | 319 | directa | direct | |
| 287 | siempre | always | ✓ | 320 | plantear | pose | |
| 288 | música | music | ✓ | 321 | dejar | leave | |
| 289 | los | those | ✓ | 322 | canción | song | ✓ |
| 290 | ambos | both | | 323 | medir | measure | |
| 291 | marca | mark | | 324 | puerta | door | ✓ |
| 292 | menudo | often | | 325 | producto | product | |
| 293 | carta | letter | ✓ | 326 | negro | black | ✓ |
| 294 | hasta | until | ✓ | 327 | corto | short | ✓ |
| 295 | milla | mile | ✓ | 328 | numeral | numeral | |
| 296 | río | river | ✓ | 329 | clase | class | ✓ |
| 297 | coche | car | ✓ | 330 | viento | wind | |
| 298 | pies | feet | ✓ | 331 | pregunta | question | ✓ |
| 299 | cuidado | care | | 332 | suceder | happen | |
| 300 | segundo | second | ✓ | 333 | completo | complete | |
| 301 | suficiente | enough | ✓ | 334 | buque | ship | |
| 302 | llano | plain | | 335 | zona | area | ✓ |

| # | Spanish | English | Acquired | # | Spanish | English | Acquired |
|---|---------|---------|----------|---|---------|---------|----------|
| 336 | medio | halt | | 370 | registro | record | |
| 337 | roca | rock | | 371 | barco | boat | |
| 338 | orden | order | | 372 | común | common | |
| 339 | fuego | fire | | 373 | oro | gold | |
| 340 | sur | south | ✓ | 374 | posible | possible | ✓ |
| 341 | problema | problem | ✓ | 375 | plano | plane | |
| 342 | pieza | piece | ✓ | 376 | lugar | stead | |
| 343 | dicho | told | | 377 | seco | dry | ✓ |
| 344 | sabía | knew | | 378 | maravilla | wonder | |
| 345 | pasar | pass | ✓ | 379 | risa | laugh | |
| 346 | desde | since | ✓ | 380 | mil | thousand | ✓ |
| 347 | cima | top | | 381 | hace | ago | |
| 348 | todo | whole | | 382 | corrió | ran | |
| 349 | rey | king | | 383 | comprobar | check | |
| 350 | calle | street | ✓ | 384 | juego | game | |
| 351 | pulgadas | inch | | 385 | forma | shape | |
| 352 | multiplicar | multiply | | 386 | equiparar | equate | |
| 353 | nada | nothing | ✓ | 387 | caliente | hot | |
| 354 | curso | course | ✓ | 388 | señorita | miss | ✓ |
| 355 | quedarse | stay | ✓ | 389 | traído | brought | |
| 356 | rueda | wheel | | 390 | calor | heat | ✓ |
| 357 | completo | full | | 391 | nieve | snow | ✓ |
| 358 | fuerza | force | | 392 | neumáticos | tire | |
| 359 | azul | blue | ✓ | 393 | traer | bring | ✓ |
| 360 | objeto | object | ✓ | 394 | sí | yes | ✓ |
| 361 | decidir | decide | ✓ | 395 | distante | distant | |
| 362 | superficie | surface | | 396 | llenar | fill | |
| 363 | profunda | deep | | 397 | al este | east | |
| 364 | luna | moon | | 398 | pintar | paint | ✓ |
| 365 | isla | island | | 399 | idioma | language | ✓ |
| 366 | pie | foot | ✓ | 400 | entre | among | |
| 367 | sistema | system | ✓ | 401 | unidad | unit | ✓ |
| 368 | ocupado | busy | ✓ | 402 | potencia | power | |
| 369 | prueba | test | | 403 | ciudad | town | ✓ |

# 500 Most Frequently Used Words

| # | Spanish | English | Acquired | # | Spanish | English | Acquired |
|---|---------|---------|----------|---|---------|---------|----------|
| 404 | fina | fine | | 437 | desarrollar | develop | |
| 405 | cierto | certain | | 438 | océano | ocean | |
| 406 | volar | fly | | 439 | caliente | warm | ✓ |
| 407 | caer | fall | | 440 | libre | free | ✓ |
| 408 | conducir | lead | | 441 | minuto | minute | ✓ |
| 409 | grito | cry | ✓ | 442 | fuerte | strong | ✓ |
| 410 | oscuro | dark | ✓ | 443 | especial | special | ✓ |
| 411 | máquina | machine | ✓ | 444 | mente | mind | ✓ |
| 412 | nota | note | ✓ | 445 | detrás | behind | |
| 413 | espere | wait | | 446 | claro | clear | ✓ |
| 414 | plan de | plan | | 447 | cola | tail | |
| 415 | figura | figure | | 448 | Produce | produce | |
| 416 | estrella | star | | 449 | hecho | fact | |
| 417 | caja | box | ✓ | 450 | espacio | space | ✓ |
| 418 | sustantivo | noun | | 451 | oído | heard | |
| 419 | campo | field | | 452 | mejor | best | ✓ |
| 420 | resto | rest | | 453 | horas | hour | ✓ |
| 421 | correcta | correct | | 454 | mejor | better | ✓ |
| 422 | capaz | able | | 455 | verdadero | true | |
| 423 | libra | pound | | 456 | durante | during | ✓ |
| 424 | hecho | done | ✓ | 457 | cien | hundred | |
| 425 | belleza | beauty | | 458 | cinco | five | ✓ |
| 426 | unidad | drive | | 459 | recordar | remember | ✓ |
| 427 | destacado | stood | | 460 | paso | step | |
| 428 | contener | contain | | 461 | temprana | early | |
| 429 | delante | front | | 462 | mantenga | hold | |
| 430 | enseñar | teach | ✓ | 463 | oeste | west | |
| 431 | semana | week | ✓ | 464 | suelo | ground | |
| 432 | último | final | ✓ | 465 | interés | interest | |
| 433 | dio | gave | | 466 | llegar | reach | |
| 434 | verde | green | ✓ | 467 | rápido | fast | ✓ |
| 435 | oh | oh | | 468 | verbo | verb | ✓ |
| 436 | rápido | quick | ✓ | 469 | cantar | sing | ✓ |

| # | Spanish | English | Acquired | # | Spanish | English | Acquired |
|---|---------|---------|----------|---|---------|---------|----------|
| 470 | escuchar | listen | ✓ | 485 | lenta | slow | ✓ |
| 471 | seis | six | ✓ | 486 | centro | center | ✓ |
| 472 | mesa | table | ✓ | 487 | amar | love | ✓ |
| 473 | viajes | travel | ✓ | 488 | persona | person | ✓ |
| 474 | menos | less | ✓ | 489 | dinero | money | ✓ |
| 475 | mañana | morning | ✓ | 490 | servir | serve | ✓ |
| 476 | diez | ten | ✓ | 491 | aparecerá | appear | ✓ |
| 477 | sencilla | simple | | 492 | carretera | road | ✓ |
| 478 | varios | several | ✓ | 493 | mapa | map | |
| 479 | vocal | vowel | | 494 | lluvia | rain | ✓ |
| 480 | hacia | toward | | 495 | regla | rule | |
| 481 | guerra | war | ✓ | 496 | gobernar | govern | ✓ |
| 482 | sentar | lay | | 497 | Halar | pull | |
| 483 | contra | against | ✓ | 498 | frío | cold | |
| 484 | patrón | pattern | | 499 | aviso | notice | ✓ |
| | | | | 500 | voz | voice | |

# WHEN TO USE WHAT FORM OF PAST TENSE

| WHEN TO USE WHAT FORM OF PAST TENSE | | |
| --- | --- | --- |
| **Present Perfect** *I've eaten* | **Past Simple (Preterite)** *I ate* | **Past (Imperfect)** *I was eating, I used to eat* |
| Today **Hoy** | Yesterday **Ayer** | Always, Almost always **Siempre, Casi siempre** |
| **Esta mañana, esta tarde, esta noche** | Last night **Anoche** | Usually **Generalmente** |
| **Esta semana, este mes, este años** | The day before yesterday **Anteayer o antes de ayer** | Every day, week, month… **Todos los días, semanas,** |
| Lately **Últimamente** | Last Monday, Tuesday… **El lunes pasado, …** | Usually **Normalmente** |
| Recently **Recientemente** | The other day **El otra día** | Frequently **Con frecuencia** |
| Never **Nunca** | Last Week **La semana pasada** | Often, A lot **A menudo, Mucho** |
| Ever **Jamás** | Last Month **El mes pasado** | Sometimes, So many times **A veces, Tantas veces** |
| Already **Ya** | (Time) ago **Hace (tiempo)** | Almost never, never **Casi nunca, Nunca** |
| Still **Todavía** | In March, in April, … **En Marzo, en Abril,…** | Many times, Various times **Muchas veces, varias veces** |
| All my life **Todos mi vida** | In 2005 **En 2005** | For awhile **Por un rato** |
| In my life **En mi vida** | 7 days/wks/mons/years **Siete días/sem/mes/añ** | At that time **En aquella época** |
| Sometime **Alguna vez** | **Durante nueve días, semanas, meses, años** | All the time **Todo el tiempo** |
| A few times **Alguna veces** | From Sunday to Tuesday **De Domingo a Martes** | Every day, week **Cada día, Cada semana** |
| Various times, # times **Varias veces, # veces** | From 1999 to 2003 **De 1999 a 2003** | Every month, Every year **Cada mes, Cada año** |
| | | From time to time **De vez en cuando** |

# WHAT TO SAY

## WHAT TO SAY IN ORDER TO START A SENTENCE

| | | |
|---|---|---|
| I want<br>**Quiero** | I just<br>**Acabo de** | I love to<br>**Me encanta** |
| I need<br>**Necesito** | I could<br>**Podría** | I would love to<br>**Me encantaría** |
| I can<br>**Puedo** | I should<br>**Debería** | I prefer<br>**Prefiero** |
| I have to<br>**Tengo que** | I like<br>**Me gusta** | I'm planning to<br>**Estoy pensando en** |
| I am going to<br>**Voy a** | I would like<br>**Me gustaría** | I was thinking about<br>**Estaba pensando en que** |
| I (he/she/it) was going to<br>**Iba a** | The truth is<br>**La verdad es que** | It's something that…<br>**Es algo que…** |
| I'm just about to<br>**Estoy a punto de** | I was just about to<br>**Estaba a punto de** | What's happening is<br>**Lo que pasa es que** |

## WHAT TO SAY IN ORDER TO CONNECT TWO SENTENCES TOGETHER

| | | |
|---|---|---|
| In spite of<br>**A pesar de** | Nearby<br>**Cerca de** | Oftentimes<br>**Muchas veces** |
| Suddenly<br>**De repente** | Night before last<br>**Antenoche** | Sometimes<br>**A veces** |
| As well<br>**As así como** | Besides<br>**Además, También** | That is (or) I mean<br>**Es decir, o sea** |
| as a result<br>**Como resultado** | As one would expect<br>**Como es de esperar** | So<br>**Con que** |
| Among<br>**Entre, en medio de** | In a way<br>**De cierta manera** | No doubt<br>**Sin duda** |
| As soon as<br>**Tan pronto como** | Briefly<br>**Brevemente** | Immediately<br>**Inmediatamente** |
| In any case<br>**En todo caso** | Consequently<br>**En consecuencia** | After, afterward<br>**Después (de)** |
| At the same time<br>**Al mismo tiempo** | At the same time<br>**Al mismo tiempo** | In a little while<br>**Al rato** |
| To measure time:<br>**Hace (días, meses, años) que...** | On the following day<br>**al (día/mes/año) siguiente** | Most of the time<br>**La mayor parte del tiempo** |

## WHAT TO SAY WHEN NEEDING TO CONNECT TWO SENTENCES TOGETHER

| | | |
|---|---|---|
| Someone<br>**Alguien** | So<br>**Así que** | Even though<br>**Aunque** |
| Somewhere<br>**En algún lado** | Nowhere / Anywhere<br>**En ningun lado** | Everywhere<br>**En todos lados** |
| Until<br>**Hasta** | Anymore<br>**Más** | Nothing / Anything<br>**Nada** |
| Never again<br>**Nunca más** | Again<br>**Otra vez** | In order to<br>**Para** |
| Therefore<br>**Por lo tanto** | However<br>**Sin embargo** | About<br>**Sobre** |
| I know that<br>**Sé que** | Also / Too<br>**Tambien** | Neither / Either<br>**Tampoco** |
| No one / anyone<br>**Nadie** | Yet<br>**Todavía** | Already<br>**Ya** |
| Me neither / either<br>**Yo Tampoco** | Myself<br>**Yo mismo** | For Example<br>**Por ejemplo** |
| In other words<br>**En otras palabras** | For this reason<br>**Por esta razón** | Meanwhile<br>**Mientras tanto** |
| In fact<br>**De hecho** | Above all<br>**Sobre todo** | On the whole<br>**En general** |

## WHAT TO SAY WHEN SPEAKING ABOUT PLACES

| | | |
|---|---|---|
| above<br>**encima de, arriba de** | among<br>**entre, en medio de** | around<br>**alrededor de** |
| below<br>**abajo** | beside<br>**al lado de** | beyond<br>**más allá, más lejos** |
| down<br>**abajo, hacia abajo** | forward<br>**adelante, hacia adelante** | from<br>**de, desde** |
| under<br>**debajo de** | in front of<br>**delante de, frente a, en frente de** | inside<br>**dentro de, adentro** |
| nearby<br>**cerca de** | next to<br>**al lado de** | on<br>**en, sobre** |
| opposite<br>**frente a** | outside<br>**afuera, hacia afuera** | through<br>**por, através de** |

## WHAT TO SAY WHEN SPEAKING ABOUT TIME

| | | |
|---|---|---|
| after, afterward<br>**después (de)** | already<br>**ya** | always<br>**siempre** |
| as soon as<br>**en cuanto, tan pronto como** | at first<br>**al principio** | at last<br>**por fin** |
| at the beginning<br>**al principio** | at the same time<br>**al mismo tiempo, a la misma vez** | at once<br>**inmediatamente** |
| before<br>**antes de (que)** | briefly<br>**brevemente, consisamente** | day before yesterday<br>**antes de ayer, antier** |
| during<br>**durante** | eventually<br>**eventualmente** | finally<br>**finalmente, por fin** |
| first<br>**primero** | frequently<br>**frecuentemente** | immediately<br>**inmediatamente** |
| in a little while<br>**al rato** | in the first place<br>**en primer lugar, en primera instancia** | in the meantime<br>**mientras tanto** |
| in the past/future<br>**en el pasado/futuro** | last night<br>**anoche** | lastly<br>**por último** |
| later<br>**después, más tarde, luego, mientras tanto** | meanwhile<br>**mientras tanto** | most of the time<br>**la mayor parte del tiempo, la mayoría del tiempo** |
| next<br>**luego** | (the) next day<br>**al otro día** | (the) next morning<br>**a la mañana siguiente** |
| never<br>**nunca** | night before last<br>**antenoche** | now<br>**ahora (entonces, pues)** |
| often<br>**muchas veces, a menudo, con frecuencia** | on the following day<br>**al (día/mes/año) siguiente** | once<br>**una vez** |
| promptly<br>**rápidamente** | rarely<br>**raramente, rara vez** | sometimes<br>**a veces, algunas veces** |
| soon<br>**pronto, dentro de poco, próximamente** | suddenly<br>**de repente, súbitamente, de golpe,** | then<br>**entonces, luego** |
| when<br>**cuando** | yesterday<br>**ayer** | to measure time:<br>**Hace (días, meses, años) que....** |

## WHAT TO SAY TO ADD AN IDEA

| | | |
|---|---|---|
| again<br>**otra vez, de nuevo, nuevamente** | also<br>**también** | as well<br>**as así como** |
| besides<br>**además, también** | for one thing<br>**para mencionar una cosa, primero** | futher, furthermore<br>**además, a más de esto** |
| in addition<br>**por añadidura, además** | in addittion to<br>**además de, a más de** | in the first place<br>**en primer lugar, en primera instancia** |
| in the second place<br>**en segundo lugar** | last(ly)<br>**por último** | likewise<br>**asimismo, igualmente, de mismo modo** |
| moreover<br>**además, es más, por otra parte** | on the other hand<br>**por otro lado** | similarly<br>**de igualmanera, semejantemente** |

## WHAT TO SAY TO ILLUSTRATE OR EXPLAIN AN IDEA

| | | |
|---|---|---|
| among them figure<br>**entre ellos/ellas figura** | as follows<br>**como sigue** | for example<br>**por ejemplo, ejemplo de esto** |
| in particular<br>**en particular** | in other words<br>**en otras palabras** | in the first instance<br>**en primer lugar, en primer término** |
| in the following way<br>**de la manera siguiente** | like<br>**como** | mainly<br>**principalmente** |
| namely<br>**es decir, a saber, o sea** | specifically<br>**específicamente** | such as<br>**como** |

## WHAT TO SAY TO COMPARE/CONTRAST IDEAS

| | | |
|---|---|---|
| although<br>**aunque** | but<br>**pero, sino** | even so<br>**aún así, no obstante** |
| conversely<br>**a la inversa,**<br>**vice-versa** | differently<br>**diferentemente,**<br>**de manera diferente** | however<br>**sin embargo, no obstante** |
| in contrast<br>**en contraste,**<br>**por el contrario** | in spite of<br>**a pesar de** | in a way<br>**de cierta manera,**<br>**hasta cierto punto,**<br>**en cierto modo** |
| nevertheless<br>**sin embargo, con todo,**<br>**no obstante,**<br>**a pesar de eso** | on the one hand<br>**por un lado** | on the other hand<br>**por otro lado,**<br>**por otra parte** |
| no doubt<br>**sin duda** | of course<br>**por supuesto, claro está**<br>**que** | on the contrary<br>**al contrario** |
| otherwise<br>**de otra manera, de otro**<br>**modo** | | |

## WHAT TO SAY TO SHOW A RESULT

| | | |
|---|---|---|
| accordingly<br>**por consiguiente, en**<br>**conformidad con** | as a result<br>**como resultado** | as one would expect<br>**como es/era de esperarse** |
| consequently<br>**en consecuencia** | for this reason<br>**por esta razón** | hence<br>**por (lo) tanto, por esto** |
| in any case<br>**en todo caso,**<br>**de cualquier modo,**<br>**de todas maneras** | logically<br>**lógicamente** | of course<br>**por supuesto** |
| then<br>**entonces, luego** | therefore<br>**por lo tanto, así que** | thus<br>**así** |
| finally<br>**finalmente** | properly<br>**correctamente** | just<br>**simplemente** |
| so<br>**con que, así que** | it follows<br>**sigue que** | unfortunately<br>**desfortunadamente** |

## WHAT TO SAY TO EMPHASIZE AN IDEA

| above all<br>**sobre todo** | equally<br>**igualmente** | especially<br>**especialmente** |
|---|---|---|
| indeed<br>**efectivamente, realmente, en verdad, de veras, en realidad** | in fact<br>**de hecho** | principally<br>**principalmente, por la mayor parte** |

## WHAT TO SAY TO SUMMARIZE

| after all<br>**al fin y al cabo, después de todo** | as has been noted<br>**como se ha notado** | finally<br>**finalmente, por fin** |
|---|---|---|
| in effect<br>**en efecto** | in the end<br>**en fin, en fin de cuentas** | in other words<br>**en otras palabras** |
| in sum<br>**en síntesis** | on the whole<br>**en general, mirándolo todo** | to summarize<br>**para resumir, en resumen** |
| that is<br>**es decir, o sea** | For these reasons<br>**Por estas razones** | That is why<br>**Por eso** |
| therefore<br>**así que** | So<br>**Entonces** | In conclusion<br>**En conclusión** |

## WHAT TO SAY WHEN AGREEING AND DISAGREEING

| I agree<br>**Estoy de acuerdo** | I disagree<br>**No estoy de acuerdo** | In my opinion<br>**En mi opinión** |
|---|---|---|
| I agree with what the author says<br>**Estoy de acuerdo con lo que dice el autor** | I believe that<br>**(Yo) creo que** | It doesn't seem to me<br>**No me parece** |
| The truth is<br>**La verdad es** | It's true<br>**Es verdad** | It seems to me<br>**Me parece** |
| I think it is a good idea<br>**Me parece bien que** | I think that<br>**(Yo) pienso que** | |

## WHAT TO SAY WHEN STATING AN OPINION

| | | |
|---|---|---|
| It's evident that<br>**Es evidente que** | It's clear that<br>**Es claro que** | It's certain that<br>**Es cierto que** |
| It's obvious that<br>**Es obvio que** | It's important that<br>**Es importante que** | It's necessary that<br>**Es necesario que** |
| It's probable that<br>**Es probable que** | It's doubtful that<br>**Es dudoso que** | |

## WHAT TO SAY WHEN SUPPORTING AN OPINION

| | | |
|---|---|---|
| According to<br>**Según** | The source<br>**La fuente** | The theme/topic<br>**El tema** |
| To show<br>**Mostrar** | To demonstrate<br>**Demostrar** | To indicate<br>**Indicar** |
| To support<br>**Apoyar** | On the other hand<br>**Por otra parte** | For this reason/That's why<br>**Por lo cual** |
| Additionally<br>**Además** | However<br>**Sin embargo** | In comparison<br>**En comparación** |
| Just like<br>**Al igual que** | (blank) as well as (blank)<br>**Tanto _____ como** | But rather<br>**Sino** |
| Without a doubt<br>**Sin duda** | Even though / Although<br>**Aunque** | |

# 16 MOST FREQUENT IRREGULAR VERBS

## 1. SER – To be. (present participle: siendo; past part.: sido)

| Person | Present | Preterite | Imperfect | Conditional | Future |
|---|---|---|---|---|---|
| Yo | Soy<br>I am | Fui<br>I was | Era<br>I was | Sería<br>I would be | Seré<br>I will be |
| Tú | Eres<br>You are | Fuiste<br>You were | Eres<br>You were | Serías<br>You would be | Serás<br>You will be |
| Él, Ella, Usted | Es<br>He is | Fue<br>He was | Era<br>He was | Sería<br>He would be | Será<br>He will be |
| Nostotros | Somos<br>We are | Fuimos<br>We were | Éramos<br>We were | Seríamos<br>We would be | Seremos<br>We will be |
| Vostotros | Sois<br>You are | Fuisteis<br>You were | Erais<br>You were | Seríais<br>You would be | Seréis<br>You will be |
| Ellas | Son<br>They are | Fueron<br>They were | Eran<br>They were | Serían<br>They would be | Serán<br>They will be |

## 2. HABER – To have. (present participle: habiendo; past part.: habido)

| Person | Present | Preterite | Imperfect | Conditional | Future |
|---|---|---|---|---|---|
| Yo | He<br>I have | Hube<br>I had | Había<br>I had, I was having | Habría<br>I would have | Habré<br>I will have |
| Tú | Has<br>You have | Hubiste<br>You had | Habías<br>You had, you were having | Habrías<br>You would have | Habrás<br>You will have |
| Él, Ella, Usted | Ha, Hay<br>He has | Hubo<br>He had | Había<br>He had, he was having | Habría<br>He would have | Habrá<br>He will have |
| Nostotros | Hemos<br>We have | Hubimos<br>We had | Habíamos<br>We had, we were having | Habríamos<br>We would have | Habremos<br>We will have |
| Vostotros | Habéis<br>You have | Hubisteis<br>You had | Habíais<br>You had | Habríais<br>You would have | Habréis<br>You will have |
| Ellas | Han<br>They give | Hubieron<br>They had | Habían<br>They had, they were having | Habrían<br>The would have | Habrán<br>They will have |

## 3. ESTAR – To be.  (present participle: estando; past part.: estado)

| Person | Present | Preterite | Imperfect | Conditional | Future |
|---|---|---|---|---|---|
| Yo | **Estoy** <br> I am | **Estuve** <br> I was | **Estaba** <br> I was | **Estaría** <br> I would be | **Estaré** <br> I will be |
| Tú | **Estás** <br> You are | **Estuviste** <br> You were | **Estabas** <br> You were | **Estarías** <br> You would be | **Estarás** <br> You will be |
| Él, Ella, Usted | **Está** <br> He is | **Estuvo** <br> He was | **Estaba** <br> He was | **Estaría** <br> He would be | **Estará** <br> He will be |
| Nostotros | **Estamos** <br> We are | **Estuvimos** <br> We were | **Estábamos** <br> We were | **Estaríamos** <br> We would be | **Estaremos** <br> We will be |
| Vostotros | **Estáis** <br> You are | **Estuvisteis** <br> You were | **Estabais** <br> You were | **Estaríais** <br> You would be | **Estaréis** <br> You will be |
| Ellas | **Están** <br> They are | **Estuvieron** <br> They were | **Estaban** <br> They were | **Estarían** <br> They would be | **Estarán** <br> They will be |

## 4. TENER – To have.  (present participle: teniendo; past part.: tenido)

| Person | Present | Preterite | Imperfect | Conditional | Future |
|---|---|---|---|---|---|
| Yo | **Tengo** <br> I have | **Tuve** <br> I had | **Tenía** <br> I had, I was having | **Tendría** <br> I would have | **Tendré** <br> I will have |
| Tú | **Tienes** <br> You have | **Tuviste** <br> You had | **Tenías** <br> You had, you were having | **Tendrías** <br> You would have | **Tendrás** <br> You will have |
| Él, Ella, Usted | **Tiene** <br> He has | **Tuvo** <br> He had | **Tenía** <br> He had, he was having | **Tendría** <br> He would have | **Tendrá** <br> He will have |
| Nostotros | **Tenemos** <br> We have | **Tuvimos** <br> We had | **Teníamos** <br> We had, we were having | **Tendríamos** <br> We would have | **Tendremos** <br> We will have |
| Vostotros | **Tenéis** <br> You have | **Tuvisteis** <br> You had | **Teníais** <br> You had | **Tendríais** <br> You would have | **Tendréis** <br> You will have |
| Ellas | **Tienen** <br> They have | **Tuvieron** <br> They had | **Tenían** <br> They had, they were having | **Tendrían** <br> We would have | **Tendrán** <br> They will have |

## 5. HACER – To make. (present participle: haciendo; past part.: hecho)

| Person | Present | Preterite | Imperfect | Conditional | Future |
|---|---|---|---|---|---|
| Yo | **Hago** I do, I make | **Hice** I did, I made | **Hacía** I was doing, I did | **Haría** I would do | **Haré** I will do |
| Tú | **Haces** You do, You make | **Hiciste** You did, you made | **Hacías** You were doing, You did | **Harías** You would do | **Harás** You will do |
| Él, Ella, Usted | **Hace** He does, He makes | **Hizo** He did, he made | **Hacía** He was doing, He did | **Haría** He would do | **Hará** He will do |
| Nostotros | **Hacemos** We do, We make | **Hicimos** We did, we made | **Hacíamos** We were doing, We did | **Haríamos** We would do | **Haremos** We will do |
| Vostotros | **Hacéis** You do | **Hicisteis** You did | **Hacíais** You were doing, You did | **Haríais** He would do | **Haréis** You will do |
| Ellas | **Hacen** They do, They make | **Hicieron** They did, they made | **Hacían** They were doing, They did | **Harían** They would do | **Harán** They will do |

## 6. PODER – To be able to. (present participle: pudiendo; past part.: podido)

| Person | Present | Preterite | Imperfect | Conditional | Future |
|---|---|---|---|---|---|
| Yo | **Puedo** I can | **Pude** I could, I was able to | **Podía** I could, I was able to | **Podría** I could be able to do | **Podré** I will be able to do |
| Tú | **Puedes** You can | **Pudiste** You could, you were able to | **Podías** You could, you were able to | **Podrías** You could be able to do | **Podrás** You will be able to do |
| Él, Ella, Usted | **Puede** He can | **Pudo** He could, he was able to | **Podía** He gave, he was giving | **Podría** He could be able to do | **Podrá** He will be able to do |
| Nostotros | **Podemos** We can | **Pudimos** We could, we were able to | **Podíamos** We could, we were able | **Podríamos** We could be able to do | **Podremos** We will be able to do |
| Vostotros | **Podéis** You can | **Pudisteis** You could, you were able to | **Podíais** You could, you were able to | **Podríais** You could be able to do | **Podréis** You will be able to do |
| Ellas | **Pueden** They can | **Pudieron** They could, they were able to | **Podían** They could, they were able to | **Podrían** They could be able to do | **Podrán** They will be able to do |

## 7. DECIR – To say.   (present participle:  diciendo; past part.: dicho)

| Person | Present | Preterite | Imperfect | Conditional | Future |
|---|---|---|---|---|---|
| Yo | **Digo** <br> I say | **Dije** <br> I said | **Decía** <br> I said, I had said | **Diría** <br> I would say | **Diré** <br> I will say |
| Tú | **Dices** <br> You say | **Dijiste** <br> You said | **Decías** <br> You said, you had said | **Dirías** <br> You would say | **Dirás** <br> You will say |
| Él, Ella, Usted | **Dice** <br> He says | **Dijo** <br> He said | **Decía** <br> He said, he had said | **Diría** <br> He would say | **Dirá** <br> He will say |
| Nostotros | **Decimos** <br> We say | **Dijimos** <br> We said | **Decíamos** <br> We said, we had said | **Diríamos** <br> We would say | **Diremos** <br> We will say |
| Vostotros | **Decís** <br> You say | **Dijisteis** <br> You said | **Decíais** <br> You said | **Diríais** <br> You would say | **Diréis** <br> You will say |
| Ellas | **Dicen** <br> They say | **Dijeron** <br> They said | **Decían** <br> They said, they had said | **Dirían** <br> They would say | **Dirán** <br> They will say |

## 8. IR – To go.   (present participle:  yendo; past part.: ido)

| Person | Present | Preterite | Imperfect | Conditional | Future |
|---|---|---|---|---|---|
| Yo | **Voy** <br> I go | **Fui** <br> I went | **Iba** <br> I went, I was going | **Iría** <br> I would go | **Iré** <br> I will go |
| Tú | **Vas** <br> You go | **Fuiste** <br> You went | **Ibas** <br> You went, you were going | **Irías** <br> You would go | **Irás** <br> You will go |
| Él, Ella, Usted | **Va** <br> He goes | **Fue** <br> He went | **Iba** <br> He went, he was going | **Iría** <br> He would go | **Irá** <br> He will go |
| Nostotros | **Vamos** <br> We go | **Fuimos** <br> We went | **Íbamos** <br> We went, we were going | **Iríamos** <br> We would go | **Iremos** <br> We will go |
| Vostotros | **Vais** <br> You go | **Fuisteis** <br> You went | **Veíais** <br> You went | **Iríais** <br> You would go | **Iréis** <br> You will go |
| Ellas | **Van** <br> They go | **Fueron** <br> They went | **Ibais** <br> They went, they were going | **Irían** <br> They would go | **Irán** <br> They will go |

## 9. VER – To see.     (present participle:  viendo; past part.: visto)

| Person | Present | Preterite | Imperfect | Conditional | Future |
|---|---|---|---|---|---|
| Yo | **Veo** I see | **Vi** I saw | **Veía** I saw, I was seeing | **Vería** I would see | **Veré** I will see |
| Tú | **Ves** You see | **Viste** You saw | **Veías** You saw, You were seeing | **Verías** I would see | **Verás** You will see |
| Él, Ella, Usted | **Ve** He sees | **Vio** He saw | **Veía** He saw, He was seeing | **Vería** I would see | **Verá** He will see |
| Nostotros | **Vemos** We see | **Vimos** We saw | **Veíamos** We saw, We were seeing | **Veríamos** I would see | **Veremos** We will see |
| Vostotros | **Veis** You see | **Visteis** You saw | **Veíais** You saw | **Veríais** I would see | **Veréis** You will see |
| Ellas | **Ven** They see | **Vieron** They saw | **Veían** They saw, they were seeing | **Verían** I would see | **Verán** They will see |

## 10. DAR – To give.  (present participle:  dando; past part.: dado)

| Person | Present | Preterite | Imperfect | Conditional | Future |
|---|---|---|---|---|---|
| Yo | **Doy** I give | **Di** I gave | **Daba** I gave, I was giving | **Daría** I would give | **Daré** I will give |
| Tú | **Das** You give | **Diste** You gave | **Dabas** You gave, you were giving | **Darías** You would give | **Darás** You will give |
| Él, Ella, Usted | **Da** He gives | **Dio** He gave | **Daba** He gave, he was giving | **Daría** He would give | **Dará** He will give |
| Nostotros | **Damos** We give | **Dimos** We gave | **Dábamos** We gave, we were giving | **Daríamos** We would give | **Daremos** We will give |
| Vostotros | **Dais** You give | **Disteis** You gave | **Dabais** You gave | **Daríais** You would give | **Daréis** He will give |
| Ellas | **Dan** They give | **Dieron** They gave | **Daban** They gave, they were giving | **Darían** They would give | **Darán** They will give |

## 11. SABER – To know    (present participle: sabiendo; past part.: sabido)

| Person | Present | Preterite | Imperfect | Conditional | Future |
|---|---|---|---|---|---|
| Yo | Sé — I know | Supe — I knew | Sabía — I knew, I was knowing | Sabría — I would know | Sabré — I will know |
| Tú | Sabes — You know | Supiste — You knew | Sabías — You knew, you were knowing | Sabrías — You would know | Sabrás — You will know |
| Él, Ella, Usted | Sabe — He knows | Supo — He knew | Sabía — He knew, he was knowing | Sabría — He would know | Sabrá — He will know |
| Nostotros | Sabemos — We know | Supimos — We knew | Sabíamos — We knew, we were knowing | Sabríamos — We would know | Sabremos — We will know |
| Vostotros | Sabéis — You know | Supisteis — You knew | Sabíais — You knew | Sabríais — You would know | Sabréis — You will know |
| Ellas | Saben — They know | Supieron — They knew | Sabían — They knew, they were knowing | Sabrían — The would know | Sabrán — They will know |

## 12. QUERER – To want, to love  (present participle: queriendo; past part.: querido)

| Person | Present | Preterite | Imperfect | Conditional | Future |
|---|---|---|---|---|---|
| Yo | Quiero — I want | Quise — I wanted | Quería — I wanted, I was wanting | Querría — I would want | Querré — I will want |
| Tú | Quieres — You want | Quisiste — You wanted | Querías — You wanted, you were wanting | Querrías — You would want | Querrás — You will want |
| Él, Ella, Usted | Quiere — He wants | Quiso — He wanted | Quería — He wanted, he was wanting | Querría — He would want | Querrá — He will want |
| Nostotros | Queremos — We want | Quisimos — We wanted | Queríamos — We wanted, we were wanting | Querríamos — We would want | Querremos — We will want |
| Vostotros | Queréis — You want | Quisisteis — You wanted | Queríais — You wanted, you were wanting | Querríais — You would want | Querréis — You will want |
| Ellas | Quieren — They want | Quisieron — They wanted | Querían — They wanted, were wanting | Querrían — They would want | Querrán — They will want |

## 13. LLEGAR – To arrive, to come. (present participle: llegando; past part.: llegado)

| Person | Present | Preterite | Imperfect | Conditional | Future |
|---|---|---|---|---|---|
| Yo | **Llego** <br> I arrive | **Llegué** <br> I arrived | **Llegaba** <br> I arrived, I was arriving | **Llegaría** <br> I would arrive | **Llegaré** <br> I will arrive |
| Tú | **Llegas** <br> You arrive | **Llegaste** <br> You arrived | **Llegabas** <br> You arrived, you were arriving | **Llegarías** <br> You would arrive | **Llegarás** <br> You will arrive |
| Él, Ella, Usted | **Llega** <br> He arrives | **Llegó** <br> He arrived | **Llegaba** <br> He arrived, he was arriving | **Llegaría** <br> He would arrive | **Llegará** <br> He will arrive |
| Nostotros | **Llegamos** <br> We arrive | **Llegamos** <br> We arrived | **Llegábamos** <br> We arrived, we were arriving | **Llegaríamos** <br> We would arrive | **Llegaremos** <br> We will arrive |
| Vostotros | **Llegáis** <br> You arrive | **Llegasteis** <br> You arrived | **Llegabais** <br> You arrived, you were arriving | **Llegaríais** <br> You would arrive | **Llegaréis** <br> You will arrive |
| Ellas | **Llegan** <br> They arrive | **Llegaron** <br> They arrived | **Llegaban** <br> They arrived, they were arriving | **Llegarían** <br> They would arrive | **Llegarán** <br> They will arrive |

## 14. PONER – To put, To place (present participle: poniendo; past part.: puesto)

| Person | Present | Preterite | Imperfect | Conditional | Future |
|---|---|---|---|---|---|
| Yo | **Pongo** <br> I put | **Puse** <br> I put | **Ponía** <br> I put, I was putting | **Pondría** <br> I would put | **Pondré** <br> I will put |
| Tú | **Pones** <br> You put | **Pusiste** <br> You put | **Ponías** <br> You put, you were putting | **Pondrías** <br> You would put | **Pondrás** <br> You will put |
| Él, Ella, Usted | **Pone** <br> He puts | **Puso** <br> He put | **Ponía** <br> He put, he was putting | **Pondría** <br> He would put | **Pondrá** <br> He will put |
| Nostotros | **Ponemos** <br> We put | **Pusimos** <br> We put | **Poníamos** <br> We put, we were putting | **Pondríamos** <br> We would put | **Pondremos** <br> We will put |
| Vostotros | **Ponéis** <br> You put | **Pusisteis** <br> You put | **Poníais** <br> You put, you were putting | **Pondríais** <br> You would put | **Pondréis** <br> You will put |
| Ellas | **Ponen** <br> They arrive | **Pusieron** <br> They put | **Ponían** <br> They put, they were putting | **Pondrían** <br> They would put | **Pondrán** <br> They will put |

## 15. PARECER – To seem  (present participle:  pareciendo; past part.: parecido)

| Person | Present | Preterite | Imperfect | Conditional | Future |
|---|---|---|---|---|---|
| Yo | **Parezco** I seem | **Perecí** I seemed | **Parecía** I seemed | **Parecería** I would seem | **Pareceré** I will seem |
| Tú | **Pareces** You seem | **Pareciste** You seemed | **Parecías** You seemed | **Parecerías** You would seem | **Parecerás** You will seem |
| Él, Ella, Usted | **Parece** He seems | **Pareció** He seemed | **Parecía** He seemed | **Parecería** He would seem | **Parecerá** He will seem |
| Nostotros | **Parecemos** We seem | **Parecimos** We seemed | **Parecíamos** We seemed | **Pareceríamos** We would seem | **Pareceremos** We will seem |
| Vostotros | **Parecéis** You seem | **Parecisteis** You seemed | **Parecíais** You seemed | **Pareceríais** You would seem | **Pareceréis** You will seem |
| Ellas | **Parecen** They seem | **Parecieron** They seemed | **Parecían** They seemed | **Parecerían** They would seem | **Parecerán** They will seem |

## 16. OÍR – To hear, to listen to  (present participle:  oyendo; past part.: oído)

| Person | Present | Preterite | Imperfect | Conditional | Future |
|---|---|---|---|---|---|
| Yo | **Oigo** I hear | **Oí** I heard | **Oía** I heard, I was hearing | **Oiría** I would hear | **Oiré** I will hear |
| Tú | **Oyes** You hear | **Oíste** You heard | **Oías** You heard, you were hearing | **Oirías** You would hear | **Oirás** You will hear |
| Él, Ella, Usted | **Oye** He hears | **Oyó** He heard | **Oía** He heard, he was hearing | **Oiría** He would hear | **Oirá** He will hear |
| Nostotros | **Oímos** We hear | **Oímos** We heard | **Oíamos** We heard, we were hearing | **Oiríamos** We would hear | **Oiremos** We will hear |
| Vostotros | **Oís** You hear | **Oísteis** You heard | **Oíais** You heared, you were hearing | **Oiríais** You would hear | **Oiréis** You will hear |
| Ellas | **Oyen** They hear | **Oyeron** They heard | **Oían** They heard, they were hearing | **Oirían** They would hear | **Oirán** They will hear |

# HOW FLUENT AM I?
# HOW FLUENT AM I, WHEN IT COMES TO LISTENING?

To help determine your level of fluency in Spanish, please select the highest level that BEST describes your honest perception of your skills. In the column "MY LEVEL" write the number of points found in the column "POINTS." Only choose one level!

| SKILL AREA: LISTENING - COMPREHENSION | | |
|---|---|---|
| Find the skill description below that BEST MATCHES your level of ability. Then copy the point value from the points column to the right. Only match ONE level. | MY LEVEL | POINTS |
| I have no difficulty in understanding any spoken language, whether live or broadcast, even when delivered at fast native speed, provided I have some time to get familiar with the accent. | | 6 |
| I can understand extended speech even when it is not clearly structured and when relationships are only implied and not signaled explicitly. I can understand television programs and films without too much effort. | | 5 |
| I can understand extended speech and lectures and follow even intricate lines of argument provided the topic is reasonably familiar. I can understand most TV news and current affairs programs. I can understand most films in standard dialect. | | 4 |
| I can understand the main points of clear standard speech on familiar matters regularly encountered in work, school, leisure, etc. I can understand the main point of many radio or TV programs on current affairs or topics of personal or professional interest when the delivery is relatively slow and precise. | 17/5/20 | 3 |
| I can understand phrases and the highest frequency vocabulary related to areas of most immediate personal relevance (e.g., very basic personal and family information, shopping, local area, employment). I can catch the main point in short, clear, simple messages and announcements. | | 2 |
| I can recognize familiar words and very basic phrases concerning myself, my family, and immediate concrete surroundings when people speak slowly and clearly. | | 1 |

# HOW FLUENT AM I, WHEN IT COMES TO READING?

To help determine your level of fluency in Spanish, please select the highest level that BEST describes your honest perception of your skills. In the column "MY LEVEL" write the number of points found in the column "POINTS." Only choose one level!

| SKILL AREA: READING - UNDERSTANDING | | |
|---|---|---|
| Find the skill description below that BEST MATCHES your level of ability. Then copy the point value from the points column to the right. Only match ONE level. | MY LEVEL | POINTS |
| I can read with ease virtually all forms of the written language, including abstract, structurally or linguistically complex texts such as manuals, specialized articles, and literary works. | | 6 |
| I can understand long and complex factual and literary texts, appreciating distinctions of style. I can understand specialized articles and longer technical instructions, even when they do not relate to my field. | | 5 |
| I can read articles and reports concerned with contemporary problems in which the writers adopt particular attitudes or viewpoints. I can understand contemporary literary prose. | | 4 |
| I can understand texts that consist mainly of high frequency every day or job-related language. I can understand the description of events, feelings, and wishes in personal letters. | 17/5/20 | 3 |
| I can read very short, simple texts. I can find specific, predictable information in simple everyday material such as advertisements, prospectuses, menus, and timetables. I can also understand short simple personal letters. | | 2 |
| I can understand familiar names, words, and very simple sentences, for example, on notices and posters or in catalogs. | | 1 |

# HOW FLUENT AM I, WHEN IT COMES TO CONVERSATIONAL SPEAKING?

To help determine your level of fluency in Spanish, please select the highest level that BEST describes your honest perception of your skills. In the column "MY LEVEL" write the number of points found in the column "POINTS." Only choose one level!

| SKILL AREA: CONVERSATIONAL SPEAKING | | |
|---|---|---|
| Find the skill description below that BEST MATCHES your level of ability. Then copy the point value from the points column to the right. Only match ONE level. | MY LEVEL | POINTS |
| I can take part effortlessly in any conversation or discussion and have a good familiarity with idiomatic expressions and colloquialisms. I can express myself fluently and convey finer shades of meaning precisely. If I do have a problem, I can backtrack and restructure around the difficulty so smoothly that other people are hardly aware of it. | | 6 |
| I can express myself fluently and spontaneously without much obvious searching for expressions. I can use language flexibly and effectively for social and professional purposes. I can formulate ideas and opinions with precision and relate my contribution skilfully to those of other speakers. | | 5 |
| I can interact with a degree of fluency and spontaneity that makes regular interaction with native speakers quite possible. I can take an active part in discussion in familiar contexts, accounting for, and sustaining my views. | | 4 |
| I can deal with most situations likely to arise while traveling in an area where the language is spoken. I can enter unprepared into conversation on familiar topics, of personal interest or pertinent to everyday life (e.g., family, hobbies, work, travel, and current events). | 17/5/20 | 3 |
| I can communicate in simple and routine tasks requiring a simple and direct exchange of information on familiar topics and activities. I can handle very short social exchanges, even though I can't usually understand enough to keep the conversation going myself. | | 2 |
| I can interact in a simple way provided the other person is prepared to repeat or rephrase things at a slower rate of speech and help me formulate what I'm trying to say. I can ask and answer simple questions in areas of immediate need or on very familiar topics. | | 1 |

# HOW FLUENT AM I, WHEN IT COMES TO GENERAL SPEAKING?

To help determine your level of fluency in Spanish, please select the highest level that BEST describes your honest perception of your skills. In the column "MY LEVEL" write the number of points found in the column "POINTS." Only choose one level!

| SKILL AREA: GENERAL SPEAKING | | |
|---|---|---|
| Find the skill description below that BEST MATCHES your level of ability. Then copy the point value from the points column to the right. Only match ONE level. | MY LEVEL | POINTS |
| I can present a clear, smoothly-flowing description or argument in a style appropriate to the context and with an effective logical structure which helps the recipient to notice and remember significant points. | | 6 |
| I can present clear, detailed descriptions of complex subjects integrating sub-themes, developing particular points, and rounding off with an appropriate conclusion. | | 5 |
| I can present clear, detailed descriptions on a wide range of subjects related to my field of interest. I can explain a viewpoint on a topical issue giving the advantages and disadvantages of various options. | | 4 |
| I can connect phrases in a simple way in order to describe experiences and events, my dreams, hopes, and ambitions. I can briefly give reasons and explanations for opinions and plans. I can narrate a story or relate the plot of a book or film and describe my reactions. | 17/5/20 | 3 |
| I can use a series of phrases and sentences to describe in simple terms my family and other people, living conditions, my educational background, and my present or most recent job. | | 2 |
| I can use simple phrases and sentences to describe where I live and the people I know. | | 1 |

# HOW FLUENT AM I, WHEN IT COMES TO WRITING?

To help determine your level of fluency in Spanish, please select the highest level that BEST describes your honest perception of your skills. In the column "MY LEVEL" write the number of points found in the column "POINTS." Only choose one level!

| SKILL AREA: WRITING | | |
|---|---|---|
| Find the skill description below that BEST MATCHES your level of ability. Then copy the point value from the points column to the right. Only match ONE level. | MY LEVEL | POINTS |
| I can write clear, smoothly-flowing text in an appropriate style. I can write complex letters, reports, or articles which present a case with an effective logical structure which helps the recipient to notice and remember significant points. I can write summaries and reviews of professional or literary works. | | 6 |
| I can express myself in clear, well-structured text, expressing points of view at some length. I can write about complex subjects in a letter, an essay or a report, underlining what I consider to be the salient issues. I can select a style appropriate to the reader in mind. | | 5 |
| I can write clear, detailed text on a wide range of subjects related to my interests. I can write an essay or report, passing on information, or giving reasons in support of or against a particular point of view. I can write letters highlighting the personal significance of events and experiences. | | 4 |
| I can write simple connected text on topics which are familiar or of personal interest. I can write personal letters describing experiences and impressions. | 17/5/20 | 3 |
| I can write short, simple notes and messages relating to matters in areas of immediate needs. I can write a very simple personal letter, for example thanking someone for something. | | 2 |
| I can write a short, simple postcard, for example sending holiday greetings. I can fill in forms with personal details, for example, entering my name, nationality, and address on a hotel registration form. | | 1 |

To help determine your current level of fluency in Spanish, transfer your scores:

| SKILL AREAS | POINTS |
|---|---|
| LISTENING - UNDERSTANDING | |
| READING - UNDERSTANDING | |
| CONVERSATIONAL SPEAKING | |
| GENERAL SPEAKING | |
| WRITING | |
| Total Your Points: | |

# FLUENCY SCORE RESULTS

| Points | Fluency Description |
|---|---|
| 30 | **Proficient User or CEFR Level C2**<br><br>Can understand with ease virtually everything heard or read. Can summarize information from different spoken and written sources, reconstructing arguments, and accounts in a coherent presentation. Can express him/herself spontaneously, very fluently and precisely, differentiating finer shades of meaning even in more complex situations. |
| 25-29 | **Proficient User or CEFR Level C1**<br><br>Can understand a wide range of demanding, longer texts, and recognize implicit meaning. Can express him/herself fluently and spontaneously without much obvious searching for expressions. Can use language flexibly and effectively for social, academic, and professional purposes. Can produce clear, well-structured, detailed text on complex subjects, showing controlled use of organizational patterns, connectors, and cohesive devices. |
| 20-24 | **Independent User or CEFR Level B2**<br><br>Can understand the main ideas of complex text on both concrete and abstract topics, including technical discussions in his/her field of specialization. Can interact with a degree of fluency and spontaneity that makes regular interaction with native speakers quite possible without strain for either party. Can produce clear, detailed text on a wide range of subjects and explain a viewpoint on a topical issue giving the advantages and disadvantages of various options. |
| 17/5/20<br><br>15-19 | **Independent User or CEFR Level B1**<br><br>Can understand the main points of clear standard input on familiar matters regularly encountered in work, school, leisure, etc. Can deal with most situations likely to arise while traveling in an area where the language is spoken. Can produce simple connected text on familiar topics. Can describe experiences and events, dreams, hopes and ambitions, and briefly give reasons and explanations for opinions and plans. |
| 10-14 | **Basic User or CEFR Level A2**<br><br>Can understand sentences and frequently used expressions related to areas of most immediate relevance (e.g., very basic personal and family information, shopping, local geography, employment). Can communicate in simple and routine tasks requiring a simple and direct exchange of information on familiar and routine matters. Can describe in simple terms aspects of his/her background, immediate environment, and matters in areas of immediate need. |
| 5-9 | **Basic User or CEFR Level A1**<br><br>Can understand and use familiar everyday expressions and very basic phrases aimed at the satisfaction of needs of a concrete type. Can introduce him/herself and others and can ask and answer questions about personal details such as where he/she lives, people he/she knows and things he/she has. Can interact in a simple way provided the other person talks slowly and clearly and is prepared to help. |

# DAILY SPANISH LANGUAGE LEARNING JOURNALS WITH WEEKLY REVIEWS

## HOW TO USE THE DAILY LANGUAGE LEARNING JOURNAL

**AT THE BEGINNING OF EACH DAY:**

Write the day and date

**DAY & DATE**

Write down your vocabulary from yesterday, from 5 days ago, and from 10 days ago

| VOCABULARY FROM 5 DAYS AGO | VOCABULARY FROM 10 DAYS AGO |
|---|---|
| 1 | 1 |
| 2 | 2 |
| 3 | 3 |

Write down your goals from yesterday

**GOALS FROM YESTERDAY**
- ☐
- ☐
- ☐

Write down the vocabulary you want to learn today

**VOCABULARY FOR TODAY**
1.
2.
3.

Write down the goals that you have for today

**GOALS FOR TODAY**
- ☐
- ☐
- ☐

## AS EACH DAY PROGRESSES:

Write down the questions that you have for your tutor, for your learning group, or to research on your own.

| THINGS I HAVE QUESTIONS ABOUT | |
|---|---|
| | |
| | |

For each 5 minutes you spend in study, shade one time box in the daily page.

| LOG YOUR STUDY TIME EACH BOX EQUALS 5 MINS. | | | | | | | | |
|---|---|---|---|---|---|---|---|---|
| | | | | | | | | |

Write down sentences that you created, read, or heard that you wish to remember or study further.

| INTERESTING THINGS FROM TODAY |
|---|
| FOUR SENTENCES THAT I READ, HEARD OR CREATED TODAY |
| 1 |
| 2 |
| 3 |
| 4 |

Learn your vocabulary for today by writing down sentences with the words or using them in spoken speech.

| VOCABULARY FOR TODAY |
|---|
| 1 |
| 2 |
| 3 |

Work on completing your learning goals for today

| GOALS FOR TODAY |
|---|
| ☐ |
| ☐ |
| ☐ |

Study the Daily Word Builder, the Verb of the Day, and the Cognate of the Day.

| SPECIAL WORDS FOR TODAY | | |
|---|---|---|
| DAILY WORD BUILDER | VERB OF THE DAY | COGNATE OF THE DAY |
| Hasta Ahora | Ir | Lamentación |
| Adverb. So far. Until now. Thus far. Up to now. | To Go /g: Yendo / pp: Ido /Irr. | Noun. From: Lamentation (TION=CIÓN) |

## AT THE END OF EACH DAY:

Rate your learning mood for the day at the top of the daily page section.

Track both your study streak and the total number of verbs you have acquired

If you have completed a learning goal for the day, mark it completed. If it isn't completed, write it down in the next day's "goals from yesterday" section

**GOALS FOR TODAY**

☐
☐
☐

Rate your satisfaction with your learning activities and jot down any special notes about each learning activities that you want to remember

| DESCRIBE YOUR ACTIVITIES IN THESE TASKS FOR TODAY | | |
|---|---|---|
| ACTIVITY | DESCRIPTION | SATISFACTION |
| READING | | ☹☹☺☺☺ |
| LISTENING | | ☹☹☺☺☺ |
| WRITING | | ☹☹☺☺☺ |
| SPEAKING | | ☹☹☺☺☺ |
| STUDYING | | ☹☹☺☺☺ |
| VOCABULARY | | ☹☹☺☺☺ |

Total your study time for the day in hours and minutes and write it at the bottom left corner of the daily pages

**TOTAL TIME**

:

# THE VALUE OF DOCUMENTING YOUR LANGUAGE LEARNING ON A DAILY BASIS

1. Daily journaling can sometimes be just the encouragement you need to study every day. It is easy to become discouraged when studying a foreign language. By documenting your daily language-learning activities as a habit, you can help keep yourself motivated.

2. Daily journaling can help you see progress over the long term that you typically would not have noticed. Without journaling, it is difficult to track the number of new verbs and words you have acquired. Journaling enables you to see the progress you have made in areas like reading, studying, listening, and writing.

3. Daily journaling helps you to monitor the impact your learning moods can have on your language-learning. Everyone has good days and not-so-good days. Journaling helps you to keep an honest track of how motivated you are to achieving your goal and oftentimes, discover what the potential causes for a poor language-learning mood may be.

4. Daily journaling helps you use scientifically proven techniques like spaced-repetition, goal setting, self-assessments, and documented achievements to ensure the subject matter you are studying is actually being acquired into long-term memory.

5. Daily journaling can be a powerful tool to share with your language teacher, tutor, or fellow language learner. By referring to your journal, you can discuss things that you have questions about, share sentences that you have created, discuss areas you have noticed where you need improvement, and receive focused help.

6. Daily journaling can help you review your progress quickly and even pick back up where you left off if you do have a time gap in your studies.

*"Just learning to think in another language allows you to see your own culturein a better viewpoint."*

- Gates McFadden

# HOW TO USE THE WEEKLY LANGUAGE LEARNING JOURNAL

**AT THE END OF WEEK:**

Write down the week number of your studies, include the date range for the week.

**WEEK NUMBER**

**THIS WEEK IN REVIEW**

List all the vocabulary that you feel you have confidently *aquired*.

**VOCABULARY ACQUIRED**

List your 6 biggest achievements of the week.

**BIGGEST ACHIEVEMENTS**

☐ ☐
☐ ☐
☐ ☐

List the top 4 areas you feel you need to improve upon.

**AREAS FOR IMPROVEMENT**

1
2
3
4

Write down the questions that you still have and don't forget to include how you will find the answers.

**THINGS THAT I STILL HAVE QUESTIONS ABOUT**

Write down the total amount of time that you have spent studying.

Write down the total number of new words you have acquired this week

| FINAL MEASUREMENTS OF THIS WEEK | | |
|---|---|---|
| TOTAL TIME THIS WEEK | TOTAL NEW VERBS | TOTAL NEW WORDS |
| | | |

Write down the total number of new verbs you have acquired this week.

Rate your satisfaction with your learning activities and jot down any special notes about each learning activities that you want to remember.

| SELF-ASSESSMENT OF MY ACTIVITIES THIS WEEK | | |
|---|---|---|
| ACTIVITIES | SPECIFIC ASSESSMENTS | SATISFACTION |
| READING | | ☹☹☺☺☺ |
| LISTENING | | ☹☹☺☺☺ |
| WRITING | | ☹☹☺☺☺ |
| SPEAKING | | ☹☹☺☺☺ |
| STUDYING | | ☹☹☺☺☺ |
| MOTIVATION | | ☹☹☺☺☺ |

For each hour you spent in study, shade one time box in the weekly page.

**LOG YOUR STUDY TIME**
**EACH BOX EQUALS 1 HOUR**

Total your study time for the week in hours and minutes and write it at the bottom left corner of the daily pages

TOTAL TIME

:

| DAY & DATE | Sun 17/5/20 | STUDY STREAK # | |
|---|---|---|---|
| LEARNING MOOD | ☹ ☹ 😐 🙂 😀 | # VERBS ACQUIRED | |

## PAST STUDIES IN REVIEW

| VOCABULARY FROM YESTERDAY | GOALS FROM YESTERDAY |
|---|---|
| 1 Llevar - to carry | ☐ |
| 2 Déjar - to leave | ☐ |
| 3 Existir - to exist | ☐ |

| VOCABULARY FROM 5 DAYS AGO | VOCABULARY FROM 10 DAYS AGO |
|---|---|
| 1 Considerar - to consider | 1 Levantar - to lift |
| 2 aceptar - to accept | 2 Interesar - to interest |
| 3 Intentar - to try | 3 Lograr - to achieve |

## PRIORITIES FOR TODAY

| VOCABULARY FOR TODAY | GOALS FOR TODAY |
|---|---|
| 1 | ☐ |
| 2 | ☐ |
| 3 | ☐ |

## DESCRIBE YOUR LEARNING EXPERIENCE FOR TODAY

## SPECIAL WORDS FOR TODAY

| DAILY WORD BUILDER | VERB OF THE DAY | COGNATE OF THE DAY |
|---|---|---|
| **Ahora** | **Abrir** | **Tradicional** |
| Adverb. Now | To Open /g: Abriendo / pp: Abierto /Irr. | Adjective. From: Traditional (AL=AL) |

## INTERESTING THINGS FROM TODAY

### FOUR SENTENCES THAT I READ, HEARD OR CREATED TODAY

**1**

**2**

**3**

**4**

## THINGS I HAVE QUESTIONS ABOUT

## DESCRIBE YOUR ACTIVITIES IN THESE TASKS FOR TODAY

| ACTIVITY | DESCRIPTION | SATISFACTION |
|---|---|---|
| READING | | ☹ 😖 😐 🙂 😃 |
| LISTENING | | ☹ 😖 😐 🙂 😃 |
| WRITING | | ☹ 😖 😐 🙂 😃 |
| SPEAKING | | ☹ 😖 😐 🙂 😃 |
| STUDYING | | ☹ 😖 😐 🙂 😃 |
| VOCABULARY | | ☹ 😖 😐 🙂 😃 |

| LOG YOUR STUDY TIME | | TOTAL TIME |
|---|---|---|
| EACH BOX EQUALS 5 MINS. | | : |

| DAY & DATE | | STUDY STREAK # |
|---|---|---|
| LEARNING MOOD | ☹ ☹ 😐 🙂 😀 | # VERBS ACQUIRED |

## PAST STUDIES IN REVIEW

| VOCABULARY FROM YESTERDAY | GOALS FROM YESTERDAY |
|---|---|
| 1 | ☐ |
| 2 | ☐ |
| 3 | ☐ |

| VOCABULARY FROM 5 DAYS AGO | VOCABULARY FROM 10 DAYS AGO |
|---|---|
| 1 | 1 |
| 2 | 2 |
| 3 | 3 |

## PRIORITIES FOR TODAY

| VOCABULARY FOR TODAY | GOALS FOR TODAY |
|---|---|
| 1 | ☐ |
| 2 | ☐ |
| 3 | ☐ |

## DESCRIBE YOUR LEARNING EXPERIENCE FOR TODAY

## SPECIAL WORDS FOR TODAY

| DAILY WORD BUILDER | VERB OF THE DAY | COGNATE OF THE DAY |
|---|---|---|
| **Hasta Ahora** | **Ir** | **Lamentación** |
| Adverb. So far. Until now. Thus far. Up to now. | To Go /g: Yendo / pp: Ido /Irr. | Noun. From: Lamentation (TION=CIÓN) |

## INTERESTING THINGS FROM TODAY

### FOUR SENTENCES THAT I READ, HEARD OR CREATED TODAY

**1**

**2**

**3**

**4**

## THINGS I HAVE QUESTIONS ABOUT

## DESCRIBE YOUR ACTIVITIES IN THESE TASKS FOR TODAY

| ACTIVITY | DESCRIPTION | SATISFACTION |
|---|---|---|
| READING | | ☹ ☹ 😐 🙂 😊 |
| LISTENING | | ☹ ☹ 😐 🙂 😊 |
| WRITING | | ☹ ☹ 😐 🙂 😊 |
| SPEAKING | | ☹ ☹ 😐 🙂 😊 |
| STUDYING | | ☹ ☹ 😐 🙂 😊 |
| VOCABULARY | | ☹ ☹ 😐 🙂 😊 |

| LOG YOUR STUDY TIME | | | | | | | | | | | | | TOTAL TIME |
|---|---|---|---|---|---|---|---|---|---|---|---|---|---|
| EACH BOX EQUALS 5 MINS. | | | | | | | | | | | | | : |

| DAY & DATE | | STUDY STREAK # |
|---|---|---|
| LEARNING MOOD | ☹ ☹ 😐 🙂 😀 | # VERBS ACQUIRED |

## PAST STUDIES IN REVIEW

| VOCABULARY FROM YESTERDAY | GOALS FROM YESTERDAY |
|---|---|
| 1 | ☐ |
| 2 | ☐ |
| 3 | ☐ |

| VOCABULARY FROM 5 DAYS AGO | VOCABULARY FROM 10 DAYS AGO |
|---|---|
| 1 | 1 |
| 2 | 2 |
| 3 | 3 |

## PRIORITIES FOR TODAY

| VOCABULARY FOR TODAY | GOALS FOR TODAY |
|---|---|
| 1 | ☐ |
| 2 | ☐ |
| 3 | ☐ |

## DESCRIBE YOUR LEARNING EXPERIENCE FOR TODAY

## SPECIAL WORDS FOR TODAY

| DAILY WORD BUILDER | VERB OF THE DAY | COGNATE OF THE DAY |
|---|---|---|
| **Por Ahora** | **Sentirse** | **Defecto** |
| Adverb. For now. For the time being. | To Feel /g: Sintiéndose / pp: Sentido /Irr. | Noun. From: Defect (CT=CTO) |

## INTERESTING THINGS FROM TODAY

### FOUR SENTENCES THAT I READ, HEARD OR CREATED TODAY

**1**

**2**

**3**

**4**

## THINGS I HAVE QUESTIONS ABOUT

## DESCRIBE YOUR ACTIVITIES IN THESE TASKS FOR TODAY

| ACTIVITY | DESCRIPTION | SATISFACTION |
|----------|-------------|--------------|
| READING | | ☹ 😟 😐 🙂 😊 |
| LISTENING | | ☹ 😟 😐 🙂 😊 |
| WRITING | | ☹ 😟 😐 🙂 😊 |
| SPEAKING | | ☹ 😟 😐 🙂 😊 |
| STUDYING | | ☹ 😟 😐 🙂 😊 |
| VOCABULARY | | ☹ 😟 😐 🙂 😊 |

| LOG YOUR STUDY TIME | | TOTAL TIME |
|---------------------|--|------------|
| EACH BOX EQUALS 5 MINS. | | : |

| DAY & DATE | | STUDY STREAK # |
|---|---|---|
| LEARNING MOOD ☹ ☹ 😐 🙂 😃 | | # VERBS ACQUIRED |

## PAST STUDIES IN REVIEW

| VOCABULARY FROM YESTERDAY | GOALS FROM YESTERDAY |
|---|---|
| 1 | ☐ |
| 2 | ☐ |
| 3 | ☐ |

| VOCABULARY FROM 5 DAYS AGO | VOCABULARY FROM 10 DAYS AGO |
|---|---|
| 1 | 1 |
| 2 | 2 |
| 3 | 3 |

## PRIORITIES FOR TODAY

| VOCABULARY FOR TODAY | GOALS FOR TODAY |
|---|---|
| 1 | ☐ |
| 2 | ☐ |
| 3 | ☐ |

## DESCRIBE YOUR LEARNING EXPERIENCE FOR TODAY

## SPECIAL WORDS FOR TODAY

| DAILY WORD BUILDER | VERB OF THE DAY | COGNATE OF THE DAY |
|---|---|---|
| **Ahora Bien** | **Cocinar** | **Balancear** |
| Adverb. That said. Meanwhile. In that case. | To Cook; To Do The Cooking /g: Cocinando / pp: Cocinado | Verb. From: Balance (E=AR OR IR) |

## INTERESTING THINGS FROM TODAY

### FOUR SENTENCES THAT I READ, HEARD OR CREATED TODAY

**1**

**2**

**3**

**4**

## THINGS I HAVE QUESTIONS ABOUT

## DESCRIBE YOUR ACTIVITIES IN THESE TASKS FOR TODAY

| ACTIVITY | DESCRIPTION | SATISFACTION |
|---|---|---|
| READING | | ☹ ☹ 😐 🙂 😊 |
| LISTENING | | ☹ ☹ 😐 🙂 😊 |
| WRITING | | ☹ ☹ 😐 🙂 😊 |
| SPEAKING | | ☹ ☹ 😐 🙂 😊 |
| STUDYING | | ☹ ☹ 😐 🙂 😊 |
| VOCABULARY | | ☹ ☹ 😐 🙂 😊 |

| LOG YOUR STUDY TIME | | | | | | | | | | | | | TOTAL TIME |
|---|---|---|---|---|---|---|---|---|---|---|---|---|---|
| EACH BOX EQUALS 5 MINS. | | | | | | | | | | | | | : |

| DAY & DATE | | STUDY STREAK # |
|---|---|---|
| LEARNING MOOD | ☹ ☹ 😐 🙂 😃 | # VERBS ACQUIRED |

## PAST STUDIES IN REVIEW

| VOCABULARY FROM YESTERDAY | GOALS FROM YESTERDAY |
|---|---|
| 1 | ☐ |
| 2 | ☐ |
| 3 | ☐ |

| VOCABULARY FROM 5 DAYS AGO | VOCABULARY FROM 10 DAYS AGO |
|---|---|
| 1 | 1 |
| 2 | 2 |
| 3 | 3 |

## PRIORITIES FOR TODAY

| VOCABULARY FOR TODAY | GOALS FOR TODAY |
|---|---|
| 1 | ☐ |
| 2 | ☐ |
| 3 | ☐ |

## DESCRIBE YOUR LEARNING EXPERIENCE FOR TODAY

## SPECIAL WORDS FOR TODAY

| DAILY WORD BUILDER | VERB OF THE DAY | COGNATE OF THE DAY |
|---|---|---|
| **A Partir De Ahora** | **Levantar** | **Dividir** |
| Adverb. From now on. From now. Henceforth | To Raise, To Lift /g: Levantando / pp: Levantado | Verb. From: Divide (E=AR OR IR) |

## INTERESTING THINGS FROM TODAY

### FOUR SENTENCES THAT I READ, HEARD OR CREATED TODAY

**1**

**2**

**3**

**4**

## THINGS I HAVE QUESTIONS ABOUT

## DESCRIBE YOUR ACTIVITIES IN THESE TASKS FOR TODAY

| ACTIVITY | DESCRIPTION | SATISFACTION |
|---|---|---|
| READING | | 😣 😟 😐 😊 😄 |
| LISTENING | | 😣 😟 😐 😊 😄 |
| WRITING | | 😣 😟 😐 😊 😄 |
| SPEAKING | | 😣 😟 😐 😊 😄 |
| STUDYING | | 😣 😟 😐 😊 😄 |
| VOCABULARY | | 😣 😟 😐 😊 😄 |

| LOG YOUR STUDY TIME | | TOTAL TIME |
|---|---|---|
| EACH BOX EQUALS 5 MINS. | | : |

| DAY & DATE | | STUDY STREAK # | |
|---|---|---|---|
| LEARNING MOOD | ☹ ☹ 😐 🙂 😃 | # VERBS ACQUIRED | |

## PAST STUDIES IN REVIEW

| VOCABULARY FROM YESTERDAY | GOALS FROM YESTERDAY |
|---|---|
| 1 | ☐ |
| 2 | ☐ |
| 3 | ☐ |

| VOCABULARY FROM 5 DAYS AGO | VOCABULARY FROM 10 DAYS AGO |
|---|---|
| 1 | 1 |
| 2 | 2 |
| 3 | 3 |

## PRIORITIES FOR TODAY

| VOCABULARY FOR TODAY | GOALS FOR TODAY |
|---|---|
| 1 | ☐ |
| 2 | ☐ |
| 3 | ☐ |

## DESCRIBE YOUR LEARNING EXPERIENCE FOR TODAY

---

## SPECIAL WORDS FOR TODAY

| DAILY WORD BUILDER | VERB OF THE DAY | COGNATE OF THE DAY |
|---|---|---|
| **Ahora Mismo** | **Tomar** | **Benevolencia** |
| Adverb. Right now. Just now. Straight away. Momentarily. | To Take, Drink /g: Tomando / pp: Tomado | Noun. From: Benevolence (ENCE=ENCIA) |

## INTERESTING THINGS FROM TODAY

### FOUR SENTENCES THAT I READ, HEARD OR CREATED TODAY

**1**

**2**

**3**

**4**

## THINGS I HAVE QUESTIONS ABOUT

## DESCRIBE YOUR ACTIVITIES IN THESE TASKS FOR TODAY

| ACTIVITY | DESCRIPTION | SATISFACTION |
|----------|-------------|--------------|
| READING | | 😣 😟 😐 😊 😃 |
| LISTENING | | 😣 😟 😐 😊 😃 |
| WRITING | | 😣 😟 😐 😊 😃 |
| SPEAKING | | 😣 😟 😐 😊 😃 |
| STUDYING | | 😣 😟 😐 😊 😃 |
| VOCABULARY | | 😣 😟 😐 😊 😃 |

| LOG YOUR STUDY TIME | | | | | | | | | | | | | | TOTAL TIME |
|---------------------|--|--|--|--|--|--|--|--|--|--|--|--|--|------------|
| EACH BOX EQUALS 5 MINS. | | | | | | | | | | | | | | : |

| DAY & DATE | | STUDY STREAK # |
|---|---|---|
| LEARNING MOOD | ☹ ☹ 😐 🙂 😃 | # VERBS ACQUIRED |

## PAST STUDIES IN REVIEW

| VOCABULARY FROM YESTERDAY | GOALS FROM YESTERDAY |
|---|---|
| 1 | ☐ |
| 2 | ☐ |
| 3 | ☐ |

| VOCABULARY FROM 5 DAYS AGO | VOCABULARY FROM 10 DAYS AGO |
|---|---|
| 1 | 1 |
| 2 | 2 |
| 3 | 3 |

## PRIORITIES FOR TODAY

| VOCABULARY FOR TODAY | GOALS FOR TODAY |
|---|---|
| 1 | ☐ |
| 2 | ☐ |
| 3 | ☐ |

## DESCRIBE YOUR LEARNING EXPERIENCE FOR TODAY

## SPECIAL WORDS FOR TODAY

| DAILY WORD BUILDER | VERB OF THE DAY | COGNATE OF THE DAY |
|---|---|---|
| **Desde Ahora** | **Arrepentirse** | **Básico** |
| Adverb. From now. From now on. | To Repent, Be Repentant /g: Arrepintiéndose / pp: Arrepentido /Irr. | Adjective. From: Basic (IC=ICO) |

## INTERESTING THINGS FROM TODAY

### FOUR SENTENCES THAT I READ, HEARD OR CREATED TODAY

**1**

**2**

**3**

**4**

## THINGS I HAVE QUESTIONS ABOUT

## DESCRIBE YOUR ACTIVITIES IN THESE TASKS FOR TODAY

| ACTIVITY | DESCRIPTION | SATISFACTION |
|---|---|---|
| READING | | ☹ ☹ 😐 🙂 😊 |
| LISTENING | | ☹ ☹ 😐 🙂 😊 |
| WRITING | | ☹ ☹ 😐 🙂 😊 |
| SPEAKING | | ☹ ☹ 😐 🙂 😊 |
| STUDYING | | ☹ ☹ 😐 🙂 😊 |
| VOCABULARY | | ☹ ☹ 😐 🙂 😊 |

| LOG YOUR STUDY TIME | | | | | | | | | | | | | TOTAL TIME |
|---|---|---|---|---|---|---|---|---|---|---|---|---|---|
| EACH BOX EQUALS 5 MINS. | | | | | | | | | | | | | : |

**WEEK NUMBER:**

## THIS WEEK IN REVIEW

### VOCABULARY ACQUIRED

### BIGGEST ACHIEVEMENTS

- [ ]
- [ ]
- [ ]
- [ ]
- [ ]
- [ ]

### AREAS FOR IMPROVEMENT

1.
2.
3.
4.

## THINGS THAT I STILL HAVE QUESTIONS ABOUT

| | |
|---|---|
| | |
| | |
| | |

## FINAL MEASUREMENTS OF THIS WEEK

| TOTAL TIME THIS WEEK | TOTAL NEW VERBS | TOTAL NEW WORDS |
|---|---|---|
| | | |

## SELF-ASSESSMENT OF MY ACTIVITIES THIS WEEK

| ACTIVITIES | SPECIFIC ASSESSMENTS | SATISFACTION |
|---|---|---|
| READING | | 😣 😟 😐 🙂 😊 |
| LISTENING | | 😣 😟 😐 🙂 😊 |
| WRITING | | 😣 😟 😐 🙂 😊 |
| SPEAKING | | 😣 😟 😐 🙂 😊 |
| STUDYING | | 😣 😟 😐 🙂 😊 |
| MOTIVATION | | 😣 😟 😐 🙂 😊 |
| LOG YOUR STUDY TIME | | TOTAL TIME |
| EACH BOX EQUALS 1 HOUR | | : |

## PAST STUDIES IN REVIEW

| VOCABULARY FROM YESTERDAY | GOALS FROM YESTERDAY |
|---|---|
| 1 | ☐ |
| 2 | ☐ |
| 3 | ☐ |

| VOCABULARY FROM 5 DAYS AGO | VOCABULARY FROM 10 DAYS AGO |
|---|---|
| 1 | 1 |
| 2 | 2 |
| 3 | 3 |

## PRIORITIES FOR TODAY

| VOCABULARY FOR TODAY | GOALS FOR TODAY |
|---|---|
| 1 | ☐ |
| 2 | ☐ |
| 3 | ☐ |

## DESCRIBE YOUR LEARNING EXPERIENCE FOR TODAY

## SPECIAL WORDS FOR TODAY

| DAILY WORD BUILDER | VERB OF THE DAY | COGNATE OF THE DAY |
|---|---|---|
| **Sencilla** | **Acordar** | **Fracción** |
| adj, m/f. Simple. Easy. Straightforward. Modest | To Decide, Resolve, Agree [On] /g: Acordando / pp: Acordado /Irr. | Noun. From: Fraction (TION=CIÓN) |

## INTERESTING THINGS FROM TODAY

### FOUR SENTENCES THAT I READ, HEARD OR CREATED TODAY

**1**

**2**

**3**

**4**

## THINGS I HAVE QUESTIONS ABOUT

## DESCRIBE YOUR ACTIVITIES IN THESE TASKS FOR TODAY

| ACTIVITY | DESCRIPTION | SATISFACTION |
|---|---|---|
| READING | | ☹ ☹ 😐 🙂 😊 |
| LISTENING | | ☹ ☹ 😐 🙂 😊 |
| WRITING | | ☹ ☹ 😐 🙂 😊 |
| SPEAKING | | ☹ ☹ 😐 🙂 😊 |
| STUDYING | | ☹ ☹ 😐 🙂 😊 |
| VOCABULARY | | ☹ ☹ 😐 🙂 😊 |
| LOG YOUR STUDY TIME | | TOTAL TIME |
| EACH BOX EQUALS 5 MINS. | | : |

| DAY & DATE | | STUDY STREAK # |
|---|---|---|
| LEARNING MOOD ☹ ☹ 😐 🙂 😀 | | # VERBS ACQUIRED |

## PAST STUDIES IN REVIEW

| VOCABULARY FROM YESTERDAY | GOALS FROM YESTERDAY |
|---|---|
| **1** | ☐ |
| **2** | ☐ |
| **3** | ☐ |

| VOCABULARY FROM 5 DAYS AGO | VOCABULARY FROM 10 DAYS AGO |
|---|---|
| **1** | **1** |
| **2** | **2** |
| **3** | **3** |

## PRIORITIES FOR TODAY

| VOCABULARY FOR TODAY | GOALS FOR TODAY |
|---|---|
| **1** | ☐ |
| **2** | ☐ |
| **3** | ☐ |

## DESCRIBE YOUR LEARNING EXPERIENCE FOR TODAY

## SPECIAL WORDS FOR TODAY

| DAILY WORD BUILDER | VERB OF THE DAY | COGNATE OF THE DAY |
|---|---|---|
| **Persona Sencilla** | **Irse** | **Cohesión** |
| n. f. Simple person | To Go Away, Leave, Depart /g: Yéndose / pp: Ido /Irr. | Noun. From: Cohesion (SION=SIÓN) |

## INTERESTING THINGS FROM TODAY

### FOUR SENTENCES THAT I READ, HEARD OR CREATED TODAY

**1**

**2**

**3**

**4**

## THINGS I HAVE QUESTIONS ABOUT

## DESCRIBE YOUR ACTIVITIES IN THESE TASKS FOR TODAY

| ACTIVITY | DESCRIPTION | SATISFACTION |
|----------|-------------|--------------|
| READING | | ☹ ☹ 😐 🙂 😊 |
| LISTENING | | ☹ ☹ 😐 🙂 😊 |
| WRITING | | ☹ ☹ 😐 🙂 😊 |
| SPEAKING | | ☹ ☹ 😐 🙂 😊 |
| STUDYING | | ☹ ☹ 😐 🙂 😊 |
| VOCABULARY | | ☹ ☹ 😐 🙂 😊 |

| LOG YOUR STUDY TIME | | | | | | | | | | | | | TOTAL TIME |
|---------------------|--|--|--|--|--|--|--|--|--|--|--|--|------------|
| EACH BOX EQUALS 5 MINS. | | | | | | | | | | | | | : |

| DAY & DATE | | STUDY STREAK # | |
|---|---|---|---|
| LEARNING MOOD | ☹ ☹ ☺ ☺ ☺ | # VERBS ACQUIRED | |

## PAST STUDIES IN REVIEW

| VOCABULARY FROM YESTERDAY | GOALS FROM YESTERDAY |
|---|---|
| 1 | ☐ |
| 2 | ☐ |
| 3 | ☐ |

| VOCABULARY FROM 5 DAYS AGO | VOCABULARY FROM 10 DAYS AGO |
|---|---|
| 1 | 1 |
| 2 | 2 |
| 3 | 3 |

## PRIORITIES FOR TODAY

| VOCABULARY FOR TODAY | GOALS FOR TODAY |
|---|---|
| 1 | ☐ |
| 2 | ☐ |
| 3 | ☐ |

## DESCRIBE YOUR LEARNING EXPERIENCE FOR TODAY

## SPECIAL WORDS FOR TODAY

| DAILY WORD BUILDER | VERB OF THE DAY | COGNATE OF THE DAY |
|---|---|---|
| **Gente Sencilla** | **Ser** | **Celebración** |
| n. f. Simple people. Simple folk. | To Be /g: Siendo / pp: Sido /Irr. | Noun. From: Celebration (TION=CIÓN) |

## INTERESTING THINGS FROM TODAY

### FOUR SENTENCES THAT I READ, HEARD OR CREATED TODAY

**1**

**2**

**3**

**4**

## THINGS I HAVE QUESTIONS ABOUT

## DESCRIBE YOUR ACTIVITIES IN THESE TASKS FOR TODAY

| ACTIVITY | DESCRIPTION | SATISFACTION |
|----------|-------------|--------------|
| READING | | ☹ ☹ 😐 🙂 😀 |
| LISTENING | | ☹ ☹ 😐 🙂 😀 |
| WRITING | | ☹ ☹ 😐 🙂 😀 |
| SPEAKING | | ☹ ☹ 😐 🙂 😀 |
| STUDYING | | ☹ ☹ 😐 🙂 😀 |
| VOCABULARY | | ☹ ☹ 😐 🙂 😀 |

| LOG YOUR STUDY TIME | | | | | | | | | | | | | | TOTAL TIME |
|---------------------|--|--|--|--|--|--|--|--|--|--|--|--|--|-----------|
| EACH BOX EQUALS 5 MINS. | | | | | | | | | | | | | | : |

| DAY & DATE | | STUDY STREAK # |
|---|---|---|
| LEARNING MOOD ☹ ☹ 😐 🙂 😃 | | # VERBS ACQUIRED |

## PAST STUDIES IN REVIEW

| VOCABULARY FROM YESTERDAY | GOALS FROM YESTERDAY |
|---|---|
| 1 | ☐ |
| 2 | ☐ |
| 3 | ☐ |

| VOCABULARY FROM 5 DAYS AGO | VOCABULARY FROM 10 DAYS AGO |
|---|---|
| 1 | 1 |
| 2 | 2 |
| 3 | 3 |

## PRIORITIES FOR TODAY

| VOCABULARY FOR TODAY | GOALS FOR TODAY |
|---|---|
| 1 | ☐ |
| 2 | ☐ |
| 3 | ☐ |

## DESCRIBE YOUR LEARNING EXPERIENCE FOR TODAY

## SPECIAL WORDS FOR TODAY

| DAILY WORD BUILDER | VERB OF THE DAY | COGNATE OF THE DAY |
|---|---|---|
| **Vida Sencilla** | **Coger** | **Fatalismo** |
| n. f. Simple life. Simple living. | To Catch, Grasp, Take Hold Of /g: Cogiendo / pp: Cogido | Noun. From: Fatalism (ISM=ISMO) |

## INTERESTING THINGS FROM TODAY

### FOUR SENTENCES THAT I READ, HEARD OR CREATED TODAY

**1**

**2**

**3**

**4**

## THINGS I HAVE QUESTIONS ABOUT

## DESCRIBE YOUR ACTIVITIES IN THESE TASKS FOR TODAY

| ACTIVITY | DESCRIPTION | SATISFACTION |
|---|---|---|
| READING | | 😧 😦 😐 🙂 😄 |
| LISTENING | | 😧 😦 😐 🙂 😄 |
| WRITING | | 😧 😦 😐 🙂 😄 |
| SPEAKING | | 😧 😦 😐 🙂 😄 |
| STUDYING | | 😧 😦 😐 🙂 😄 |
| VOCABULARY | | 😧 😦 😐 🙂 😄 |

| LOG YOUR STUDY TIME | | | | | | | | | | | | | TOTAL TIME |
|---|---|---|---|---|---|---|---|---|---|---|---|---|---|
| EACH BOX EQUALS 5 MINS. | | | | | | | | | | | | | : |

| DAY & DATE | | | STUDY STREAK # |
|---|---|---|---|
| LEARNING MOOD | ☹ ☹ 😐 🙂 😀 | | # VERBS ACQUIRED |

## PAST STUDIES IN REVIEW

| VOCABULARY FROM YESTERDAY | GOALS FROM YESTERDAY |
|---|---|
| 1 | ☐ |
| 2 | ☐ |
| 3 | ☐ |

| VOCABULARY FROM 5 DAYS AGO | VOCABULARY FROM 10 DAYS AGO |
|---|---|
| 1 | 1 |
| 2 | 2 |
| 3 | 3 |

## PRIORITIES FOR TODAY

| VOCABULARY FOR TODAY | GOALS FOR TODAY |
|---|---|
| 1 | ☐ |
| 2 | ☐ |
| 3 | ☐ |

## DESCRIBE YOUR LEARNING EXPERIENCE FOR TODAY

## SPECIAL WORDS FOR TODAY

| DAILY WORD BUILDER | VERB OF THE DAY | COGNATE OF THE DAY |
|---|---|---|
| **Forma Sencilla** | **Limpiar** | **Exportar** |
| n. f. Simple way. Easy way. | To Clean /g: Limpiando / pp: Limpiado | Verb. From: Export (ADDING AR OR IR) |

## INTERESTING THINGS FROM TODAY

### FOUR SENTENCES THAT I READ, HEARD OR CREATED TODAY

**1**

**2**

**3**

**4**

## THINGS I HAVE QUESTIONS ABOUT

## DESCRIBE YOUR ACTIVITIES IN THESE TASKS FOR TODAY

| ACTIVITY | DESCRIPTION | SATISFACTION |
|---|---|---|
| READING | | ☹ 🙁 😐 🙂 😃 |
| LISTENING | | ☹ 🙁 😐 🙂 😃 |
| WRITING | | ☹ 🙁 😐 🙂 😃 |
| SPEAKING | | ☹ 🙁 😐 🙂 😃 |
| STUDYING | | ☹ 🙁 😐 🙂 😃 |
| VOCABULARY | | ☹ 🙁 😐 🙂 😃 |
| LOG YOUR STUDY TIME | | TOTAL TIME |
| EACH BOX EQUALS 5 MINS. | | : |

| DAY & DATE | | STUDY STREAK # |
|---|---|---|
| LEARNING MOOD ☹ ☹ 😐 🙂 😃 | | # VERBS ACQUIRED |

## PAST STUDIES IN REVIEW

| VOCABULARY FROM YESTERDAY | GOALS FROM YESTERDAY |
|---|---|
| 1 | ☐ |
| 2 | ☐ |
| 3 | ☐ |

| VOCABULARY FROM 5 DAYS AGO | VOCABULARY FROM 10 DAYS AGO |
|---|---|
| 1 | 1 |
| 2 | 2 |
| 3 | 3 |

## PRIORITIES FOR TODAY

| VOCABULARY FOR TODAY | GOALS FOR TODAY |
|---|---|
| 1 | ☐ |
| 2 | ☐ |
| 3 | ☐ |

## DESCRIBE YOUR LEARNING EXPERIENCE FOR TODAY

## SPECIAL WORDS FOR TODAY

| DAILY WORD BUILDER | VERB OF THE DAY | COGNATE OF THE DAY |
|---|---|---|
| **Manera Sencilla** | **Trabajar** | **Singular** |
| n. f. Simple way. Simple manner. Easy way. | To Work /g: Trabajando / pp: Trabajado | Adjective. From: Singular (AR=AR) |

## INTERESTING THINGS FROM TODAY

### FOUR SENTENCES THAT I READ, HEARD OR CREATED TODAY

**1**

**2**

**3**

**4**

### THINGS I HAVE QUESTIONS ABOUT

### DESCRIBE YOUR ACTIVITIES IN THESE TASKS FOR TODAY

| ACTIVITY | DESCRIPTION | SATISFACTION |
|---|---|---|
| READING | | 😫 😖 😐 😊 😄 |
| LISTENING | | 😫 😖 😐 😊 😄 |
| WRITING | | 😫 😖 😐 😊 😄 |
| SPEAKING | | 😫 😖 😐 😊 😄 |
| STUDYING | | 😫 😖 😐 😊 😄 |
| VOCABULARY | | 😫 😖 😐 😊 😄 |
| LOG YOUR STUDY TIME | | TOTAL TIME |
| EACH BOX EQUALS 5 MINS. | | : |

| DAY & DATE | | STUDY STREAK # |
|---|---|---|
| LEARNING MOOD | 😧 😦 😐 😊 😃 | # VERBS ACQUIRED |

## PAST STUDIES IN REVIEW

| VOCABULARY FROM YESTERDAY | GOALS FROM YESTERDAY |
|---|---|
| 1 | ☐ |
| 2 | ☐ |
| 3 | ☐ |

| VOCABULARY FROM 5 DAYS AGO | VOCABULARY FROM 10 DAYS AGO |
|---|---|
| 1 | 1 |
| 2 | 2 |
| 3 | 3 |

## PRIORITIES FOR TODAY

| VOCABULARY FOR TODAY | GOALS FOR TODAY |
|---|---|
| 1 | ☐ |
| 2 | ☐ |
| 3 | ☐ |

## DESCRIBE YOUR LEARNING EXPERIENCE FOR TODAY

## SPECIAL WORDS FOR TODAY

| DAILY WORD BUILDER | VERB OF THE DAY | COGNATE OF THE DAY |
|---|---|---|
| **Estructura Sencilla** | **Atacar** | **Elefante** |
| n. f. Simple structure. | To Attack /g: Atacando / pp: Atacado /Irr. | Noun. From: Elephant (NT=NTE) |

## INTERESTING THINGS FROM TODAY

### FOUR SENTENCES THAT I READ, HEARD OR CREATED TODAY

**1**

**2**

**3**

**4**

## THINGS I HAVE QUESTIONS ABOUT

## DESCRIBE YOUR ACTIVITIES IN THESE TASKS FOR TODAY

| ACTIVITY | DESCRIPTION | SATISFACTION |
|---|---|---|
| READING | | ☹ 😟 😐 🙂 😄 |
| LISTENING | | ☹ 😟 😐 🙂 😄 |
| WRITING | | ☹ 😟 😐 🙂 😄 |
| SPEAKING | | ☹ 😟 😐 🙂 😄 |
| STUDYING | | ☹ 😟 😐 🙂 😄 |
| VOCABULARY | | ☹ 😟 😐 🙂 😄 |
| LOG YOUR STUDY TIME | | TOTAL TIME |
| EACH BOX EQUALS 5 MINS. | | : |

## THIS WEEK IN REVIEW

### VOCABULARY ACQUIRED

### BIGGEST ACHIEVEMENTS

☐        ☐

☐        ☐

☐        ☐

### AREAS FOR IMPROVEMENT

**1**

**2**

**3**

**4**

## THINGS THAT I STILL HAVE QUESTIONS ABOUT

## FINAL MEASUREMENTS OF THIS WEEK

| TOTAL TIME THIS WEEK | TOTAL NEW VERBS | TOTAL NEW WORDS |
|---|---|---|
| | | |

## SELF-ASSESSMENT OF MY ACTIVITIES THIS WEEK

| ACTIVITIES | SPECIFIC ASSESSMENTS | SATISFACTION |
|---|---|---|
| READING | | ☹ ☹ 😐 ☺ 😃 |
| LISTENING | | ☹ ☹ 😐 ☺ 😃 |
| WRITING | | ☹ ☹ 😐 ☺ 😃 |
| SPEAKING | | ☹ ☹ 😐 ☺ 😃 |
| STUDYING | | ☹ ☹ 😐 ☺ 😃 |
| MOTIVATION | | ☹ ☹ 😐 ☺ 😃 |

| LOG YOUR STUDY TIME | | | | | | | | | | | | | TOTAL TIME |
|---|---|---|---|---|---|---|---|---|---|---|---|---|---|
| EACH BOX EQUALS 1 HOUR | | | | | | | | | | | | | : |

| DAY & DATE | | STUDY STREAK # |
|---|---|---|
| LEARNING MOOD  ☹ ☹ 😐 🙂 😀 | | # VERBS ACQUIRED |

## PAST STUDIES IN REVIEW

| VOCABULARY FROM YESTERDAY | GOALS FROM YESTERDAY |
|---|---|
| **1** | ☐ |
| **2** | ☐ |
| **3** | ☐ |

| VOCABULARY FROM 5 DAYS AGO | VOCABULARY FROM 10 DAYS AGO |
|---|---|
| **1** | **1** |
| **2** | **2** |
| **3** | **3** |

## PRIORITIES FOR TODAY

| VOCABULARY FOR TODAY | GOALS FOR TODAY |
|---|---|
| **1** | ☐ |
| **2** | ☐ |
| **3** | ☐ |

## DESCRIBE YOUR LEARNING EXPERIENCE FOR TODAY

_____

_____

_____

_____

## SPECIAL WORDS FOR TODAY

| DAILY WORD BUILDER | VERB OF THE DAY | COGNATE OF THE DAY |
|---|---|---|
| **Cargo** | **Acostar** | **Fabuloso** |
| n. m. Charge. Position. Care. Office. Job. Expense. | To Put To Bed /g: Acostando / pp: Acostado /Irr. | Adjective. From: Fabulous (OUS=OSO) |

## INTERESTING THINGS FROM TODAY
### FOUR SENTENCES THAT I READ, HEARD OR CREATED TODAY

1

2

3

4

## THINGS I HAVE QUESTIONS ABOUT

## DESCRIBE YOUR ACTIVITIES IN THESE TASKS FOR TODAY

| ACTIVITY | DESCRIPTION | SATISFACTION |
|---|---|---|
| READING | | ☹ ☹ 😐 🙂 😄 |
| LISTENING | | ☹ ☹ 😐 🙂 😄 |
| WRITING | | ☹ ☹ 😐 🙂 😄 |
| SPEAKING | | ☹ ☹ 😐 🙂 😄 |
| STUDYING | | ☹ ☹ 😐 🙂 😄 |
| VOCABULARY | | ☹ ☹ 😐 🙂 😄 |
| LOG YOUR STUDY TIME | | TOTAL TIME |
| EACH BOX EQUALS 5 MINS. | | : |

| DAY & DATE | | STUDY STREAK # |
|---|---|---|
| LEARNING MOOD | ☹ ☹ 😐 🙂 😀 | # VERBS ACQUIRED |

## PAST STUDIES IN REVIEW

| VOCABULARY FROM YESTERDAY | GOALS FROM YESTERDAY |
|---|---|
| **1** | ☐ |
| **2** | ☐ |
| **3** | ☐ |

| VOCABULARY FROM 5 DAYS AGO | VOCABULARY FROM 10 DAYS AGO |
|---|---|
| **1** | **1** |
| **2** | **2** |
| **3** | **3** |

## PRIORITIES FOR TODAY

| VOCABULARY FOR TODAY | GOALS FOR TODAY |
|---|---|
| **1** | ☐ |
| **2** | ☐ |
| **3** | ☐ |

## DESCRIBE YOUR LEARNING EXPERIENCE FOR TODAY

## SPECIAL WORDS FOR TODAY

| DAILY WORD BUILDER | VERB OF THE DAY | COGNATE OF THE DAY |
|---|---|---|
| **A Su Cargo** | **Jugar** | **Documento** |
| adv. At X's expense. | To Play /g: Jugando / pp: Jugado /Irr. | Noun. From: Document (MENT=MENTO) |

## INTERESTING THINGS FROM TODAY

### FOUR SENTENCES THAT I READ, HEARD OR CREATED TODAY

**1**

**2**

**3**

**4**

## THINGS I HAVE QUESTIONS ABOUT

## DESCRIBE YOUR ACTIVITIES IN THESE TASKS FOR TODAY

| ACTIVITY | DESCRIPTION | SATISFACTION |
|---|---|---|
| READING | | 😫 😠 😐 😊 😀 |
| LISTENING | | 😫 😠 😐 😊 😀 |
| WRITING | | 😫 😠 😐 😊 😀 |
| SPEAKING | | 😫 😠 😐 😊 😀 |
| STUDYING | | 😫 😠 😐 😊 😀 |
| VOCABULARY | | 😫 😠 😐 😊 😀 |

| LOG YOUR STUDY TIME | | | | | | | | | | | | | | TOTAL TIME |
|---|---|---|---|---|---|---|---|---|---|---|---|---|---|---|
| EACH BOX EQUALS 5 MINS. | | | | | | | | | | | | | | : |

| DAY & DATE | | STUDY STREAK # |
|---|---|---|
| LEARNING MOOD | ☹ ☹ 😐 🙂 😃 | # VERBS ACQUIRED |

## PAST STUDIES IN REVIEW

| VOCABULARY FROM YESTERDAY | GOALS FROM YESTERDAY |
|---|---|
| 1 | ☐ |
| 2 | ☐ |
| 3 | ☐ |

| VOCABULARY FROM 5 DAYS AGO | VOCABULARY FROM 10 DAYS AGO |
|---|---|
| 1 | 1 |
| 2 | 2 |
| 3 | 3 |

## PRIORITIES FOR TODAY

| VOCABULARY FOR TODAY | GOALS FOR TODAY |
|---|---|
| 1 | ☐ |
| 2 | ☐ |
| 3 | ☐ |

## DESCRIBE YOUR LEARNING EXPERIENCE FOR TODAY

## SPECIAL WORDS FOR TODAY

| DAILY WORD BUILDER | VERB OF THE DAY | COGNATE OF THE DAY |
|---|---|---|
| **Hacerse Cargo** | **Significar** | **Aceleración** |
| v. Take over. Deal with. | To Signify, Mean /g: Significando / pp: Significado /Irr. | Noun. From: Acceleration (TION=CIÓN) |

## INTERESTING THINGS FROM TODAY

### FOUR SENTENCES THAT I READ, HEARD OR CREATED TODAY

**1**

**2**

**3**

**4**

## THINGS I HAVE QUESTIONS ABOUT

## DESCRIBE YOUR ACTIVITIES IN THESE TASKS FOR TODAY

| ACTIVITY | DESCRIPTION | SATISFACTION |
|----------|-------------|--------------|
| READING | | ☹ 🙁 😐 🙂 😃 |
| LISTENING | | ☹ 🙁 😐 🙂 😃 |
| WRITING | | ☹ 🙁 😐 🙂 😃 |
| SPEAKING | | ☹ 🙁 😐 🙂 😃 |
| STUDYING | | ☹ 🙁 😐 🙂 😃 |
| VOCABULARY | | ☹ 🙁 😐 🙂 😃 |

| LOG YOUR STUDY TIME | | | | | | | | | | | | | TOTAL TIME |
|---|---|---|---|---|---|---|---|---|---|---|---|---|---|
| EACH BOX EQUALS 5 MINS. | | | | | | | | | | | | | : |

| DAY & DATE | | STUDY STREAK # | |
|---|---|---|---|
| LEARNING MOOD | ☹ ☹ 😐 🙂 😃 | # VERBS ACQUIRED | |

## PAST STUDIES IN REVIEW

| VOCABULARY FROM YESTERDAY | GOALS FROM YESTERDAY |
|---|---|
| ① | ☐ |
| ② | ☐ |
| ③ | ☐ |

| VOCABULARY FROM 5 DAYS AGO | VOCABULARY FROM 10 DAYS AGO |
|---|---|
| ① | ① |
| ② | ② |
| ③ | ③ |

## PRIORITIES FOR TODAY

| VOCABULARY FOR TODAY | GOALS FOR TODAY |
|---|---|
| ① | ☐ |
| ② | ☐ |
| ③ | ☐ |

## DESCRIBE YOUR LEARNING EXPERIENCE FOR TODAY

## SPECIAL WORDS FOR TODAY

| DAILY WORD BUILDER | VERB OF THE DAY | COGNATE OF THE DAY |
|---|---|---|
| **Altos Cargos** | **Comer** | **Urgencia** |
| n. m. pl. High position. | To Eat /g: Comiendo / pp: Comido | Noun. From: Urgency (Y=IA OR ÍA) |

## INTERESTING THINGS FROM TODAY

### FOUR SENTENCES THAT I READ, HEARD OR CREATED TODAY

**1**

**2**

**3**

**4**

## THINGS I HAVE QUESTIONS ABOUT

## DESCRIBE YOUR ACTIVITIES IN THESE TASKS FOR TODAY

| ACTIVITY | DESCRIPTION | SATISFACTION |
|----------|-------------|--------------|
| READING | | ☹ ☹ ☺ ☺ ☺ |
| LISTENING | | ☹ ☹ ☺ ☺ ☺ |
| WRITING | | ☹ ☹ ☺ ☺ ☺ |
| SPEAKING | | ☹ ☹ ☺ ☺ ☺ |
| STUDYING | | ☹ ☹ ☺ ☺ ☺ |
| VOCABULARY | | ☹ ☹ ☺ ☺ ☺ |

| LOG YOUR STUDY TIME | | TOTAL TIME |
|---------------------|---|------------|
| EACH BOX EQUALS 5 MINS. | | : |

| DAY & DATE | | STUDY STREAK # | |
|---|---|---|---|
| LEARNING MOOD | ☹ ☹ 😐 🙂 😃 | # VERBS ACQUIRED | |

## PAST STUDIES IN REVIEW

| VOCABULARY FROM YESTERDAY | GOALS FROM YESTERDAY |
|---|---|
| 1 | ☐ |
| 2 | ☐ |
| 3 | ☐ |

| VOCABULARY FROM 5 DAYS AGO | VOCABULARY FROM 10 DAYS AGO |
|---|---|
| 1 | 1 |
| 2 | 2 |
| 3 | 3 |

## PRIORITIES FOR TODAY

| VOCABULARY FOR TODAY | GOALS FOR TODAY |
|---|---|
| 1 | ☐ |
| 2 | ☐ |
| 3 | ☐ |

## DESCRIBE YOUR LEARNING EXPERIENCE FOR TODAY

## SPECIAL WORDS FOR TODAY

| DAILY WORD BUILDER | VERB OF THE DAY | COGNATE OF THE DAY |
|---|---|---|
| **Sin Cargo** | **Llamar** | **Diferenciación** |
| adv. Free of charge. | To Call, To Name /g: Llamando / pp: Llamado | Noun. From: Differentiation (TION=CIÓN) |

## INTERESTING THINGS FROM TODAY
### FOUR SENTENCES THAT I READ, HEARD OR CREATED TODAY

**1**

**2**

**3**

**4**

## THINGS I HAVE QUESTIONS ABOUT

## DESCRIBE YOUR ACTIVITIES IN THESE TASKS FOR TODAY

| ACTIVITY | DESCRIPTION | SATISFACTION |
|---|---|---|
| READING | | 😧 😟 😐 😊 😀 |
| LISTENING | | 😧 😟 😐 😊 😀 |
| WRITING | | 😧 😟 😐 😊 😀 |
| SPEAKING | | 😧 😟 😐 😊 😀 |
| STUDYING | | 😧 😟 😐 😊 😀 |
| VOCABULARY | | 😧 😟 😐 😊 😀 |
| LOG YOUR STUDY TIME | | TOTAL TIME |
| EACH BOX EQUALS 5 MINS. | | : |

| DAY & DATE | | STUDY STREAK # | |
|---|---|---|---|
| LEARNING MOOD | 😫 😞 😐 🙂 😀 | # VERBS ACQUIRED | |

## PAST STUDIES IN REVIEW

| VOCABULARY FROM YESTERDAY | GOALS FROM YESTERDAY |
|---|---|
| 1 | ☐ |
| 2 | ☐ |
| 3 | ☐ |

| VOCABULARY FROM 5 DAYS AGO | VOCABULARY FROM 10 DAYS AGO |
|---|---|
| 1 | 1 |
| 2 | 2 |
| 3 | 3 |

## PRIORITIES FOR TODAY

| VOCABULARY FOR TODAY | GOALS FOR TODAY |
|---|---|
| 1 | ☐ |
| 2 | ☐ |
| 3 | ☐ |

## DESCRIBE YOUR LEARNING EXPERIENCE FOR TODAY

## SPECIAL WORDS FOR TODAY

| DAILY WORD BUILDER | VERB OF THE DAY | COGNATE OF THE DAY |
|---|---|---|
| **Estar A Cargo** | **Tratar** | **Favorable** |
| v. To be in charge | To Treat, Handle /g: Tratando / pp: Tratado | Adjective. From: Favorable (BLE=BLE) |

## INTERESTING THINGS FROM TODAY

### FOUR SENTENCES THAT I READ, HEARD OR CREATED TODAY

**1**

**2**

**3**

**4**

## THINGS I HAVE QUESTIONS ABOUT

## DESCRIBE YOUR ACTIVITIES IN THESE TASKS FOR TODAY

| ACTIVITY | DESCRIPTION | SATISFACTION |
|----------|-------------|--------------|
| READING | | ☹ ☹ 😐 🙂 😊 |
| LISTENING | | ☹ ☹ 😐 🙂 😊 |
| WRITING | | ☹ ☹ 😐 🙂 😊 |
| SPEAKING | | ☹ ☹ 😐 🙂 😊 |
| STUDYING | | ☹ ☹ 😐 🙂 😊 |
| VOCABULARY | | ☹ ☹ 😐 🙂 😊 |

| LOG YOUR STUDY TIME | | | | | | | | | | | | | | | TOTAL TIME |
|---------------------|--|--|--|--|--|--|--|--|--|--|--|--|--|--|------------|
| EACH BOX EQUALS 5 MINS. | | | | | | | | | | | | | | | : |

| DAY & DATE | | STUDY STREAK # |
|---|---|---|
| LEARNING MOOD ☹ ☹ 😐 🙂 😃 | | # VERBS ACQUIRED |

## PAST STUDIES IN REVIEW

| VOCABULARY FROM YESTERDAY | GOALS FROM YESTERDAY |
|---|---|
| 1 | ☐ |
| 2 | ☐ |
| 3 | ☐ |

| VOCABULARY FROM 5 DAYS AGO | VOCABULARY FROM 10 DAYS AGO |
|---|---|
| 1 | 1 |
| 2 | 2 |
| 3 | 3 |

## PRIORITIES FOR TODAY

| VOCABULARY FOR TODAY | GOALS FOR TODAY |
|---|---|
| 1 | ☐ |
| 2 | ☐ |
| 3 | ☐ |

## DESCRIBE YOUR LEARNING EXPERIENCE FOR TODAY

_____

_____

_____

_____

## SPECIAL WORDS FOR TODAY

| DAILY WORD BUILDER | VERB OF THE DAY | COGNATE OF THE DAY |
|---|---|---|
| **Carga de Trabajo** | **Atender** | **Tolerable** |
| n. f. Work load. Working load. Work burden. | To Attend To, Pay Attention To /g: Atendiendo / pp: Atendido /Irr. | Adjective. From: Tolerable (BLE=BLE) |

## INTERESTING THINGS FROM TODAY

### FOUR SENTENCES THAT I READ, HEARD OR CREATED TODAY

**1**

**2**

**3**

**4**

## THINGS I HAVE QUESTIONS ABOUT

## DESCRIBE YOUR ACTIVITIES IN THESE TASKS FOR TODAY

| ACTIVITY | DESCRIPTION | SATISFACTION |
|---|---|---|
| READING | | 😞 😟 😐 🙂 😊 |
| LISTENING | | 😞 😟 😐 🙂 😊 |
| WRITING | | 😞 😟 😐 🙂 😊 |
| SPEAKING | | 😞 😟 😐 🙂 😊 |
| STUDYING | | 😞 😟 😐 🙂 😊 |
| VOCABULARY | | 😞 😟 😐 🙂 😊 |
| LOG YOUR STUDY TIME | | TOTAL TIME |
| EACH BOX EQUALS 5 MINS. | | : |

## THIS WEEK IN REVIEW

### VOCABULARY ACQUIRED

### BIGGEST ACHIEVEMENTS

☐          ☐

☐          ☐

☐          ☐

### AREAS FOR IMPROVEMENT

1

2

3

4

## THINGS THAT I STILL HAVE QUESTIONS ABOUT

|  |  |
|  |  |
|  |  |

## FINAL MEASUREMENTS OF THIS WEEK

| TOTAL TIME THIS WEEK | TOTAL NEW VERBS | TOTAL NEW WORDS |
|---|---|---|
|  |  |  |

## SELF-ASSESSMENT OF MY ACTIVITIES THIS WEEK

| ACTIVITIES | SPECIFIC ASSESSMENTS | SATISFACTION |
|---|---|---|
| READING |  | ☹ ☹ 😐 🙂 😃 |
| LISTENING |  | ☹ ☹ 😐 🙂 😃 |
| WRITING |  | ☹ ☹ 😐 🙂 😃 |
| SPEAKING |  | ☹ ☹ 😐 🙂 😃 |
| STUDYING |  | ☹ ☹ 😐 🙂 😃 |
| MOTIVATION |  | ☹ ☹ 😐 🙂 😃 |

| LOG YOUR STUDY TIME |  |  |  |  |  |  |  |  |  |  | TOTAL TIME |
|---|---|---|---|---|---|---|---|---|---|---|---|
| EACH BOX EQUALS 1 HOUR |  |  |  |  |  |  |  |  |  |  | : |

| DAY & DATE | | STUDY STREAK # |
|---|---|---|
| LEARNING MOOD | ☹ ☹ 😐 🙂 😀 | # VERBS ACQUIRED |

## PAST STUDIES IN REVIEW

| VOCABULARY FROM YESTERDAY | GOALS FROM YESTERDAY |
|---|---|
| 1 | ☐ |
| 2 | ☐ |
| 3 | ☐ |

| VOCABULARY FROM 5 DAYS AGO | VOCABULARY FROM 10 DAYS AGO |
|---|---|
| 1 | 1 |
| 2 | 2 |
| 3 | 3 |

## PRIORITIES FOR TODAY

| VOCABULARY FOR TODAY | GOALS FOR TODAY |
|---|---|
| 1 | ☐ |
| 2 | ☐ |
| 3 | ☐ |

## DESCRIBE YOUR LEARNING EXPERIENCE FOR TODAY

_____

_____

_____

_____

## SPECIAL WORDS FOR TODAY

| DAILY WORD BUILDER | VERB OF THE DAY | COGNATE OF THE DAY |
|---|---|---|
| **Medio** | **Almorzar** | **Protestar** |
| adj. m. Middle. Medium. | To Lunch, Eat Lunch, Have Lunch /g: Almorzando / pp: Almorzado /Irr. | Verb. From: Protest (V+C+T=TIR OR TAR) |

## INTERESTING THINGS FROM TODAY

### FOUR SENTENCES THAT I READ, HEARD OR CREATED TODAY

**1**

**2**

**3**

**4**

## THINGS I HAVE QUESTIONS ABOUT

## DESCRIBE YOUR ACTIVITIES IN THESE TASKS FOR TODAY

| ACTIVITY | DESCRIPTION | SATISFACTION |
|----------|-------------|--------------|
| READING | | 😞 😟 😐 🙂 😀 |
| LISTENING | | 😞 😟 😐 🙂 😀 |
| WRITING | | 😞 😟 😐 🙂 😀 |
| SPEAKING | | 😞 😟 😐 🙂 😀 |
| STUDYING | | 😞 😟 😐 🙂 😀 |
| VOCABULARY | | 😞 😟 😐 🙂 😀 |
| LOG YOUR STUDY TIME | | TOTAL TIME |
| EACH BOX EQUALS 5 MINS. | | : |

| DAY & DATE | | STUDY STREAK # |
|---|---|---|
| LEARNING MOOD ☹ ☹ 😐 🙂 😃 | | # VERBS ACQUIRED |

## PAST STUDIES IN REVIEW

| VOCABULARY FROM YESTERDAY | GOALS FROM YESTERDAY |
|---|---|
| 1 | ☐ |
| 2 | ☐ |
| 3 | ☐ |

| VOCABULARY FROM 5 DAYS AGO | VOCABULARY FROM 10 DAYS AGO |
|---|---|
| 1 | 1 |
| 2 | 2 |
| 3 | 3 |

## PRIORITIES FOR TODAY

| VOCABULARY FOR TODAY | GOALS FOR TODAY |
|---|---|
| 1 | ☐ |
| 2 | ☐ |
| 3 | ☐ |

## DESCRIBE YOUR LEARNING EXPERIENCE FOR TODAY

## SPECIAL WORDS FOR TODAY

| DAILY WORD BUILDER | VERB OF THE DAY | COGNATE OF THE DAY |
|---|---|---|
| **Medio Ambiente** | **Leer** | **Agonía** |
| n. Environment. | To Read /g: Leyendo / pp: Leído /Irr. | Noun. From: Agony (Y=IA OR ÍA) |

## INTERESTING THINGS FROM TODAY

### FOUR SENTENCES THAT I READ, HEARD OR CREATED TODAY

**1**

**2**

**3**

**4**

## THINGS I HAVE QUESTIONS ABOUT

## DESCRIBE YOUR ACTIVITIES IN THESE TASKS FOR TODAY

| ACTIVITY | DESCRIPTION | SATISFACTION |
|----------|-------------|--------------|
| READING | | ☹ ☹ 😐 🙂 😄 |
| LISTENING | | ☹ ☹ 😐 🙂 😄 |
| WRITING | | ☹ ☹ 😐 🙂 😄 |
| SPEAKING | | ☹ ☹ 😐 🙂 😄 |
| STUDYING | | ☹ ☹ 😐 🙂 😄 |
| VOCABULARY | | ☹ ☹ 😐 🙂 😄 |

| LOG YOUR STUDY TIME | | TOTAL TIME |
|---------------------|--|------------|
| EACH BOX EQUALS 5 MINS. | | : |

| DAY & DATE | | STUDY STREAK # |
|---|---|---|
| LEARNING MOOD ☹ ☹ 😐 🙂 😄 | | # VERBS ACQUIRED |

## PAST STUDIES IN REVIEW

| VOCABULARY FROM YESTERDAY | GOALS FROM YESTERDAY |
|---|---|
| 1 | ☐ |
| 2 | ☐ |
| 3 | ☐ |

| VOCABULARY FROM 5 DAYS AGO | VOCABULARY FROM 10 DAYS AGO |
|---|---|
| 1 | 1 |
| 2 | 2 |
| 3 | 3 |

## PRIORITIES FOR TODAY

| VOCABULARY FOR TODAY | GOALS FOR TODAY |
|---|---|
| 1 | ☐ |
| 2 | ☐ |
| 3 | ☐ |

## DESCRIBE YOUR LEARNING EXPERIENCE FOR TODAY

_____

_____

_____

_____

## SPECIAL WORDS FOR TODAY

| DAILY WORD BUILDER | VERB OF THE DAY | COGNATE OF THE DAY |
|---|---|---|
| **Por Medio De** | **Suponer** | **Honorable** |
| prep. By means of | To Suppose /g: Suponiendo / pp: Supuesto /Irr. | Adjective. From: Honorable (BLE=BLE) |

## INTERESTING THINGS FROM TODAY

### FOUR SENTENCES THAT I READ, HEARD OR CREATED TODAY

**1**

**2**

**3**

**4**

## THINGS I HAVE QUESTIONS ABOUT

## DESCRIBE YOUR ACTIVITIES IN THESE TASKS FOR TODAY

| ACTIVITY | DESCRIPTION | SATISFACTION |
|----------|-------------|--------------|
| READING | | 😞 😟 😐 🙂 😀 |
| LISTENING | | 😞 😟 😐 🙂 😀 |
| WRITING | | 😞 😟 😐 🙂 😀 |
| SPEAKING | | 😞 😟 😐 🙂 😀 |
| STUDYING | | 😞 😟 😐 🙂 😀 |
| VOCABULARY | | 😞 😟 😐 🙂 😀 |

| LOG YOUR STUDY TIME | | TOTAL TIME |
|---------------------|--|------------|
| EACH BOX EQUALS 5 MINS. | | : |

| DAY & DATE | | STUDY STREAK # |
|---|---|---|
| LEARNING MOOD  ☹ ☹ ☺ ☺ 😀 | | # VERBS ACQUIRED |

## PAST STUDIES IN REVIEW

| VOCABULARY FROM YESTERDAY | GOALS FROM YESTERDAY |
|---|---|
| 1 | ☐ |
| 2 | ☐ |
| 3 | ☐ |

| VOCABULARY FROM 5 DAYS AGO | VOCABULARY FROM 10 DAYS AGO |
|---|---|
| 1 | 1 |
| 2 | 2 |
| 3 | 3 |

## PRIORITIES FOR TODAY

| VOCABULARY FOR TODAY | GOALS FOR TODAY |
|---|---|
| 1 | ☐ |
| 2 | ☐ |
| 3 | ☐ |

## DESCRIBE YOUR LEARNING EXPERIENCE FOR TODAY

## SPECIAL WORDS FOR TODAY

| DAILY WORD BUILDER | VERB OF THE DAY | COGNATE OF THE DAY |
|---|---|---|
| **Medios de** | **Comprar** | **Hospitalidad** |
| n. m. pl. Media. Mass media. Media outlets. News media | To Buy, Purchase /g: Comprando / pp: Comprado | Noun. From: Hospitality (TY=IDAD) |

## INTERESTING THINGS FROM TODAY

### FOUR SENTENCES THAT I READ, HEARD OR CREATED TODAY

**1**

**2**

**3**

**4**

## THINGS I HAVE QUESTIONS ABOUT

## DESCRIBE YOUR ACTIVITIES IN THESE TASKS FOR TODAY

| ACTIVITY | DESCRIPTION | SATISFACTION |
|---|---|---|
| READING | | ☹ 😟 😐 🙂 😊 |
| LISTENING | | ☹ 😟 😐 🙂 😊 |
| WRITING | | ☹ 😟 😐 🙂 😊 |
| SPEAKING | | ☹ 😟 😐 🙂 😊 |
| STUDYING | | ☹ 😟 😐 🙂 😊 |
| VOCABULARY | | ☹ 😟 😐 🙂 😊 |

| LOG YOUR STUDY TIME | | TOTAL TIME |
|---|---|---|
| EACH BOX EQUALS 5 MINS. | | : |

| DAY & DATE | | STUDY STREAK # |
| --- | --- | --- |
| LEARNING MOOD | ☹ ☹ 😐 🙂 😃 | # VERBS ACQUIRED |

## PAST STUDIES IN REVIEW

| VOCABULARY FROM YESTERDAY | GOALS FROM YESTERDAY |
| --- | --- |
| 1 | ☐ |
| 2 | ☐ |
| 3 | ☐ |

| VOCABULARY FROM 5 DAYS AGO | VOCABULARY FROM 10 DAYS AGO |
| --- | --- |
| 1 | 1 |
| 2 | 2 |
| 3 | 3 |

## PRIORITIES FOR TODAY

| VOCABULARY FOR TODAY | GOALS FOR TODAY |
| --- | --- |
| 1 | ☐ |
| 2 | ☐ |
| 3 | ☐ |

## DESCRIBE YOUR LEARNING EXPERIENCE FOR TODAY

## SPECIAL WORDS FOR TODAY

| DAILY WORD BUILDER | VERB OF THE DAY | COGNATE OF THE DAY |
| --- | --- | --- |
| **Medios de Transporte** | **Llevar** | **Contrastar** |
| n. m. pl. Means of transport. Transport methods. | To Carry, Bring /g: Llevando / pp: Llevado | Verb. From: Contrast (V+C+T=TIR OR TAR) |

## INTERESTING THINGS FROM TODAY
### FOUR SENTENCES THAT I READ, HEARD OR CREATED TODAY

**1**

**2**

**3**

**4**

## THINGS I HAVE QUESTIONS ABOUT

## DESCRIBE YOUR ACTIVITIES IN THESE TASKS FOR TODAY

| ACTIVITY | DESCRIPTION | SATISFACTION |
|---|---|---|
| READING | | ☹ 😖 😐 🙂 😄 |
| LISTENING | | ☹ 😖 😐 🙂 😄 |
| WRITING | | ☹ 😖 😐 🙂 😄 |
| SPEAKING | | ☹ 😖 😐 🙂 😄 |
| STUDYING | | ☹ 😖 😐 🙂 😄 |
| VOCABULARY | | ☹ 😖 😐 🙂 😄 |

| LOG YOUR STUDY TIME | | | | | | | | | | | | | TOTAL TIME |
|---|---|---|---|---|---|---|---|---|---|---|---|---|---|
| EACH BOX EQUALS 5 MINS. | | | | | | | | | | | | | : |

| DAY & DATE | | STUDY STREAK # | |
|---|---|---|---|
| LEARNING MOOD | ☹ ☹ 😐 🙂 😄 | # VERBS ACQUIRED | |

## PAST STUDIES IN REVIEW

| VOCABULARY FROM YESTERDAY | GOALS FROM YESTERDAY |
|---|---|
| 1 | ☐ |
| 2 | ☐ |
| 3 | ☐ |

| VOCABULARY FROM 5 DAYS AGO | VOCABULARY FROM 10 DAYS AGO |
|---|---|
| 1 | 1 |
| 2 | 2 |
| 3 | 3 |

## PRIORITIES FOR TODAY

| VOCABULARY FOR TODAY | GOALS FOR TODAY |
|---|---|
| 1 | ☐ |
| 2 | ☐ |
| 3 | ☐ |

## DESCRIBE YOUR LEARNING EXPERIENCE FOR TODAY

## SPECIAL WORDS FOR TODAY

| DAILY WORD BUILDER | VERB OF THE DAY | COGNATE OF THE DAY |
|---|---|---|
| **Medios de Pago** | **Vender** | **Describir** |
| n. m. pl. Means of payment. Payment methods or options. | To Sell /g: Vendiendo / pp: Vendido | Verb. From: Describe (E=AR OR IR) |

## INTERESTING THINGS FROM TODAY

### FOUR SENTENCES THAT I READ, HEARD OR CREATED TODAY

**1**

**2**

**3**

**4**

## THINGS I HAVE QUESTIONS ABOUT

## DESCRIBE YOUR ACTIVITIES IN THESE TASKS FOR TODAY

| ACTIVITY | DESCRIPTION | SATISFACTION |
|---|---|---|
| READING | | 😕 😣 😐 😊 😃 |
| LISTENING | | 😕 😣 😐 😊 😃 |
| WRITING | | 😕 😣 😐 😊 😃 |
| SPEAKING | | 😕 😣 😐 😊 😃 |
| STUDYING | | 😕 😣 😐 😊 😃 |
| VOCABULARY | | 😕 😣 😐 😊 😃 |

| LOG YOUR STUDY TIME | | | | | | | | | | | | | | TOTAL TIME |
|---|---|---|---|---|---|---|---|---|---|---|---|---|---|---|
| EACH BOX EQUALS 5 MINS. | | | | | | | | | | | | | | : |

| DAY & DATE | | | STUDY STREAK # | |
|---|---|---|---|---|
| LEARNING MOOD | ☹ ☹ 😐 🙂 😃 | | # VERBS ACQUIRED | |

## PAST STUDIES IN REVIEW

| VOCABULARY FROM YESTERDAY | GOALS FROM YESTERDAY |
|---|---|
| 1 | ☐ |
| 2 | ☐ |
| 3 | ☐ |

| VOCABULARY FROM 5 DAYS AGO | VOCABULARY FROM 10 DAYS AGO |
|---|---|
| 1 | 1 |
| 2 | 2 |
| 3 | 3 |

## PRIORITIES FOR TODAY

| VOCABULARY FOR TODAY | GOALS FOR TODAY |
|---|---|
| 1 | ☐ |
| 2 | ☐ |
| 3 | ☐ |

## DESCRIBE YOUR LEARNING EXPERIENCE FOR TODAY

## SPECIAL WORDS FOR TODAY

| DAILY WORD BUILDER | VERB OF THE DAY | COGNATE OF THE DAY |
|---|---|---|
| **Medios de Vida** | **Atraer** | **Abdominal** |
| n. m. pl. Livelihoods. Means of living. | To Attract, Draw, Lure /g: Atrayendo / pp: Atraído /Irr. | Adjective. From: Abdominal (AL=AL) |

## INTERESTING THINGS FROM TODAY

### FOUR SENTENCES THAT I READ, HEARD OR CREATED TODAY

**1**

**2**

**3**

**4**

## THINGS I HAVE QUESTIONS ABOUT

## DESCRIBE YOUR ACTIVITIES IN THESE TASKS FOR TODAY

| ACTIVITY | DESCRIPTION | SATISFACTION |
|---|---|---|
| READING | | ☹ ☹ ☺ ☺ ☺ |
| LISTENING | | ☹ ☹ ☺ ☺ ☺ |
| WRITING | | ☹ ☹ ☺ ☺ ☺ |
| SPEAKING | | ☹ ☹ ☺ ☺ ☺ |
| STUDYING | | ☹ ☹ ☺ ☺ ☺ |
| VOCABULARY | | ☹ ☹ ☺ ☺ ☺ |
| LOG YOUR STUDY TIME | | TOTAL TIME |
| EACH BOX EQUALS 5 MINS. | | : |

**WEEK NUMBER:**

## THIS WEEK IN REVIEW

### VOCABULARY ACQUIRED

### BIGGEST ACHIEVEMENTS

☐　　　　　　　　　　　　☐

☐　　　　　　　　　　　　☐

☐　　　　　　　　　　　　☐

### AREAS FOR IMPROVEMENT

1

2

3

4

## THINGS THAT I STILL HAVE QUESTIONS ABOUT

|  |  |
|--|--|
|  |  |
|  |  |
|  |  |

## FINAL MEASUREMENTS OF THIS WEEK

| TOTAL TIME THIS WEEK | TOTAL NEW VERBS | TOTAL NEW WORDS |
|---|---|---|
|  |  |  |

## SELF-ASSESSMENT OF MY ACTIVITIES THIS WEEK

| ACTIVITIES | SPECIFIC ASSESSMENTS | SATISFACTION |
|---|---|---|
| READING |  | ☹ ☹ 😐 🙂 😊 |
| LISTENING |  | ☹ ☹ 😐 🙂 😊 |
| WRITING |  | ☹ ☹ 😐 🙂 😊 |
| SPEAKING |  | ☹ ☹ 😐 🙂 😊 |
| STUDYING |  | ☹ ☹ 😐 🙂 😊 |
| MOTIVATION |  | ☹ ☹ 😐 🙂 😊 |

| LOG YOUR STUDY TIME |  |  |  |  |  |  |  |  |  |  | TOTAL TIME |
|---|---|---|---|---|---|---|---|---|---|---|---|
| EACH BOX EQUALS 1 HOUR |  |  |  |  |  |  |  |  |  |  | : |

| DAY & DATE | | STUDY STREAK # | |
|---|---|---|---|
| LEARNING MOOD | ☹ ☹ 😐 🙂 😄 | # VERBS ACQUIRED | |

## PAST STUDIES IN REVIEW

| VOCABULARY FROM YESTERDAY | GOALS FROM YESTERDAY |
|---|---|
| 1 | ☐ |
| 2 | ☐ |
| 3 | ☐ |

| VOCABULARY FROM 5 DAYS AGO | VOCABULARY FROM 10 DAYS AGO |
|---|---|
| 1 | 1 |
| 2 | 2 |
| 3 | 3 |

## PRIORITIES FOR TODAY

| VOCABULARY FOR TODAY | GOALS FOR TODAY |
|---|---|
| 1 | ☐ |
| 2 | ☐ |
| 3 | ☐ |

## DESCRIBE YOUR LEARNING EXPERIENCE FOR TODAY

## SPECIAL WORDS FOR TODAY

| DAILY WORD BUILDER | VERB OF THE DAY | COGNATE OF THE DAY |
|---|---|---|
| **Dios** | **Andar** | **Convencional** |
| n. God. | To Walk, Go /g: Andando / pp: Andado /Irr. | Adjective. From: Conventional (AL=AL) |

## INTERESTING THINGS FROM TODAY

### FOUR SENTENCES THAT I READ, HEARD OR CREATED TODAY

**1**

**2**

**3**

**4**

## THINGS I HAVE QUESTIONS ABOUT

## DESCRIBE YOUR ACTIVITIES IN THESE TASKS FOR TODAY

| ACTIVITY | DESCRIPTION | SATISFACTION |
|---|---|---|
| READING | | ☹ 😟 😐 🙂 😊 |
| LISTENING | | ☹ 😟 😐 🙂 😊 |
| WRITING | | ☹ 😟 😐 🙂 😊 |
| SPEAKING | | ☹ 😟 😐 🙂 😊 |
| STUDYING | | ☹ 😟 😐 🙂 😊 |
| VOCABULARY | | ☹ 😟 😐 🙂 😊 |
| LOG YOUR STUDY TIME | | TOTAL TIME |
| EACH BOX EQUALS 5 MINS. | | : |

| DAY & DATE | | | STUDY STREAK # |
|---|---|---|---|
| LEARNING MOOD | ☹ ☹ 😐 🙂 😀 | | # VERBS ACQUIRED |

## PAST STUDIES IN REVIEW

| VOCABULARY FROM YESTERDAY | GOALS FROM YESTERDAY |
|---|---|
| 1 | ☐ |
| 2 | ☐ |
| 3 | ☐ |

| VOCABULARY FROM 5 DAYS AGO | VOCABULARY FROM 10 DAYS AGO |
|---|---|
| 1 | 1 |
| 2 | 2 |
| 3 | 3 |

## PRIORITIES FOR TODAY

| VOCABULARY FOR TODAY | GOALS FOR TODAY |
|---|---|
| 1 | ☐ |
| 2 | ☐ |
| 3 | ☐ |

## DESCRIBE YOUR LEARNING EXPERIENCE FOR TODAY

## SPECIAL WORDS FOR TODAY

| DAILY WORD BUILDER | VERB OF THE DAY | COGNATE OF THE DAY |
|---|---|---|
| **Dios No Lo Quiera** | **Llegar** | **Eventualmente** |
| intj. God forbid. | To Arrive, Come, Reach; To Bring Up, Bring Over; To Gather Together /g: Llegando / pp: Llegado /Irr. | Adverb. From: Eventually (LY=MENTE) |

## INTERESTING THINGS FROM TODAY

### FOUR SENTENCES THAT I READ, HEARD OR CREATED TODAY

**1**

**2**

**3**

**4**

## THINGS I HAVE QUESTIONS ABOUT

## DESCRIBE YOUR ACTIVITIES IN THESE TASKS FOR TODAY

| ACTIVITY | DESCRIPTION | SATISFACTION |
|----------|-------------|--------------|
| READING | | ☹ 😣 😐 🙂 😊 |
| LISTENING | | ☹ 😣 😐 🙂 😊 |
| WRITING | | ☹ 😣 😐 🙂 😊 |
| SPEAKING | | ☹ 😣 😐 🙂 😊 |
| STUDYING | | ☹ 😣 😐 🙂 😊 |
| VOCABULARY | | ☹ 😣 😐 🙂 😊 |

| LOG YOUR STUDY TIME | | | | | | | | | | | | | TOTAL TIME |
|---------------------|--|--|--|--|--|--|--|--|--|--|--|--|------------|
| EACH BOX EQUALS 5 MINS. | | | | | | | | | | | | | : |

| DAY & DATE | | | STUDY STREAK # | |
|---|---|---|---|---|
| LEARNING MOOD | ☹ ☹ 😐 🙂 😃 | | # VERBS ACQUIRED | |

## PAST STUDIES IN REVIEW

| VOCABULARY FROM YESTERDAY | GOALS FROM YESTERDAY |
|---|---|
| 1 | ☐ |
| 2 | ☐ |
| 3 | ☐ |

| VOCABULARY FROM 5 DAYS AGO | VOCABULARY FROM 10 DAYS AGO |
|---|---|
| 1 | 1 |
| 2 | 2 |
| 3 | 3 |

## PRIORITIES FOR TODAY

| VOCABULARY FOR TODAY | GOALS FOR TODAY |
|---|---|
| 1 | ☐ |
| 2 | ☐ |
| 3 | ☐ |

## DESCRIBE YOUR LEARNING EXPERIENCE FOR TODAY

## SPECIAL WORDS FOR TODAY

| DAILY WORD BUILDER | VERB OF THE DAY | COGNATE OF THE DAY |
|---|---|---|
| **Regalo de Dios** | **Tener** | **Coeficiente** |
| n. m. Gift of God. Godsend. | To Have /g: Teniendo / pp: Tenido /Irr. | Noun. From: Coefficient (NT=NTE) |

## INTERESTING THINGS FROM TODAY

### FOUR SENTENCES THAT I READ, HEARD OR CREATED TODAY

**1**

**2**

**3**

**4**

## THINGS I HAVE QUESTIONS ABOUT

## DESCRIBE YOUR ACTIVITIES IN THESE TASKS FOR TODAY

| ACTIVITY | DESCRIPTION | SATISFACTION |
|---|---|---|
| READING | | ☹ 🙁 😐 🙂 😃 |
| LISTENING | | ☹ 🙁 😐 🙂 😃 |
| WRITING | | ☹ 🙁 😐 🙂 😃 |
| SPEAKING | | ☹ 🙁 😐 🙂 😃 |
| STUDYING | | ☹ 🙁 😐 🙂 😃 |
| VOCABULARY | | ☹ 🙁 😐 🙂 😃 |

| LOG YOUR STUDY TIME | | TOTAL TIME |
|---|---|---|
| EACH BOX EQUALS 5 MINS. | | : |

| DAY & DATE | | STUDY STREAK # |
|---|---|---|
| LEARNING MOOD | ☹ ☹ 😐 🙂 😀 | # VERBS ACQUIRED |

## PAST STUDIES IN REVIEW

| VOCABULARY FROM YESTERDAY | GOALS FROM YESTERDAY |
|---|---|
| **1** | ☐ |
| **2** | ☐ |
| **3** | ☐ |

| VOCABULARY FROM 5 DAYS AGO | VOCABULARY FROM 10 DAYS AGO |
|---|---|
| **1** | **1** |
| **2** | **2** |
| **3** | **3** |

## PRIORITIES FOR TODAY

| VOCABULARY FOR TODAY | GOALS FOR TODAY |
|---|---|
| **1** | ☐ |
| **2** | ☐ |
| **3** | ☐ |

## DESCRIBE YOUR LEARNING EXPERIENCE FOR TODAY

_____

_____

_____

_____

## SPECIAL WORDS FOR TODAY

| DAILY WORD BUILDER | VERB OF THE DAY | COGNATE OF THE DAY |
|---|---|---|
| **Fe en Dios** | **Contestar** | **Tecnología** |
| n. f. Faith in God. Belief in God. | To Answer /g: Contestando / pp: Contestado | Noun. From: Technology (Y=IA OR ÍA) |

## INTERESTING THINGS FROM TODAY

### FOUR SENTENCES THAT I READ, HEARD OR CREATED TODAY

**1**

**2**

**3**

**4**

## THINGS I HAVE QUESTIONS ABOUT

## DESCRIBE YOUR ACTIVITIES IN THESE TASKS FOR TODAY

| ACTIVITY | DESCRIPTION | SATISFACTION |
|---|---|---|
| READING | | ☹ 🙁 😐 🙂 😊 |
| LISTENING | | ☹ 🙁 😐 🙂 😊 |
| WRITING | | ☹ 🙁 😐 🙂 😊 |
| SPEAKING | | ☹ 🙁 😐 🙂 😊 |
| STUDYING | | ☹ 🙁 😐 🙂 😊 |
| VOCABULARY | | ☹ 🙁 😐 🙂 😊 |

| LOG YOUR STUDY TIME | | | | | | | | | | | | | TOTAL TIME |
|---|---|---|---|---|---|---|---|---|---|---|---|---|---|
| EACH BOX EQUALS 5 MINS. | | | | | | | | | | | | | : |

| DAY & DATE | | STUDY STREAK # | |
|---|---|---|---|
| LEARNING MOOD | 😣 😦 😐 🙂 😃 | # VERBS ACQUIRED | |

## PAST STUDIES IN REVIEW

| VOCABULARY FROM YESTERDAY | GOALS FROM YESTERDAY |
|---|---|
| 1 | ☐ |
| 2 | ☐ |
| 3 | ☐ |

| VOCABULARY FROM 5 DAYS AGO | VOCABULARY FROM 10 DAYS AGO |
|---|---|
| 1 | 1 |
| 2 | 2 |
| 3 | 3 |

## PRIORITIES FOR TODAY

| VOCABULARY FOR TODAY | GOALS FOR TODAY |
|---|---|
| 1 | ☐ |
| 2 | ☐ |
| 3 | ☐ |

## DESCRIBE YOUR LEARNING EXPERIENCE FOR TODAY

## SPECIAL WORDS FOR TODAY

| DAILY WORD BUILDER | VERB OF THE DAY | COGNATE OF THE DAY |
|---|---|---|
| **Hombre de Dios** | **Lograr** | **Lunático** |
| n. m. Man of God | To Get, Obtain; To Achieve, Attain /g: Logrando / pp: Logrado | Noun. From: Lunatic (IC=ICO) |

## INTERESTING THINGS FROM TODAY

### FOUR SENTENCES THAT I READ, HEARD OR CREATED TODAY

**1**

**2**

**3**

**4**

## THINGS I HAVE QUESTIONS ABOUT

## DESCRIBE YOUR ACTIVITIES IN THESE TASKS FOR TODAY

| ACTIVITY | DESCRIPTION | SATISFACTION |
|----------|-------------|--------------|
| READING | | 😞😟😐😊😀 |
| LISTENING | | 😞😟😐😊😀 |
| WRITING | | 😞😟😐😊😀 |
| SPEAKING | | 😞😟😐😊😀 |
| STUDYING | | 😞😟😐😊😀 |
| VOCABULARY | | 😞😟😐😊😀 |

| LOG YOUR STUDY TIME | | TOTAL TIME |
|---------------------|--|------------|
| EACH BOX EQUALS 5 MINS. | | : |

| DAY & DATE | | | STUDY STREAK # | |
|---|---|---|---|---|
| LEARNING MOOD | ☹ ☹ 😐 🙂 😀 | | # VERBS ACQUIRED | |

## PAST STUDIES IN REVIEW

| VOCABULARY FROM YESTERDAY | GOALS FROM YESTERDAY |
|---|---|
| **1** | ☐ |
| **2** | ☐ |
| **3** | ☐ |

| VOCABULARY FROM 5 DAYS AGO | VOCABULARY FROM 10 DAYS AGO |
|---|---|
| **1** | **1** |
| **2** | **2** |
| **3** | **3** |

## PRIORITIES FOR TODAY

| VOCABULARY FOR TODAY | GOALS FOR TODAY |
|---|---|
| **1** | ☐ |
| **2** | ☐ |
| **3** | ☐ |

## DESCRIBE YOUR LEARNING EXPERIENCE FOR TODAY

## SPECIAL WORDS FOR TODAY

| DAILY WORD BUILDER | VERB OF THE DAY | COGNATE OF THE DAY |
|---|---|---|
| **Amor de Dios** | **Viajar** | **Muscular** |
| n. m. Love of God | To Travel, Journey /g: Viajando / pp: Viajado | Adjective. From: Muscular (AR=AR) |

## INTERESTING THINGS FROM TODAY

### FOUR SENTENCES THAT I READ, HEARD OR CREATED TODAY

**1**

**2**

**3**

**4**

## THINGS I HAVE QUESTIONS ABOUT

## DESCRIBE YOUR ACTIVITIES IN THESE TASKS FOR TODAY

| ACTIVITY | DESCRIPTION | SATISFACTION |
|---|---|---|
| READING | | ☹ 😕 😐 🙂 😊 |
| LISTENING | | ☹ 😕 😐 🙂 😊 |
| WRITING | | ☹ 😕 😐 🙂 😊 |
| SPEAKING | | ☹ 😕 😐 🙂 😊 |
| STUDYING | | ☹ 😕 😐 🙂 😊 |
| VOCABULARY | | ☹ 😕 😐 🙂 😊 |
| LOG YOUR STUDY TIME | | TOTAL TIME |
| EACH BOX EQUALS 5 MINS. | | : |

| DAY & DATE | | STUDY STREAK # | |
|---|---|---|---|
| LEARNING MOOD | ☹ ☹ 😐 🙂 😀 | # VERBS ACQUIRED | |

## PAST STUDIES IN REVIEW

| VOCABULARY FROM YESTERDAY | GOALS FROM YESTERDAY |
|---|---|
| 1 | ☐ |
| 2 | ☐ |
| 3 | ☐ |

| VOCABULARY FROM 5 DAYS AGO | VOCABULARY FROM 10 DAYS AGO |
|---|---|
| 1 | 1 |
| 2 | 2 |
| 3 | 3 |

## PRIORITIES FOR TODAY

| VOCABULARY FOR TODAY | GOALS FOR TODAY |
|---|---|
| 1 | ☐ |
| 2 | ☐ |
| 3 | ☐ |

## DESCRIBE YOUR LEARNING EXPERIENCE FOR TODAY

## SPECIAL WORDS FOR TODAY

| DAILY WORD BUILDER | VERB OF THE DAY | COGNATE OF THE DAY |
|---|---|---|
| **Temeroso de Dios** | **Atravesar** | **Abolicionista** |
| n. m. Fear of God. God-fearing. | To Cross, Cross Over, Go Across, Go Over, Pass Through /g: Atravesando / pp: Atravesado /Irr. | Adjective. From: Abolitionist (IST=ISTA) |

## INTERESTING THINGS FROM TODAY

### FOUR SENTENCES THAT I READ, HEARD OR CREATED TODAY

**1**

**2**

**3**

**4**

## THINGS I HAVE QUESTIONS ABOUT

## DESCRIBE YOUR ACTIVITIES IN THESE TASKS FOR TODAY

| ACTIVITY | DESCRIPTION | SATISFACTION |
|---|---|---|
| READING | | ☹ 🙁 😐 🙂 😃 |
| LISTENING | | ☹ 🙁 😐 🙂 😃 |
| WRITING | | ☹ 🙁 😐 🙂 😃 |
| SPEAKING | | ☹ 🙁 😐 🙂 😃 |
| STUDYING | | ☹ 🙁 😐 🙂 😃 |
| VOCABULARY | | ☹ 🙁 😐 🙂 😃 |

| LOG YOUR STUDY TIME | | | | | | | | | | | | | | TOTAL TIME |
|---|---|---|---|---|---|---|---|---|---|---|---|---|---|---|
| EACH BOX EQUALS 5 MINS. | | | | | | | | | | | | | | : |

**WEEK NUMBER:**

## THIS WEEK IN REVIEW

### VOCABULARY ACQUIRED

### BIGGEST ACHIEVEMENTS

☐                          ☐

☐                          ☐

☐                          ☐

### AREAS FOR IMPROVEMENT

1

2

3

4

## THINGS THAT I STILL HAVE QUESTIONS ABOUT

|  |  |
|---|---|
|  |  |
|  |  |
|  |  |

## FINAL MEASUREMENTS OF THIS WEEK

| TOTAL TIME THIS WEEK | TOTAL NEW VERBS | TOTAL NEW WORDS |
|---|---|---|
|  |  |  |

## SELF-ASSESSMENT OF MY ACTIVITIES THIS WEEK

| ACTIVITIES | SPECIFIC ASSESSMENTS | SATISFACTION |
|---|---|---|
| READING |  | ☹ ☹ 😐 ☺ ☺ |
| LISTENING |  | ☹ ☹ 😐 ☺ ☺ |
| WRITING |  | ☹ ☹ 😐 ☺ ☺ |
| SPEAKING |  | ☹ ☹ 😐 ☺ ☺ |
| STUDYING |  | ☹ ☹ 😐 ☺ ☺ |
| MOTIVATION |  | ☹ ☹ 😐 ☺ ☺ |

| LOG YOUR STUDY TIME | TOTAL TIME |
|---|---|
| EACH BOX EQUALS 1 HOUR | : |

| DAY & DATE | | | STUDY STREAK # | |
|---|---|---|---|---|
| LEARNING MOOD | ☹ ☹ 😐 🙂 😀 | | # VERBS ACQUIRED | |

## PAST STUDIES IN REVIEW

| VOCABULARY FROM YESTERDAY | GOALS FROM YESTERDAY |
|---|---|
| 1 | ☐ |
| 2 | ☐ |
| 3 | ☐ |

| VOCABULARY FROM 5 DAYS AGO | VOCABULARY FROM 10 DAYS AGO |
|---|---|
| 1 | 1 |
| 2 | 2 |
| 3 | 3 |

## PRIORITIES FOR TODAY

| VOCABULARY FOR TODAY | GOALS FOR TODAY |
|---|---|
| 1 | ☐ |
| 2 | ☐ |
| 3 | ☐ |

## DESCRIBE YOUR LEARNING EXPERIENCE FOR TODAY

## SPECIAL WORDS FOR TODAY

| DAILY WORD BUILDER | VERB OF THE DAY | COGNATE OF THE DAY |
|---|---|---|
| **Pago** | **Apagar** | **Afortunadamente** |
| n. m. Payment. Payout. Fee. Paying | To Extinguish, Put Out, Turn Off /g: Apagando / pp: Apagado /Irr. | Adverb. From: Fortunately (LY=MENTE) |

## INTERESTING THINGS FROM TODAY

### FOUR SENTENCES THAT I READ, HEARD OR CREATED TODAY

**1**

**2**

**3**

**4**

## THINGS I HAVE QUESTIONS ABOUT

## DESCRIBE YOUR ACTIVITIES IN THESE TASKS FOR TODAY

| ACTIVITY | DESCRIPTION | SATISFACTION |
|---|---|---|
| READING | | 😞 😟 😐 😊 😃 |
| LISTENING | | 😞 😟 😐 😊 😃 |
| WRITING | | 😞 😟 😐 😊 😃 |
| SPEAKING | | 😞 😟 😐 😊 😃 |
| STUDYING | | 😞 😟 😐 😊 😃 |
| VOCABULARY | | 😞 😟 😐 😊 😃 |

| LOG YOUR STUDY TIME | | TOTAL TIME |
|---|---|---|
| EACH BOX EQUALS 5 MINS. | | : |

| DAY & DATE | | STUDY STREAK # |
|---|---|---|
| LEARNING MOOD  ☹ ☹ 😐 🙂 😀 | | # VERBS ACQUIRED |

## PAST STUDIES IN REVIEW

| VOCABULARY FROM YESTERDAY | GOALS FROM YESTERDAY |
|---|---|
| 1 | ☐ |
| 2 | ☐ |
| 3 | ☐ |

| VOCABULARY FROM 5 DAYS AGO | VOCABULARY FROM 10 DAYS AGO |
|---|---|
| 1 | 1 |
| 2 | 2 |
| 3 | 3 |

## PRIORITIES FOR TODAY

| VOCABULARY FOR TODAY | GOALS FOR TODAY |
|---|---|
| 1 | ☐ |
| 2 | ☐ |
| 3 | ☐ |

## DESCRIBE YOUR LEARNING EXPERIENCE FOR TODAY

## SPECIAL WORDS FOR TODAY

| DAILY WORD BUILDER | VERB OF THE DAY | COGNATE OF THE DAY |
|---|---|---|
| **Forma de Pago** | **Llover** | **Obediente** |
| n. f. Form of payment. Payment method, mode. | To Rain /g: Lloviendo / pp: Llovido /Irr. | Adjective. From: Obedient (NT=NTE) |

## INTERESTING THINGS FROM TODAY

### FOUR SENTENCES THAT I READ, HEARD OR CREATED TODAY

**1**

**2**

**3**

**4**

## THINGS I HAVE QUESTIONS ABOUT

## DESCRIBE YOUR ACTIVITIES IN THESE TASKS FOR TODAY

| ACTIVITY | DESCRIPTION | SATISFACTION |
|---|---|---|
| READING | | 😫 😖 😐 😊 😄 |
| LISTENING | | 😫 😖 😐 😊 😄 |
| WRITING | | 😫 😖 😐 😊 😄 |
| SPEAKING | | 😫 😖 😐 😊 😄 |
| STUDYING | | 😫 😖 😐 😊 😄 |
| VOCABULARY | | 😫 😖 😐 😊 😄 |

| LOG YOUR STUDY TIME | | | | | | | | | | | | | | | TOTAL TIME |
|---|---|---|---|---|---|---|---|---|---|---|---|---|---|---|---|
| EACH BOX EQUALS 5 MINS. | | | | | | | | | | | | | | | : |

| LEARNING MOOD | ☹ ☹ 😐 🙂 😃 | # VERBS ACQUIRED |

## PAST STUDIES IN REVIEW

| VOCABULARY FROM YESTERDAY | GOALS FROM YESTERDAY |
| --- | --- |
| 1 | ☐ |
| 2 | ☐ |
| 3 | ☐ |

| VOCABULARY FROM 5 DAYS AGO | VOCABULARY FROM 10 DAYS AGO |
| --- | --- |
| 1 | 1 |
| 2 | 2 |
| 3 | 3 |

## PRIORITIES FOR TODAY

| VOCABULARY FOR TODAY | GOALS FOR TODAY |
| --- | --- |
| 1 | ☐ |
| 2 | ☐ |
| 3 | ☐ |

## DESCRIBE YOUR LEARNING EXPERIENCE FOR TODAY

## SPECIAL WORDS FOR TODAY

| DAILY WORD BUILDER | VERB OF THE DAY | COGNATE OF THE DAY |
| --- | --- | --- |
| **Comprobante de Pago** | **Tocar** | **Eficiente** |
| n. m. Proof of payment. Receipt. | To Touch; To Play /g: Tocando / pp: Tocado /Irr. | Adjective. From: Efficient (NT=NTE) |

## INTERESTING THINGS FROM TODAY

### FOUR SENTENCES THAT I READ, HEARD OR CREATED TODAY

**1**

**2**

**3**

**4**

## THINGS I HAVE QUESTIONS ABOUT

## DESCRIBE YOUR ACTIVITIES IN THESE TASKS FOR TODAY

| ACTIVITY | DESCRIPTION | SATISFACTION |
|---|---|---|
| READING | | ☹ ☹ 😐 😊 😄 |
| LISTENING | | ☹ ☹ 😐 😊 😄 |
| WRITING | | ☹ ☹ 😐 😊 😄 |
| SPEAKING | | ☹ ☹ 😐 😊 😄 |
| STUDYING | | ☹ ☹ 😐 😊 😄 |
| VOCABULARY | | ☹ ☹ 😐 😊 😄 |
| LOG YOUR STUDY TIME | | TOTAL TIME |
| EACH BOX EQUALS 5 MINS. | | : |

| DAY & DATE | | STUDY STREAK # |
|---|---|---|
| LEARNING MOOD | ☹ ☹ 😐 🙂 😀 | # VERBS ACQUIRED |

## PAST STUDIES IN REVIEW

| VOCABULARY FROM YESTERDAY | GOALS FROM YESTERDAY |
|---|---|
| 1 | ☐ |
| 2 | ☐ |
| 3 | ☐ |

| VOCABULARY FROM 5 DAYS AGO | VOCABULARY FROM 10 DAYS AGO |
|---|---|
| 1 | 1 |
| 2 | 2 |
| 3 | 3 |

## PRIORITIES FOR TODAY

| VOCABULARY FOR TODAY | GOALS FOR TODAY |
|---|---|
| 1 | ☐ |
| 2 | ☐ |
| 3 | ☐ |

## DESCRIBE YOUR LEARNING EXPERIENCE FOR TODAY

_____

_____

_____

_____

## SPECIAL WORDS FOR TODAY

| DAILY WORD BUILDER | VERB OF THE DAY | COGNATE OF THE DAY |
|---|---|---|
| **Carta de Pago** | **Correr** | **Glorioso** |
| n. f. Paying-in-slip. Payment card. | To Run /g: Corriendo / pp: Corrido | Adjective. From: Glorious (OUS=OSO) |

## INTERESTING THINGS FROM TODAY

### FOUR SENTENCES THAT I READ, HEARD OR CREATED TODAY

**1**

**2**

**3**

**4**

## THINGS I HAVE QUESTIONS ABOUT

## DESCRIBE YOUR ACTIVITIES IN THESE TASKS FOR TODAY

| ACTIVITY | DESCRIPTION | SATISFACTION |
|---|---|---|
| READING | | ☹️ 🙁 😐 🙂 😃 |
| LISTENING | | ☹️ 🙁 😐 🙂 😃 |
| WRITING | | ☹️ 🙁 😐 🙂 😃 |
| SPEAKING | | ☹️ 🙁 😐 🙂 😃 |
| STUDYING | | ☹️ 🙁 😐 🙂 😃 |
| VOCABULARY | | ☹️ 🙁 😐 🙂 😃 |
| LOG YOUR STUDY TIME | | TOTAL TIME |
| EACH BOX EQUALS 5 MINS. | | : |

| DAY & DATE | | STUDY STREAK # |
|---|---|---|
| LEARNING MOOD | ☹ ☹ 😐 🙂 😀 | # VERBS ACQUIRED |

## PAST STUDIES IN REVIEW

| VOCABULARY FROM YESTERDAY | GOALS FROM YESTERDAY |
|---|---|
| 1 | ☐ |
| 2 | ☐ |
| 3 | ☐ |

| VOCABULARY FROM 5 DAYS AGO | VOCABULARY FROM 10 DAYS AGO |
|---|---|
| 1 | 1 |
| 2 | 2 |
| 3 | 3 |

## PRIORITIES FOR TODAY

| VOCABULARY FOR TODAY | GOALS FOR TODAY |
|---|---|
| 1 | ☐ |
| 2 | ☐ |
| 3 | ☐ |

## DESCRIBE YOUR LEARNING EXPERIENCE FOR TODAY

## SPECIAL WORDS FOR TODAY

| DAILY WORD BUILDER | VERB OF THE DAY | COGNATE OF THE DAY |
|---|---|---|
| **Justificante de Pago** | **Manejar** | **Contribución** |
| n. m. Proof of payment. Receipt | To Drive /g: Manejando / pp: Manejado | Noun. From: Contribution (TION=CIÓN) |

## INTERESTING THINGS FROM TODAY

### FOUR SENTENCES THAT I READ, HEARD OR CREATED TODAY

**1**

**2**

**3**

**4**

## THINGS I HAVE QUESTIONS ABOUT

## DESCRIBE YOUR ACTIVITIES IN THESE TASKS FOR TODAY

| ACTIVITY | DESCRIPTION | SATISFACTION |
|----------|-------------|--------------|
| READING | | ☹ ☹ 😐 🙂 😄 |
| LISTENING | | ☹ ☹ 😐 🙂 😄 |
| WRITING | | ☹ ☹ 😐 🙂 😄 |
| SPEAKING | | ☹ ☹ 😐 🙂 😄 |
| STUDYING | | ☹ ☹ 😐 🙂 😄 |
| VOCABULARY | | ☹ ☹ 😐 🙂 😄 |

| LOG YOUR STUDY TIME | | | | | | | | | | | | | | TOTAL TIME |
|---------------------|--|--|--|--|--|--|--|--|--|--|--|--|--|------------|
| EACH BOX EQUALS 5 MINS. | | | | | | | | | | | | | | : |

| DAY & DATE | | | | STUDY STREAK # | |
|---|---|---|---|---|---|
| LEARNING MOOD | ☹ ☹ 😐 🙂 😀 | | | # VERBS ACQUIRED | |

## PAST STUDIES IN REVIEW

| VOCABULARY FROM YESTERDAY | GOALS FROM YESTERDAY |
|---|---|
| 1 | ☐ |
| 2 | ☐ |
| 3 | ☐ |

| VOCABULARY FROM 5 DAYS AGO | VOCABULARY FROM 10 DAYS AGO |
|---|---|
| 1 | 1 |
| 2 | 2 |
| 3 | 3 |

## PRIORITIES FOR TODAY

| VOCABULARY FOR TODAY | GOALS FOR TODAY |
|---|---|
| 1 | ☐ |
| 2 | ☐ |
| 3 | ☐ |

## DESCRIBE YOUR LEARNING EXPERIENCE FOR TODAY

## SPECIAL WORDS FOR TODAY

| DAILY WORD BUILDER | VERB OF THE DAY | COGNATE OF THE DAY |
|---|---|---|
| **Condiciones de Pago** | **Vivir** | **Distribución** |
| n. f. Payment terms. Repayment terms. | To Live /g: Viviendo / pp: Vivido | Noun. From: Distribution (TION=CIÓN) |

## INTERESTING THINGS FROM TODAY

### FOUR SENTENCES THAT I READ, HEARD OR CREATED TODAY

**1**

**2**

**3**

**4**

## THINGS I HAVE QUESTIONS ABOUT

## DESCRIBE YOUR ACTIVITIES IN THESE TASKS FOR TODAY

| ACTIVITY | DESCRIPTION | SATISFACTION |
|---|---|---|
| READING | | ☹ ☹ 😐 🙂 😄 |
| LISTENING | | ☹ ☹ 😐 🙂 😄 |
| WRITING | | ☹ ☹ 😐 🙂 😄 |
| SPEAKING | | ☹ ☹ 😐 🙂 😄 |
| STUDYING | | ☹ ☹ 😐 🙂 😄 |
| VOCABULARY | | ☹ ☹ 😐 🙂 😄 |

| LOG YOUR STUDY TIME | | TOTAL TIME |
|---|---|---|
| EACH BOX EQUALS 5 MINS. | | : |

| DAY & DATE | | STUDY STREAK # | |
|---|---|---|---|
| LEARNING MOOD | ☹ ☹ ☺ ☺ ☺ | # VERBS ACQUIRED | |

## PAST STUDIES IN REVIEW

| VOCABULARY FROM YESTERDAY | GOALS FROM YESTERDAY |
|---|---|
| 1 | ☐ |
| 2 | ☐ |
| 3 | ☐ |

| VOCABULARY FROM 5 DAYS AGO | VOCABULARY FROM 10 DAYS AGO |
|---|---|
| 1 | 1 |
| 2 | 2 |
| 3 | 3 |

## PRIORITIES FOR TODAY

| VOCABULARY FOR TODAY | GOALS FOR TODAY |
|---|---|
| 1 | ☐ |
| 2 | ☐ |
| 3 | ☐ |

## DESCRIBE YOUR LEARNING EXPERIENCE FOR TODAY

## SPECIAL WORDS FOR TODAY

| DAILY WORD BUILDER | VERB OF THE DAY | COGNATE OF THE DAY |
|---|---|---|
| **Recibo de Pago** | **Avanzar** | **Arrogante** |
| n. m. Payment receipt. Receipt tape. | To Advance, Move Forward /g: Avanzando / pp: Avanzado /Irr. | Adjective. From: Arrogant (NT=NTE) |

## INTERESTING THINGS FROM TODAY

### FOUR SENTENCES THAT I READ, HEARD OR CREATED TODAY

**1**

**2**

**3**

**4**

## THINGS I HAVE QUESTIONS ABOUT

## DESCRIBE YOUR ACTIVITIES IN THESE TASKS FOR TODAY

| ACTIVITY | DESCRIPTION | SATISFACTION |
|---|---|---|
| READING | | 😟 😣 😐 🙂 😃 |
| LISTENING | | 😟 😣 😐 🙂 😃 |
| WRITING | | 😟 😣 😐 🙂 😃 |
| SPEAKING | | 😟 😣 😐 🙂 😃 |
| STUDYING | | 😟 😣 😐 🙂 😃 |
| VOCABULARY | | 😟 😣 😐 🙂 😃 |

| LOG YOUR STUDY TIME | | | | | | | | | | | | | TOTAL TIME |
|---|---|---|---|---|---|---|---|---|---|---|---|---|---|
| EACH BOX EQUALS 5 MINS. | | | | | | | | | | | | | : |

## THIS WEEK IN REVIEW

### VOCABULARY ACQUIRED

### BIGGEST ACHIEVEMENTS

☐ | ☐
☐ | ☐
☐ | ☐

### AREAS FOR IMPROVEMENT

1
2
3
4

## THINGS THAT I STILL HAVE QUESTIONS ABOUT

| | |
|---|---|
| | |
| | |
| | |

## FINAL MEASUREMENTS OF THIS WEEK

| TOTAL TIME THIS WEEK | TOTAL NEW VERBS | TOTAL NEW WORDS |
|---|---|---|
| | | |

## SELF-ASSESSMENT OF MY ACTIVITIES THIS WEEK

| ACTIVITIES | SPECIFIC ASSESSMENTS | SATISFACTION |
|---|---|---|
| READING | | ☹ ☹ 😐 ☺ ☺ |
| LISTENING | | ☹ ☹ 😐 ☺ ☺ |
| WRITING | | ☹ ☹ 😐 ☺ ☺ |
| SPEAKING | | ☹ ☹ 😐 ☺ ☺ |
| STUDYING | | ☹ ☹ 😐 ☺ ☺ |
| MOTIVATION | | ☹ ☹ 😐 ☺ ☺ |
| LOG YOUR STUDY TIME | | TOTAL TIME |
| EACH BOX EQUALS 1 HOUR | | : |

| DAY & DATE | | STUDY STREAK # |
| --- | --- | --- |
| LEARNING MOOD | ☹ ☹ 😐 🙂 😄 | # VERBS ACQUIRED |

## PAST STUDIES IN REVIEW

| VOCABULARY FROM YESTERDAY | GOALS FROM YESTERDAY |
| --- | --- |
| 1 | ☐ |
| 2 | ☐ |
| 3 | ☐ |

| VOCABULARY FROM 5 DAYS AGO | VOCABULARY FROM 10 DAYS AGO |
| --- | --- |
| 1 | 1 |
| 2 | 2 |
| 3 | 3 |

## PRIORITIES FOR TODAY

| VOCABULARY FOR TODAY | GOALS FOR TODAY |
| --- | --- |
| 1 | ☐ |
| 2 | ☐ |
| 3 | ☐ |

## DESCRIBE YOUR LEARNING EXPERIENCE FOR TODAY

## SPECIAL WORDS FOR TODAY

| DAILY WORD BUILDER | VERB OF THE DAY | COGNATE OF THE DAY |
| --- | --- | --- |
| **Semana** | **Buscar** | **Aumentar** |
| n. f. Week. | To Search For, Look For /g: Buscando / pp: Buscado /Irr. | Verb. From: Augment (ADDING AR OR IR) |

## INTERESTING THINGS FROM TODAY

### FOUR SENTENCES THAT I READ, HEARD OR CREATED TODAY

**1**

**2**

**3**

**4**

## THINGS I HAVE QUESTIONS ABOUT

## DESCRIBE YOUR ACTIVITIES IN THESE TASKS FOR TODAY

| ACTIVITY | DESCRIPTION | SATISFACTION |
|---|---|---|
| READING | | 😖😟😐🙂😄 |
| LISTENING | | 😖😟😐🙂😄 |
| WRITING | | 😖😟😐🙂😄 |
| SPEAKING | | 😖😟😐🙂😄 |
| STUDYING | | 😖😟😐🙂😄 |
| VOCABULARY | | 😖😟😐🙂😄 |

| LOG YOUR STUDY TIME | | TOTAL TIME |
|---|---|---|
| EACH BOX EQUALS 5 MINS. | | : |

| LEARNING MOOD | 😧 😦 😐 🙂 😃 | # VERBS ACQUIRED |

## PAST STUDIES IN REVIEW

| VOCABULARY FROM YESTERDAY | GOALS FROM YESTERDAY |
|---|---|
| **1** | ☐ |
| **2** | ☐ |
| **3** | ☐ |

| VOCABULARY FROM 5 DAYS AGO | VOCABULARY FROM 10 DAYS AGO |
|---|---|
| **1** | **1** |
| **2** | **2** |
| **3** | **3** |

## PRIORITIES FOR TODAY

| VOCABULARY FOR TODAY | GOALS FOR TODAY |
|---|---|
| **1** | ☐ |
| **2** | ☐ |
| **3** | ☐ |

## DESCRIBE YOUR LEARNING EXPERIENCE FOR TODAY

## SPECIAL WORDS FOR TODAY

| DAILY WORD BUILDER | VERB OF THE DAY | COGNATE OF THE DAY |
|---|---|---|
| **Semana Santa** | **Mentir** | **Equivalente** |
| n. f. Easter. Holy Week. | To Lie /g: Mintiendo / pp: Mentido /Irr. | Adjective. From: Equivalent (NT=NTE) |

## INTERESTING THINGS FROM TODAY

### FOUR SENTENCES THAT I READ, HEARD OR CREATED TODAY

**1**

**2**

**3**

**4**

## THINGS I HAVE QUESTIONS ABOUT

## DESCRIBE YOUR ACTIVITIES IN THESE TASKS FOR TODAY

| ACTIVITY | DESCRIPTION | SATISFACTION |
|---|---|---|
| READING | | ☹ ☹ 😐 🙂 😊 |
| LISTENING | | ☹ ☹ 😐 🙂 😊 |
| WRITING | | ☹ ☹ 😐 🙂 😊 |
| SPEAKING | | ☹ ☹ 😐 🙂 😊 |
| STUDYING | | ☹ ☹ 😐 🙂 😊 |
| VOCABULARY | | ☹ ☹ 😐 🙂 😊 |

| LOG YOUR STUDY TIME | | | | | | | | | | | | | TOTAL TIME |
|---|---|---|---|---|---|---|---|---|---|---|---|---|---|
| EACH BOX EQUALS 5 MINS. | | | | | | | | | | | | | : |

| DAY & DATE | | | STUDY STREAK # | |
|---|---|---|---|---|
| LEARNING MOOD | ☹ ☹ 😐 🙂 😀 | | # VERBS ACQUIRED | |

## PAST STUDIES IN REVIEW

| VOCABULARY FROM YESTERDAY | GOALS FROM YESTERDAY |
|---|---|
| 1 | ☐ |
| 2 | ☐ |
| 3 | ☐ |

| VOCABULARY FROM 5 DAYS AGO | VOCABULARY FROM 10 DAYS AGO |
|---|---|
| 1 | 1 |
| 2 | 2 |
| 3 | 3 |

## PRIORITIES FOR TODAY

| VOCABULARY FOR TODAY | GOALS FOR TODAY |
|---|---|
| 1 | ☐ |
| 2 | ☐ |
| 3 | ☐ |

## DESCRIBE YOUR LEARNING EXPERIENCE FOR TODAY

## SPECIAL WORDS FOR TODAY

| DAILY WORD BUILDER | VERB OF THE DAY | COGNATE OF THE DAY |
|---|---|---|
| **Entre Semana** | **Traer** | **Válido** |
| adv. Midweek. | To Bring; To Get, Fetch; To Carry /g: Trayendo / pp: Traído /Irr. | Adjective. From: Timid (ID=IDO) |

# INTERESTING THINGS FROM TODAY

## FOUR SENTENCES THAT I READ, HEARD OR CREATED TODAY

**1**

**2**

**3**

**4**

# THINGS I HAVE QUESTIONS ABOUT

# DESCRIBE YOUR ACTIVITIES IN THESE TASKS FOR TODAY

| ACTIVITY | DESCRIPTION | SATISFACTION |
|---|---|---|
| READING | | 😞😟😐😊😃 |
| LISTENING | | 😞😟😐😊😃 |
| WRITING | | 😞😟😐😊😃 |
| SPEAKING | | 😞😟😐😊😃 |
| STUDYING | | 😞😟😐😊😃 |
| VOCABULARY | | 😞😟😐😊😃 |

| LOG YOUR STUDY TIME | | | | | | | | | | | | | | | TOTAL TIME |
|---|---|---|---|---|---|---|---|---|---|---|---|---|---|---|---|
| EACH BOX EQUALS 5 MINS. | | | | | | | | | | | | | | | : |

## PAST STUDIES IN REVIEW

| VOCABULARY FROM YESTERDAY | GOALS FROM YESTERDAY |
|---|---|
| **1** | ☐ |
| **2** | ☐ |
| **3** | ☐ |

| VOCABULARY FROM 5 DAYS AGO | VOCABULARY FROM 10 DAYS AGO |
|---|---|
| **1** | **1** |
| **2** | **2** |
| **3** | **3** |

## PRIORITIES FOR TODAY

| VOCABULARY FOR TODAY | GOALS FOR TODAY |
|---|---|
| **1** | ☐ |
| **2** | ☐ |
| **3** | ☐ |

## DESCRIBE YOUR LEARNING EXPERIENCE FOR TODAY

## SPECIAL WORDS FOR TODAY

| DAILY WORD BUILDER | VERB OF THE DAY | COGNATE OF THE DAY |
|---|---|---|
| **Semanal** | **Cuidar** | **Radiador** |
| adj. m. Weekly. Weekly paper | To Take Care Of, Look After /g: Cuidando / pp: Cuidado | Noun. From: Radiator (OR=OR) |

## INTERESTING THINGS FROM TODAY

### FOUR SENTENCES THAT I READ, HEARD OR CREATED TODAY

**1**

**2**

**3**

**4**

## THINGS I HAVE QUESTIONS ABOUT

## DESCRIBE YOUR ACTIVITIES IN THESE TASKS FOR TODAY

| ACTIVITY | DESCRIPTION | SATISFACTION |
|---|---|---|
| READING | | ☹ ☹ 😐 🙂 😄 |
| LISTENING | | ☹ ☹ 😐 🙂 😄 |
| WRITING | | ☹ ☹ 😐 🙂 😄 |
| SPEAKING | | ☹ ☹ 😐 🙂 😄 |
| STUDYING | | ☹ ☹ 😐 🙂 😄 |
| VOCABULARY | | ☹ ☹ 😐 🙂 😄 |

| LOG YOUR STUDY TIME | | | | | | | | | | | | | | TOTAL TIME |
|---|---|---|---|---|---|---|---|---|---|---|---|---|---|---|
| EACH BOX EQUALS 5 MINS. | | | | | | | | | | | | | | : |

| DAY & DATE | | STUDY STREAK # |
|---|---|---|
| LEARNING MOOD ☹ ☹ 😐 🙂 😃 | | # VERBS ACQUIRED |

## PAST STUDIES IN REVIEW

| VOCABULARY FROM YESTERDAY | GOALS FROM YESTERDAY |
|---|---|
| 1 | ☐ |
| 2 | ☐ |
| 3 | ☐ |

| VOCABULARY FROM 5 DAYS AGO | VOCABULARY FROM 10 DAYS AGO |
|---|---|
| 1 | 1 |
| 2 | 2 |
| 3 | 3 |

## PRIORITIES FOR TODAY

| VOCABULARY FOR TODAY | GOALS FOR TODAY |
|---|---|
| 1 | ☐ |
| 2 | ☐ |
| 3 | ☐ |

## DESCRIBE YOUR LEARNING EXPERIENCE FOR TODAY

## SPECIAL WORDS FOR TODAY

| DAILY WORD BUILDER | VERB OF THE DAY | COGNATE OF THE DAY |
|---|---|---|
| **Semanalente** | **Matar** | **Expresionismo** |
| adv. Weekly | To Kill, Slay, Slaughter /g: Matando / pp: Matado | Noun. From: Expressionism (ISM=ISMO) |

## INTERESTING THINGS FROM TODAY

### FOUR SENTENCES THAT I READ, HEARD OR CREATED TODAY

**1**

**2**

**3**

**4**

## THINGS I HAVE QUESTIONS ABOUT

## DESCRIBE YOUR ACTIVITIES IN THESE TASKS FOR TODAY

| ACTIVITY | DESCRIPTION | SATISFACTION |
|---|---|---|
| READING | | ☹ 🙁 😐 🙂 😃 |
| LISTENING | | ☹ 🙁 😐 🙂 😃 |
| WRITING | | ☹ 🙁 😐 🙂 😃 |
| SPEAKING | | ☹ 🙁 😐 🙂 😃 |
| STUDYING | | ☹ 🙁 😐 🙂 😃 |
| VOCABULARY | | ☹ 🙁 😐 🙂 😃 |

| LOG YOUR STUDY TIME | | TOTAL TIME |
|---|---|---|
| EACH BOX EQUALS 5 MINS. | | : |

| DAY & DATE | | STUDY STREAK # |
|---|---|---|
| LEARNING MOOD | ☹ ☹ 😐 🙂 😀 | # VERBS ACQUIRED |

## PAST STUDIES IN REVIEW

| VOCABULARY FROM YESTERDAY | GOALS FROM YESTERDAY |
|---|---|
| **1** | ☐ |
| **2** | ☐ |
| **3** | ☐ |

| VOCABULARY FROM 5 DAYS AGO | VOCABULARY FROM 10 DAYS AGO |
|---|---|
| **1** | **1** |
| **2** | **2** |
| **3** | **3** |

## PRIORITIES FOR TODAY

| VOCABULARY FOR TODAY | GOALS FOR TODAY |
|---|---|
| **1** | ☐ |
| **2** | ☐ |
| **3** | ☐ |

## DESCRIBE YOUR LEARNING EXPERIENCE FOR TODAY

## SPECIAL WORDS FOR TODAY

| DAILY WORD BUILDER | VERB OF THE DAY | COGNATE OF THE DAY |
|---|---|---|
| **Toda la Semana** | **Abrazar** | **Identidad** |
| n. f. Entire week | To Hug, Embrace /g: Abrazando / pp: Abrazado /Irr. | Noun. From: Identity (TY=IDAD) |

## INTERESTING THINGS FROM TODAY

### FOUR SENTENCES THAT I READ, HEARD OR CREATED TODAY

**1**

**2**

**3**

**4**

## THINGS I HAVE QUESTIONS ABOUT

## DESCRIBE YOUR ACTIVITIES IN THESE TASKS FOR TODAY

| ACTIVITY | DESCRIPTION | SATISFACTION |
|----------|-------------|--------------|
| READING | | 😩 😟 😐 😊 😃 |
| LISTENING | | 😩 😟 😐 😊 😃 |
| WRITING | | 😩 😟 😐 😊 😃 |
| SPEAKING | | 😩 😟 😐 😊 😃 |
| STUDYING | | 😩 😟 😐 😊 😃 |
| VOCABULARY | | 😩 😟 😐 😊 😃 |

| LOG YOUR STUDY TIME | | | | | | | | | | | | | | | TOTAL TIME |
|---|---|---|---|---|---|---|---|---|---|---|---|---|---|---|---|
| EACH BOX EQUALS 5 MINS. | | | | | | | | | | | | | | | : |

| DAY & DATE | | STUDY STREAK # |
|---|---|---|
| LEARNING MOOD | ☹ ☹ 😐 🙂 😀 | # VERBS ACQUIRED |

## PAST STUDIES IN REVIEW

| VOCABULARY FROM YESTERDAY | GOALS FROM YESTERDAY |
|---|---|
| 1 | ☐ |
| 2 | ☐ |
| 3 | ☐ |

| VOCABULARY FROM 5 DAYS AGO | VOCABULARY FROM 10 DAYS AGO |
|---|---|
| 1 | 1 |
| 2 | 2 |
| 3 | 3 |

## PRIORITIES FOR TODAY

| VOCABULARY FOR TODAY | GOALS FOR TODAY |
|---|---|
| 1 | ☐ |
| 2 | ☐ |
| 3 | ☐ |

## DESCRIBE YOUR LEARNING EXPERIENCE FOR TODAY

## SPECIAL WORDS FOR TODAY

| DAILY WORD BUILDER | VERB OF THE DAY | COGNATE OF THE DAY |
|---|---|---|
| **Semanario** | **Bautizar** | **Lunar** |
| n. m. Weekly. Weekly newspaper. | To Baptize, Christen /g: Bautizando / pp: Bautizado /Irr. | Noun. From: Lunar (AR=AR) |

## INTERESTING THINGS FROM TODAY

### FOUR SENTENCES THAT I READ, HEARD OR CREATED TODAY

**1**

**2**

**3**

**4**

## THINGS I HAVE QUESTIONS ABOUT

## DESCRIBE YOUR ACTIVITIES IN THESE TASKS FOR TODAY

| ACTIVITY | DESCRIPTION | SATISFACTION |
|----------|-------------|--------------|
| READING | | ☹️ 🙁 😐 🙂 😊 |
| LISTENING | | ☹️ 🙁 😐 🙂 😊 |
| WRITING | | ☹️ 🙁 😐 🙂 😊 |
| SPEAKING | | ☹️ 🙁 😐 🙂 😊 |
| STUDYING | | ☹️ 🙁 😐 🙂 😊 |
| VOCABULARY | | ☹️ 🙁 😐 🙂 😊 |
| LOG YOUR STUDY TIME | | TOTAL TIME |
| EACH BOX EQUALS 5 MINS. | | : |

## THIS WEEK IN REVIEW

### VOCABULARY ACQUIRED

### BIGGEST ACHIEVEMENTS

- [ ]                          - [ ]
- [ ]                          - [ ]
- [ ]                          - [ ]

### AREAS FOR IMPROVEMENT

1. 
2. 
3. 
4.

## THINGS THAT I STILL HAVE QUESTIONS ABOUT

| | |
|---|---|
| | |
| | |
| | |

## FINAL MEASUREMENTS OF THIS WEEK

| TOTAL TIME THIS WEEK | TOTAL NEW VERBS | TOTAL NEW WORDS |
|---|---|---|
| | | |

## SELF-ASSESSMENT OF MY ACTIVITIES THIS WEEK

| ACTIVITIES | SPECIFIC ASSESSMENTS | SATISFACTION |
|---|---|---|
| READING | | ☹ ☹ 😐 ☺ ☺ |
| LISTENING | | ☹ ☹ 😐 ☺ ☺ |
| WRITING | | ☹ ☹ 😐 ☺ ☺ |
| SPEAKING | | ☹ ☹ 😐 ☺ ☺ |
| STUDYING | | ☹ ☹ 😐 ☺ ☺ |
| MOTIVATION | | ☹ ☹ 😐 ☺ ☺ |
| LOG YOUR STUDY TIME | | TOTAL TIME |
| EACH BOX EQUALS 1 HOUR | | : |

| DAY & DATE | | STUDY STREAK # |
|---|---|---|
| LEARNING MOOD | ☹ 😟 😐 🙂 😀 | # VERBS ACQUIRED |

## PAST STUDIES IN REVIEW

| VOCABULARY FROM YESTERDAY | GOALS FROM YESTERDAY |
|---|---|
| 1 | ☐ |
| 2 | ☐ |
| 3 | ☐ |

| VOCABULARY FROM 5 DAYS AGO | VOCABULARY FROM 10 DAYS AGO |
|---|---|
| 1 | 1 |
| 2 | 2 |
| 3 | 3 |

## PRIORITIES FOR TODAY

| VOCABULARY FOR TODAY | GOALS FOR TODAY |
|---|---|
| 1 | ☐ |
| 2 | ☐ |
| 3 | ☐ |

## DESCRIBE YOUR LEARNING EXPERIENCE FOR TODAY

## SPECIAL WORDS FOR TODAY

| DAILY WORD BUILDER | VERB OF THE DAY | COGNATE OF THE DAY |
|---|---|---|
| **Abierto** | **Caber** | **Plácido** |
| adj. m. Abierta, f. Open. Running. Upfront. | To Fit /g: Cabiendo / pp: Cabido /Irr | Adjective. From: Placid (ID=IDO) |

## INTERESTING THINGS FROM TODAY

### FOUR SENTENCES THAT I READ, HEARD OR CREATED TODAY

**1**

**2**

**3**

**4**

## THINGS I HAVE QUESTIONS ABOUT

## DESCRIBE YOUR ACTIVITIES IN THESE TASKS FOR TODAY

| ACTIVITY | DESCRIPTION | SATISFACTION |
|----------|-------------|--------------|
| READING | | ☹ 🙁 😐 🙂 😀 |
| LISTENING | | ☹ 🙁 😐 🙂 😀 |
| WRITING | | ☹ 🙁 😐 🙂 😀 |
| SPEAKING | | ☹ 🙁 😐 🙂 😀 |
| STUDYING | | ☹ 🙁 😐 🙂 😀 |
| VOCABULARY | | ☹ 🙁 😐 🙂 😀 |

| LOG YOUR STUDY TIME | | | | | | | | | | | | | TOTAL TIME |
|---------------------|--|--|--|--|--|--|--|--|--|--|--|--|------------|
| EACH BOX EQUALS 5 MINS. | | | | | | | | | | | | | : |

| DAY & DATE | | STUDY STREAK # | |
|---|---|---|---|
| LEARNING MOOD | ☹ ☹ 😐 🙂 😀 | # VERBS ACQUIRED | |

## PAST STUDIES IN REVIEW

| VOCABULARY FROM YESTERDAY | GOALS FROM YESTERDAY |
|---|---|
| 1 | ☐ |
| 2 | ☐ |
| 3 | ☐ |

| VOCABULARY FROM 5 DAYS AGO | VOCABULARY FROM 10 DAYS AGO |
|---|---|
| 1 | 1 |
| 2 | 2 |
| 3 | 3 |

## PRIORITIES FOR TODAY

| VOCABULARY FOR TODAY | GOALS FOR TODAY |
|---|---|
| 1 | ☐ |
| 2 | ☐ |
| 3 | ☐ |

## DESCRIBE YOUR LEARNING EXPERIENCE FOR TODAY

## SPECIAL WORDS FOR TODAY

| DAILY WORD BUILDER | VERB OF THE DAY | COGNATE OF THE DAY |
|---|---|---|
| **Mente Abierta** | **Oír** | **Batería** |
| n. f. Open mind. | To Hear /g: Oyendo / pp: Oído /Irr. | Noun. From: Battery (Y=IA OR ÍA) |

## INTERESTING THINGS FROM TODAY

### FOUR SENTENCES THAT I READ, HEARD OR CREATED TODAY

**1**

**2**

**3**

**4**

## THINGS I HAVE QUESTIONS ABOUT

## DESCRIBE YOUR ACTIVITIES IN THESE TASKS FOR TODAY

| ACTIVITY | DESCRIPTION | SATISFACTION |
|---|---|---|
| READING | | ☹ 😦 😐 🙂 😊 |
| LISTENING | | ☹ 😦 😐 🙂 😊 |
| WRITING | | ☹ 😦 😐 🙂 😊 |
| SPEAKING | | ☹ 😦 😐 🙂 😊 |
| STUDYING | | ☹ 😦 😐 🙂 😊 |
| VOCABULARY | | ☹ 😦 😐 🙂 😊 |

| LOG YOUR STUDY TIME | | | | | | | | | | | | | TOTAL TIME |
|---|---|---|---|---|---|---|---|---|---|---|---|---|---|
| EACH BOX EQUALS 5 MINS. | | | | | | | | | | | | | : |

| DAY & DATE | | | STUDY STREAK # | |
|---|---|---|---|---|
| LEARNING MOOD | ☹ ☹ 😐 🙂 😄 | | # VERBS ACQUIRED | |

## PAST STUDIES IN REVIEW

| VOCABULARY FROM YESTERDAY | GOALS FROM YESTERDAY |
|---|---|
| 1 | ☐ |
| 2 | ☐ |
| 3 | ☐ |

| VOCABULARY FROM 5 DAYS AGO | VOCABULARY FROM 10 DAYS AGO |
|---|---|
| 1 | 1 |
| 2 | 2 |
| 3 | 3 |

## PRIORITIES FOR TODAY

| VOCABULARY FOR TODAY | GOALS FOR TODAY |
|---|---|
| 1 | ☐ |
| 2 | ☐ |
| 3 | ☐ |

## DESCRIBE YOUR LEARNING EXPERIENCE FOR TODAY

## SPECIAL WORDS FOR TODAY

| DAILY WORD BUILDER | VERB OF THE DAY | COGNATE OF THE DAY |
|---|---|---|
| **Puertas Abiertas** | **Ubicar** | **Usar** |
| n. f. pl. Doors open. | To Place, Locate; To Be Located, Be Situated /g: Ubicando / pp: Ubicado /Irr. | Verb. From: Use (E=AR OR IR) |

## INTERESTING THINGS FROM TODAY

### FOUR SENTENCES THAT I READ, HEARD OR CREATED TODAY

**1**

**2**

**3**

**4**

## THINGS I HAVE QUESTIONS ABOUT

## DESCRIBE YOUR ACTIVITIES IN THESE TASKS FOR TODAY

| ACTIVITY | DESCRIPTION | SATISFACTION |
|---|---|---|
| READING | | 😣 😟 😐 🙂 😃 |
| LISTENING | | 😣 😟 😐 🙂 😃 |
| WRITING | | 😣 😟 😐 🙂 😃 |
| SPEAKING | | 😣 😟 😐 🙂 😃 |
| STUDYING | | 😣 😟 😐 🙂 😃 |
| VOCABULARY | | 😣 😟 😐 🙂 😃 |

| LOG YOUR STUDY TIME | | | | | | | | | | | | | TOTAL TIME |
|---|---|---|---|---|---|---|---|---|---|---|---|---|---|
| EACH BOX EQUALS 5 MINS. | | | | | | | | | | | | | : |

| DAY & DATE | | STUDY STREAK # | |
|---|---|---|---|
| LEARNING MOOD | ☹ ☹ 😐 🙂 😄 | # VERBS ACQUIRED | |

## PAST STUDIES IN REVIEW

| VOCABULARY FROM YESTERDAY | GOALS FROM YESTERDAY |
|---|---|
| ❶ | ☐ |
| ❷ | ☐ |
| ❸ | ☐ |

| VOCABULARY FROM 5 DAYS AGO | VOCABULARY FROM 10 DAYS AGO |
|---|---|
| ❶ | ❶ |
| ❷ | ❷ |
| ❸ | ❸ |

## PRIORITIES FOR TODAY

| VOCABULARY FOR TODAY | GOALS FOR TODAY |
|---|---|
| ❶ | ☐ |
| ❷ | ☐ |
| ❸ | ☐ |

## DESCRIBE YOUR LEARNING EXPERIENCE FOR TODAY

## SPECIAL WORDS FOR TODAY

| DAILY WORD BUILDER | VERB OF THE DAY | COGNATE OF THE DAY |
|---|---|---|
| **Preguntas Abiertas** | **Deber** | **Asociación** |
| n. f. pl. Open-ended questions. Open questions. | To Owe; Must, Should, Ought To /g: Debiendo / pp: Debido | Noun. From: Association (TION=CIÓN) |

## INTERESTING THINGS FROM TODAY

### FOUR SENTENCES THAT I READ, HEARD OR CREATED TODAY

**1**

**2**

**3**

**4**

## THINGS I HAVE QUESTIONS ABOUT

## DESCRIBE YOUR ACTIVITIES IN THESE TASKS FOR TODAY

| ACTIVITY | DESCRIPTION | SATISFACTION |
|---|---|---|
| READING | | 😫 😣 😐 😊 😄 |
| LISTENING | | 😫 😣 😐 😊 😄 |
| WRITING | | 😫 😣 😐 😊 😄 |
| SPEAKING | | 😫 😣 😐 😊 😄 |
| STUDYING | | 😫 😣 😐 😊 😄 |
| VOCABULARY | | 😫 😣 😐 😊 😄 |

| LOG YOUR STUDY TIME | | | | | | | | | | | | | | TOTAL TIME |
|---|---|---|---|---|---|---|---|---|---|---|---|---|---|---|
| EACH BOX EQUALS 5 MINS. | | | | | | | | | | | | | | : |

| DAY & DATE | | STUDY STREAK # |
|---|---|---|
| LEARNING MOOD | ☹ ☹ 😐 🙂 😃 | # VERBS ACQUIRED |

## PAST STUDIES IN REVIEW

| VOCABULARY FROM YESTERDAY | GOALS FROM YESTERDAY |
|---|---|
| 1 | ☐ |
| 2 | ☐ |
| 3 | ☐ |

| VOCABULARY FROM 5 DAYS AGO | VOCABULARY FROM 10 DAYS AGO |
|---|---|
| 1 | 1 |
| 2 | 2 |
| 3 | 3 |

## PRIORITIES FOR TODAY

| VOCABULARY FOR TODAY | GOALS FOR TODAY |
|---|---|
| 1 | ☐ |
| 2 | ☐ |
| 3 | ☐ |

## DESCRIBE YOUR LEARNING EXPERIENCE FOR TODAY

## SPECIAL WORDS FOR TODAY

| DAILY WORD BUILDER | VERB OF THE DAY | COGNATE OF THE DAY |
|---|---|---|
| **Partidas Abiertas** | **Meter** | **Vital** |
| n. f. Open positions. | To Put [In], Place, Insert /g: Metiendo / pp: Metido | Adjective. From: Vital (AL=AL) |

## INTERESTING THINGS FROM TODAY

### FOUR SENTENCES THAT I READ, HEARD OR CREATED TODAY

**1**

**2**

**3**

**4**

## THINGS I HAVE QUESTIONS ABOUT

## DESCRIBE YOUR ACTIVITIES IN THESE TASKS FOR TODAY

| ACTIVITY | DESCRIPTION | SATISFACTION |
|---|---|---|
| READING | | 😞 😟 😐 😊 😃 |
| LISTENING | | 😞 😟 😐 😊 😃 |
| WRITING | | 😞 😟 😐 😊 😃 |
| SPEAKING | | 😞 😟 😐 😊 😃 |
| STUDYING | | 😞 😟 😐 😊 😃 |
| VOCABULARY | | 😞 😟 😐 😊 😃 |

| LOG YOUR STUDY TIME | | | | | | | | | | | | TOTAL TIME |
|---|---|---|---|---|---|---|---|---|---|---|---|---|
| EACH BOX EQUALS 5 MINS. | | | | | | | | | | | | : |

| DAY & DATE | | | STUDY STREAK # |
|---|---|---|---|
| LEARNING MOOD | ☹ ☹ 😐 🙂 😃 | | # VERBS ACQUIRED |

## PAST STUDIES IN REVIEW

| VOCABULARY FROM YESTERDAY | GOALS FROM YESTERDAY |
|---|---|
| 1 | ☐ |
| 2 | ☐ |
| 3 | ☐ |

| VOCABULARY FROM 5 DAYS AGO | VOCABULARY FROM 10 DAYS AGO |
|---|---|
| 1 | 1 |
| 2 | 2 |
| 3 | 3 |

## PRIORITIES FOR TODAY

| VOCABULARY FOR TODAY | GOALS FOR TODAY |
|---|---|
| 1 | ☐ |
| 2 | ☐ |
| 3 | ☐ |

## DESCRIBE YOUR LEARNING EXPERIENCE FOR TODAY

## SPECIAL WORDS FOR TODAY

| DAILY WORD BUILDER | VERB OF THE DAY | COGNATE OF THE DAY |
|---|---|---|
| **Inscripciones Abiertas** | **Acercar** | **Acelerar** |
| n. f. Open enrollment. | To Bring Near[Er], Move [Something] Nearer /g: Acercando / pp: Acercado | Verb. From: Accelerate (ATE=AR) |

## INTERESTING THINGS FROM TODAY

### FOUR SENTENCES THAT I READ, HEARD OR CREATED TODAY

**1**

**2**

**3**

**4**

## THINGS I HAVE QUESTIONS ABOUT

## DESCRIBE YOUR ACTIVITIES IN THESE TASKS FOR TODAY

| ACTIVITY | DESCRIPTION | SATISFACTION |
|---|---|---|
| READING | | ☹ ☹ 😐 🙂 😊 |
| LISTENING | | ☹ ☹ 😐 🙂 😊 |
| WRITING | | ☹ ☹ 😐 🙂 😊 |
| SPEAKING | | ☹ ☹ 😐 🙂 😊 |
| STUDYING | | ☹ ☹ 😐 🙂 😊 |
| VOCABULARY | | ☹ ☹ 😐 🙂 😊 |
| LOG YOUR STUDY TIME | | TOTAL TIME |
| EACH BOX EQUALS 5 MINS. | | : |

| DAY & DATE | | STUDY STREAK # | |
|---|---|---|---|
| LEARNING MOOD | ☹ ☹ 😐 🙂 😀 | # VERBS ACQUIRED | |

## PAST STUDIES IN REVIEW

| VOCABULARY FROM YESTERDAY | GOALS FROM YESTERDAY |
|---|---|
| **1** | ☐ |
| **2** | ☐ |
| **3** | ☐ |

| VOCABULARY FROM 5 DAYS AGO | VOCABULARY FROM 10 DAYS AGO |
|---|---|
| **1** | **1** |
| **2** | **2** |
| **3** | **3** |

## PRIORITIES FOR TODAY

| VOCABULARY FOR TODAY | GOALS FOR TODAY |
|---|---|
| **1** | ☐ |
| **2** | ☐ |
| **3** | ☐ |

## DESCRIBE YOUR LEARNING EXPERIENCE FOR TODAY

_____

_____

_____

_____

## SPECIAL WORDS FOR TODAY

| DAILY WORD BUILDER | VERB OF THE DAY | COGNATE OF THE DAY |
|---|---|---|
| **Fuentes Abiertas** | **Bendecir** | **Liquidar** |
| n. f. Open sources. | To Bless, Foretell, Forecast /g: Bendiciendo / pp: Bendito /Irr. | Verb. From: Liquidate (ATE=AR) |

## INTERESTING THINGS FROM TODAY

### FOUR SENTENCES THAT I READ, HEARD OR CREATED TODAY

**1**

**2**

**3**

**4**

## THINGS I HAVE QUESTIONS ABOUT

## DESCRIBE YOUR ACTIVITIES IN THESE TASKS FOR TODAY

| ACTIVITY | DESCRIPTION | SATISFACTION |
|----------|-------------|--------------|
| READING | | 😫 😟 😐 😊 😄 |
| LISTENING | | 😫 😟 😐 😊 😄 |
| WRITING | | 😫 😟 😐 😊 😄 |
| SPEAKING | | 😫 😟 😐 😊 😄 |
| STUDYING | | 😫 😟 😐 😊 😄 |
| VOCABULARY | | 😫 😟 😐 😊 😄 |

| LOG YOUR STUDY TIME | | | | | | | | | | | | | TOTAL TIME |
|---|---|---|---|---|---|---|---|---|---|---|---|---|---|
| EACH BOX EQUALS 5 MINS. | | | | | | | | | | | | | : |

**WEEK NUMBER:**

## THIS WEEK IN REVIEW

### VOCABULARY ACQUIRED

### BIGGEST ACHIEVEMENTS

☐ | ☐
☐ | ☐
☐ | ☐

### AREAS FOR IMPROVEMENT

1.
2.
3.
4.

## THINGS THAT I STILL HAVE QUESTIONS ABOUT

| | |
|---|---|
| | |
| | |
| | |

## FINAL MEASUREMENTS OF THIS WEEK

| TOTAL TIME THIS WEEK | TOTAL NEW VERBS | TOTAL NEW WORDS |
|---|---|---|
| | | |

## SELF-ASSESSMENT OF MY ACTIVITIES THIS WEEK

| ACTIVITIES | SPECIFIC ASSESSMENTS | SATISFACTION |
|---|---|---|
| READING | | ☹ ☹ 😐 🙂 😊 |
| LISTENING | | ☹ ☹ 😐 🙂 😊 |
| WRITING | | ☹ ☹ 😐 🙂 😊 |
| SPEAKING | | ☹ ☹ 😐 🙂 😊 |
| STUDYING | | ☹ ☹ 😐 🙂 😊 |
| MOTIVATION | | ☹ ☹ 😐 🙂 😊 |

| LOG YOUR STUDY TIME | | | | | | | | | | | | TOTAL TIME |
|---|---|---|---|---|---|---|---|---|---|---|---|---|
| EACH BOX EQUALS 1 HOUR | | | | | | | | | | | | : |

| LEARNING MOOD | ☹ 😠 😐 🙂 😀 | # VERBS ACQUIRED |

## PAST STUDIES IN REVIEW

| VOCABULARY FROM YESTERDAY | GOALS FROM YESTERDAY |
|---|---|
| 1 | ☐ |
| 2 | ☐ |
| 3 | ☐ |

| VOCABULARY FROM 5 DAYS AGO | VOCABULARY FROM 10 DAYS AGO |
|---|---|
| 1 | 1 |
| 2 | 2 |
| 3 | 3 |

## PRIORITIES FOR TODAY

| VOCABULARY FOR TODAY | GOALS FOR TODAY |
|---|---|
| 1 | ☐ |
| 2 | ☐ |
| 3 | ☐ |

## DESCRIBE YOUR LEARNING EXPERIENCE FOR TODAY

## SPECIAL WORDS FOR TODAY

| DAILY WORD BUILDER | VERB OF THE DAY | COGNATE OF THE DAY |
|---|---|---|
| **Hecho** | **Caer** | **Abandonar** |
| n. m. Fact. Event. Occurrence. Deed. | To Fall /g: Cayendo / pp: Caído /Irr. | Verb. From: Abandon (ADDING AR OR IR) |

## INTERESTING THINGS FROM TODAY

### FOUR SENTENCES THAT I READ, HEARD OR CREATED TODAY

**1**

**2**

**3**

**4**

## THINGS I HAVE QUESTIONS ABOUT

## DESCRIBE YOUR ACTIVITIES IN THESE TASKS FOR TODAY

| ACTIVITY | DESCRIPTION | SATISFACTION |
|----------|-------------|--------------|
| READING | | 😣 😟 😐 😊 😃 |
| LISTENING | | 😣 😟 😐 😊 😃 |
| WRITING | | 😣 😟 😐 😊 😃 |
| SPEAKING | | 😣 😟 😐 😊 😃 |
| STUDYING | | 😣 😟 😐 😊 😃 |
| VOCABULARY | | 😣 😟 😐 😊 😃 |

| LOG YOUR STUDY TIME | | | | | | | | | | | | | TOTAL TIME |
|---------------------|--|--|--|--|--|--|--|--|--|--|--|--|------------|
| EACH BOX EQUALS 5 MINS. | | | | | | | | | | | | | : |

| DAY & DATE | | | STUDY STREAK # | |
|---|---|---|---|---|
| LEARNING MOOD | ☹ ☹ 😐 🙂 😀 | | # VERBS ACQUIRED | |

## PAST STUDIES IN REVIEW

| VOCABULARY FROM YESTERDAY | GOALS FROM YESTERDAY |
|---|---|
| 1 | ☐ |
| 2 | ☐ |
| 3 | ☐ |

| VOCABULARY FROM 5 DAYS AGO | VOCABULARY FROM 10 DAYS AGO |
|---|---|
| 1 | 1 |
| 2 | 2 |
| 3 | 3 |

## PRIORITIES FOR TODAY

| VOCABULARY FOR TODAY | GOALS FOR TODAY |
|---|---|
| 1 | ☐ |
| 2 | ☐ |
| 3 | ☐ |

## DESCRIBE YOUR LEARNING EXPERIENCE FOR TODAY

## SPECIAL WORDS FOR TODAY

| DAILY WORD BUILDER | VERB OF THE DAY | COGNATE OF THE DAY |
|---|---|---|
| **De Hecho** | **Oler** | **Monumento** |
| adj. Factual. adv. In Fact. Indeed. As a matter of fact. | To Smell /g: Oliendo / pp: Olido /Irr. | Noun. From: Monument (MENT=MENTO) |

## INTERESTING THINGS FROM TODAY

### FOUR SENTENCES THAT I READ, HEARD OR CREATED TODAY

**1**

**2**

**3**

**4**

## THINGS I HAVE QUESTIONS ABOUT

## DESCRIBE YOUR ACTIVITIES IN THESE TASKS FOR TODAY

| ACTIVITY | DESCRIPTION | SATISFACTION |
|---|---|---|
| READING | | 😣😟😐😊😄 |
| LISTENING | | 😣😟😐😊😄 |
| WRITING | | 😣😟😐😊😄 |
| SPEAKING | | 😣😟😐😊😄 |
| STUDYING | | 😣😟😐😊😄 |
| VOCABULARY | | 😣😟😐😊😄 |
| LOG YOUR STUDY TIME | | TOTAL TIME |
| EACH BOX EQUALS 5 MINS. | | : |

| DAY & DATE | | | STUDY STREAK # |
|---|---|---|---|
| LEARNING MOOD | ☹ ☹ 😐 🙂 😃 | | # VERBS ACQUIRED |

## PAST STUDIES IN REVIEW

| VOCABULARY FROM YESTERDAY | GOALS FROM YESTERDAY |
|---|---|
| 1 | ☐ |
| 2 | ☐ |
| 3 | ☐ |

| VOCABULARY FROM 5 DAYS AGO | VOCABULARY FROM 10 DAYS AGO |
|---|---|
| 1 | 1 |
| 2 | 2 |
| 3 | 3 |

## PRIORITIES FOR TODAY

| VOCABULARY FOR TODAY | GOALS FOR TODAY |
|---|---|
| 1 | ☐ |
| 2 | ☐ |
| 3 | ☐ |

## DESCRIBE YOUR LEARNING EXPERIENCE FOR TODAY

## SPECIAL WORDS FOR TODAY

| DAILY WORD BUILDER | VERB OF THE DAY | COGNATE OF THE DAY |
|---|---|---|
| **Pareja de Hecho** | **Utilizar** | **La** |
| n. f. Unmarried partner. | To Use, Utilize /g: Utilizando / pp: Utilizado /Irr. | Verb. From: Combine (E=AR OR IR) |

## INTERESTING THINGS FROM TODAY

### FOUR SENTENCES THAT I READ, HEARD OR CREATED TODAY

**1**

**2**

**3**

**4**

## THINGS I HAVE QUESTIONS ABOUT

## DESCRIBE YOUR ACTIVITIES IN THESE TASKS FOR TODAY

| ACTIVITY | DESCRIPTION | SATISFACTION |
|---|---|---|
| READING | | ☹ ☹ 😐 🙂 😀 |
| LISTENING | | ☹ ☹ 😐 🙂 😀 |
| WRITING | | ☹ ☹ 😐 🙂 😀 |
| SPEAKING | | ☹ ☹ 😐 🙂 😀 |
| STUDYING | | ☹ ☹ 😐 🙂 😀 |
| VOCABULARY | | ☹ ☹ 😐 🙂 😀 |

| LOG YOUR STUDY TIME | | | | | | | | | | | | | | TOTAL TIME |
|---|---|---|---|---|---|---|---|---|---|---|---|---|---|---|
| EACH BOX EQUALS 5 MINS. | | | | | | | | | | | | | | : |

| DAY & DATE | | STUDY STREAK # |
|---|---|---|
| LEARNING MOOD | ☹ ☹ ☺ ☺ ☺ | # VERBS ACQUIRED |

## PAST STUDIES IN REVIEW

| VOCABULARY FROM YESTERDAY | GOALS FROM YESTERDAY |
|---|---|
| 1 | ☐ |
| 2 | ☐ |
| 3 | ☐ |

| VOCABULARY FROM 5 DAYS AGO | VOCABULARY FROM 10 DAYS AGO |
|---|---|
| 1 | 1 |
| 2 | 2 |
| 3 | 3 |

## PRIORITIES FOR TODAY

| VOCABULARY FOR TODAY | GOALS FOR TODAY |
|---|---|
| 1 | ☐ |
| 2 | ☐ |
| 3 | ☐ |

## DESCRIBE YOUR LEARNING EXPERIENCE FOR TODAY

## SPECIAL WORDS FOR TODAY

| DAILY WORD BUILDER | VERB OF THE DAY | COGNATE OF THE DAY |
|---|---|---|
| **Dar por Hecho** | **Dejar** | **Coherente** |
| v. Take for granted. | To Leave, Abandon; To Let, Allow /g: Dejando / pp: Dejado | Adjective. From: Coherent (NT=NTE) |

## INTERESTING THINGS FROM TODAY

### FOUR SENTENCES THAT I READ, HEARD OR CREATED TODAY

**1**

**2**

**3**

**4**

## THINGS I HAVE QUESTIONS ABOUT

## DESCRIBE YOUR ACTIVITIES IN THESE TASKS FOR TODAY

| ACTIVITY | DESCRIPTION | SATISFACTION |
|---|---|---|
| READING | | ☹ ☹ 😐 🙂 😊 |
| LISTENING | | ☹ ☹ 😐 🙂 😊 |
| WRITING | | ☹ ☹ 😐 🙂 😊 |
| SPEAKING | | ☹ ☹ 😐 🙂 😊 |
| STUDYING | | ☹ ☹ 😐 🙂 😊 |
| VOCABULARY | | ☹ ☹ 😐 🙂 😊 |

| LOG YOUR STUDY TIME | | | | | | | | | | | | | TOTAL TIME |
|---|---|---|---|---|---|---|---|---|---|---|---|---|---|
| EACH BOX EQUALS 5 MINS. | | | | | | | | | | | | | : |

| DAY & DATE | | STUDY STREAK # | |
|---|---|---|---|
| LEARNING MOOD | ☹ ☹ 😐 🙂 😀 | # VERBS ACQUIRED | |

## PAST STUDIES IN REVIEW

| VOCABULARY FROM YESTERDAY | GOALS FROM YESTERDAY |
|---|---|
| **1** | ☐ |
| **2** | ☐ |
| **3** | ☐ |

| VOCABULARY FROM 5 DAYS AGO | VOCABULARY FROM 10 DAYS AGO |
|---|---|
| **1** | **1** |
| **2** | **2** |
| **3** | **3** |

## PRIORITIES FOR TODAY

| VOCABULARY FOR TODAY | GOALS FOR TODAY |
|---|---|
| **1** | ☐ |
| **2** | ☐ |
| **3** | ☐ |

## DESCRIBE YOUR LEARNING EXPERIENCE FOR TODAY

_____

_____

_____

_____

## SPECIAL WORDS FOR TODAY

| DAILY WORD BUILDER | VERB OF THE DAY | COGNATE OF THE DAY |
|---|---|---|
| **Hecho a medida** | **Mirar** | **Binario** |
| adj. Custom-made | To Watch, Look At /g: Mirando / pp: Mirado | Adjective. From: Binary (Y=IO) |

## INTERESTING THINGS FROM TODAY

### FOUR SENTENCES THAT I READ, HEARD OR CREATED TODAY

**1**

**2**

**3**

**4**

## THINGS I HAVE QUESTIONS ABOUT

## DESCRIBE YOUR ACTIVITIES IN THESE TASKS FOR TODAY

| ACTIVITY | DESCRIPTION | SATISFACTION |
|---|---|---|
| READING | | ☹ ☹ 😐 🙂 😊 |
| LISTENING | | ☹ ☹ 😐 🙂 😊 |
| WRITING | | ☹ ☹ 😐 🙂 😊 |
| SPEAKING | | ☹ ☹ 😐 🙂 😊 |
| STUDYING | | ☹ ☹ 😐 🙂 😊 |
| VOCABULARY | | ☹ ☹ 😐 🙂 😊 |

| LOG YOUR STUDY TIME | | | | | | | | | | | | | TOTAL TIME |
|---|---|---|---|---|---|---|---|---|---|---|---|---|---|
| EACH BOX EQUALS 5 MINS. | | | | | | | | | | | | | : |

| DAY & DATE | | STUDY STREAK # |
|---|---|---|
| LEARNING MOOD  ☹ ☹ 😐 🙂 😀 | | # VERBS ACQUIRED |

## PAST STUDIES IN REVIEW

| VOCABULARY FROM YESTERDAY | GOALS FROM YESTERDAY |
|---|---|
| 1 | ☐ |
| 2 | ☐ |
| 3 | ☐ |

| VOCABULARY FROM 5 DAYS AGO | VOCABULARY FROM 10 DAYS AGO |
|---|---|
| 1 | 1 |
| 2 | 2 |
| 3 | 3 |

## PRIORITIES FOR TODAY

| VOCABULARY FOR TODAY | GOALS FOR TODAY |
|---|---|
| 1 | ☐ |
| 2 | ☐ |
| 3 | ☐ |

## DESCRIBE YOUR LEARNING EXPERIENCE FOR TODAY

## SPECIAL WORDS FOR TODAY

| DAILY WORD BUILDER | VERB OF THE DAY | COGNATE OF THE DAY |
|---|---|---|
| **Hecho imponible** | **Acontecer** | **Activar** |
| n. m. Taxable transaction. Taxable event. | To Happen, Occur, Come About /g: Aconteciendo / pp: Acontecido /Irr. | Verb. From: Activate (ATE=AR) |

## INTERESTING THINGS FROM TODAY
### FOUR SENTENCES THAT I READ, HEARD OR CREATED TODAY

**1**

**2**

**3**

**4**

## THINGS I HAVE QUESTIONS ABOUT

## DESCRIBE YOUR ACTIVITIES IN THESE TASKS FOR TODAY

| ACTIVITY | DESCRIPTION | SATISFACTION |
|---|---|---|
| READING | | 😖 😣 😐 😊 😄 |
| LISTENING | | 😖 😣 😐 😊 😄 |
| WRITING | | 😖 😣 😐 😊 😄 |
| SPEAKING | | 😖 😣 😐 😊 😄 |
| STUDYING | | 😖 😣 😐 😊 😄 |
| VOCABULARY | | 😖 😣 😐 😊 😄 |

| LOG YOUR STUDY TIME | | | | | | | | | | | | | | TOTAL TIME |
|---|---|---|---|---|---|---|---|---|---|---|---|---|---|---|
| EACH BOX EQUALS 5 MINS. | | | | | | | | | | | | | | : |

| DAY & DATE | | STUDY STREAK # | |
|---|---|---|---|
| LEARNING MOOD | ☹ ☹ 😐 🙂 😄 | # VERBS ACQUIRED | |

## PAST STUDIES IN REVIEW

| VOCABULARY FROM YESTERDAY | GOALS FROM YESTERDAY |
|---|---|
| ❶ | ☐ |
| ❷ | ☐ |
| ❸ | ☐ |

| VOCABULARY FROM 5 DAYS AGO | VOCABULARY FROM 10 DAYS AGO |
|---|---|
| ❶ | ❶ |
| ❷ | ❷ |
| ❸ | ❸ |

## PRIORITIES FOR TODAY

| VOCABULARY FOR TODAY | GOALS FOR TODAY |
|---|---|
| ❶ | ☐ |
| ❷ | ☐ |
| ❸ | ☐ |

## DESCRIBE YOUR LEARNING EXPERIENCE FOR TODAY

## SPECIAL WORDS FOR TODAY

| DAILY WORD BUILDER | VERB OF THE DAY | COGNATE OF THE DAY |
|---|---|---|
| **Hecho a Mano** | **Calentarse** | **Clarificar** |
| adj. Handmade | To Heat Up, Warm Up /g: Calentándose / pp: Calentado /Irr. | Verb. From: Clarify (IFY=IFICAR) |

## INTERESTING THINGS FROM TODAY

### FOUR SENTENCES THAT I READ, HEARD OR CREATED TODAY

**1**

**2**

**3**

**4**

## THINGS I HAVE QUESTIONS ABOUT

## DESCRIBE YOUR ACTIVITIES IN THESE TASKS FOR TODAY

| ACTIVITY | DESCRIPTION | SATISFACTION |
|---|---|---|
| READING | | 😟 😣 😐 🙂 😃 |
| LISTENING | | 😟 😣 😐 🙂 😃 |
| WRITING | | 😟 😣 😐 🙂 😃 |
| SPEAKING | | 😟 😣 😐 🙂 😃 |
| STUDYING | | 😟 😣 😐 🙂 😃 |
| VOCABULARY | | 😟 😣 😐 🙂 😃 |

| LOG YOUR STUDY TIME | | | | | | | | | | | | | TOTAL TIME |
|---|---|---|---|---|---|---|---|---|---|---|---|---|---|
| EACH BOX EQUALS 5 MINS. | | | | | | | | | | | | | : |

## THIS WEEK IN REVIEW

### VOCABULARY ACQUIRED

### BIGGEST ACHIEVEMENTS

- [ ]      [ ]
- [ ]      [ ]
- [ ]      [ ]

### AREAS FOR IMPROVEMENT

1.
2.
3.
4.

## THINGS THAT I STILL HAVE QUESTIONS ABOUT

| | |
|---|---|
| | |
| | |
| | |

## FINAL MEASUREMENTS OF THIS WEEK

| TOTAL TIME THIS WEEK | TOTAL NEW VERBS | TOTAL NEW WORDS |
|---|---|---|
| | | |

## SELF-ASSESSMENT OF MY ACTIVITIES THIS WEEK

| ACTIVITIES | SPECIFIC ASSESSMENTS | SATISFACTION |
|---|---|---|
| READING | | 😞 😟 😐 🙂 😊 |
| LISTENING | | 😞 😟 😐 🙂 😊 |
| WRITING | | 😞 😟 😐 🙂 😊 |
| SPEAKING | | 😞 😟 😐 🙂 😊 |
| STUDYING | | 😞 😟 😐 🙂 😊 |
| MOTIVATION | | 😞 😟 😐 🙂 😊 |

| LOG YOUR STUDY TIME | | | | | | | | | | | | TOTAL TIME |
|---|---|---|---|---|---|---|---|---|---|---|---|---|
| EACH BOX EQUALS 1 HOUR | | | | | | | | | | | | : |

| DAY & DATE | | STUDY STREAK # |
| LEARNING MOOD | ☹ ☹ 😐 🙂 😀 | # VERBS ACQUIRED |

## PAST STUDIES IN REVIEW

| VOCABULARY FROM YESTERDAY | GOALS FROM YESTERDAY |
|---|---|
| 1 | ☐ |
| 2 | ☐ |
| 3 | ☐ |

| VOCABULARY FROM 5 DAYS AGO | VOCABULARY FROM 10 DAYS AGO |
|---|---|
| 1 | 1 |
| 2 | 2 |
| 3 | 3 |

## PRIORITIES FOR TODAY

| VOCABULARY FOR TODAY | GOALS FOR TODAY |
|---|---|
| 1 | ☐ |
| 2 | ☐ |
| 3 | ☐ |

## DESCRIBE YOUR LEARNING EXPERIENCE FOR TODAY

## SPECIAL WORDS FOR TODAY

| DAILY WORD BUILDER | VERB OF THE DAY | COGNATE OF THE DAY |
|---|---|---|
| **Rueda** | **Calentar** | **Afirmación** |
| n. f. Wheel. Tire. | To Heat [Up], Warm [Up] /g: Calentando / pp: Calentado /Irr. | Noun. From: Affirmation (TION=CIÓN) |

## INTERESTING THINGS FROM TODAY

### FOUR SENTENCES THAT I READ, HEARD OR CREATED TODAY

**1**

**2**

**3**

**4**

## THINGS I HAVE QUESTIONS ABOUT

## DESCRIBE YOUR ACTIVITIES IN THESE TASKS FOR TODAY

| ACTIVITY | DESCRIPTION | SATISFACTION |
|---|---|---|
| READING | | 😣 😞 😐 😊 😃 |
| LISTENING | | 😣 😞 😐 😊 😃 |
| WRITING | | 😣 😞 😐 😊 😃 |
| SPEAKING | | 😣 😞 😐 😊 😃 |
| STUDYING | | 😣 😞 😐 😊 😃 |
| VOCABULARY | | 😣 😞 😐 😊 😃 |

| LOG YOUR STUDY TIME | | | | | | | | | | | | | TOTAL TIME |
|---|---|---|---|---|---|---|---|---|---|---|---|---|---|
| EACH BOX EQUALS 5 MINS. | | | | | | | | | | | | | : |

## PAST STUDIES IN REVIEW

| VOCABULARY FROM YESTERDAY | GOALS FROM YESTERDAY |
|---|---|
| 1 | ☐ |
| 2 | ☐ |
| 3 | ☐ |

| VOCABULARY FROM 5 DAYS AGO | VOCABULARY FROM 10 DAYS AGO |
|---|---|
| 1 | 1 |
| 2 | 2 |
| 3 | 3 |

## PRIORITIES FOR TODAY

| VOCABULARY FOR TODAY | GOALS FOR TODAY |
|---|---|
| 1 | ☐ |
| 2 | ☐ |
| 3 | ☐ |

## DESCRIBE YOUR LEARNING EXPERIENCE FOR TODAY

## SPECIAL WORDS FOR TODAY

| DAILY WORD BUILDER | VERB OF THE DAY | COGNATE OF THE DAY |
|---|---|---|
| **Rueda De Prensa** | **Pagar** | **Convención** |
| n. f. Press conference. | To Pay, Pay For /g: Pagando / pp: Pagado /Irr. | Noun. From: Convention (TION=CIÓN) |

## INTERESTING THINGS FROM TODAY

### FOUR SENTENCES THAT I READ, HEARD OR CREATED TODAY

**1**

**2**

**3**

**4**

## THINGS I HAVE QUESTIONS ABOUT

## DESCRIBE YOUR ACTIVITIES IN THESE TASKS FOR TODAY

| ACTIVITY | DESCRIPTION | SATISFACTION |
|----------|-------------|--------------|
| READING | | ☹ 😟 😐 🙂 😊 |
| LISTENING | | ☹ 😟 😐 🙂 😊 |
| WRITING | | ☹ 😟 😐 🙂 😊 |
| SPEAKING | | ☹ 😟 😐 🙂 😊 |
| STUDYING | | ☹ 😟 😐 🙂 😊 |
| VOCABULARY | | ☹ 😟 😐 🙂 😊 |

| LOG YOUR STUDY TIME | | TOTAL TIME |
|---------------------|--|------------|
| EACH BOX EQUALS 5 MINS. | | : |

| DAY & DATE | | STUDY STREAK # | |
|---|---|---|---|
| LEARNING MOOD | ☹ ☹ 😐 🙂 😀 | # VERBS ACQUIRED | |

## PAST STUDIES IN REVIEW

| VOCABULARY FROM YESTERDAY | GOALS FROM YESTERDAY |
|---|---|
| 1 | ☐ |
| 2 | ☐ |
| 3 | ☐ |

| VOCABULARY FROM 5 DAYS AGO | VOCABULARY FROM 10 DAYS AGO |
|---|---|
| 1 | 1 |
| 2 | 2 |
| 3 | 3 |

## PRIORITIES FOR TODAY

| VOCABULARY FOR TODAY | GOALS FOR TODAY |
|---|---|
| 1 | ☐ |
| 2 | ☐ |
| 3 | ☐ |

## DESCRIBE YOUR LEARNING EXPERIENCE FOR TODAY

## SPECIAL WORDS FOR TODAY

| DAILY WORD BUILDER | VERB OF THE DAY | COGNATE OF THE DAY |
|---|---|---|
| **Silla De Ruedas** | **Venir** | **Zoología** |
| n. f. Wheelchair. | To Come /g: Viniendo / pp: Venido /Irr. | Noun. From: Zoology (Y=IA OR ÍA) |

## INTERESTING THINGS FROM TODAY

### FOUR SENTENCES THAT I READ, HEARD OR CREATED TODAY

**1**

**2**

**3**

**4**

## THINGS I HAVE QUESTIONS ABOUT

## DESCRIBE YOUR ACTIVITIES IN THESE TASKS FOR TODAY

| ACTIVITY | DESCRIPTION | SATISFACTION |
|---|---|---|
| READING | | 😫 😠 😐 🙂 😀 |
| LISTENING | | 😫 😠 😐 🙂 😀 |
| WRITING | | 😫 😠 😐 🙂 😀 |
| SPEAKING | | 😫 😠 😐 🙂 😀 |
| STUDYING | | 😫 😠 😐 🙂 😀 |
| VOCABULARY | | 😫 😠 😐 🙂 😀 |

| LOG YOUR STUDY TIME | | | | | | | | | | | | | TOTAL TIME |
|---|---|---|---|---|---|---|---|---|---|---|---|---|---|
| EACH BOX EQUALS 5 MINS. | | | | | | | | | | | | | : |

| DAY & DATE | | | STUDY STREAK # | |
|---|---|---|---|---|
| LEARNING MOOD | ☹ ☹ 😐 🙂 😄 | | # VERBS ACQUIRED | |

## PAST STUDIES IN REVIEW

| VOCABULARY FROM YESTERDAY | GOALS FROM YESTERDAY |
|---|---|
| **1** | ☐ |
| **2** | ☐ |
| **3** | ☐ |

| VOCABULARY FROM 5 DAYS AGO | VOCABULARY FROM 10 DAYS AGO |
|---|---|
| **1** | **1** |
| **2** | **2** |
| **3** | **3** |

## PRIORITIES FOR TODAY

| VOCABULARY FOR TODAY | GOALS FOR TODAY |
|---|---|
| **1** | ☐ |
| **2** | ☐ |
| **3** | ☐ |

## DESCRIBE YOUR LEARNING EXPERIENCE FOR TODAY

## SPECIAL WORDS FOR TODAY

| DAILY WORD BUILDER | VERB OF THE DAY | COGNATE OF THE DAY |
|---|---|---|
| **Rueda Traseras** | **Descansar** | **Imposible** |
| n. f. pl. Rear wheels | To Rest, Take A Rest; To Support, Lean [On /g: Descansando / pp: | Adjective. From: Impossible (BLE=BLE) |

## INTERESTING THINGS FROM TODAY

### FOUR SENTENCES THAT I READ, HEARD OR CREATED TODAY

**1**

**2**

**3**

**4**

## THINGS I HAVE QUESTIONS ABOUT

## DESCRIBE YOUR ACTIVITIES IN THESE TASKS FOR TODAY

| ACTIVITY | DESCRIPTION | SATISFACTION |
|---|---|---|
| READING | | 😣 😖 😐 😊 😄 |
| LISTENING | | 😣 😖 😐 😊 😄 |
| WRITING | | 😣 😖 😐 😊 😄 |
| SPEAKING | | 😣 😖 😐 😊 😄 |
| STUDYING | | 😣 😖 😐 😊 😄 |
| VOCABULARY | | 😣 😖 😐 😊 😄 |

| LOG YOUR STUDY TIME | | TOTAL TIME |
|---|---|---|
| EACH BOX EQUALS 5 MINS. | | : |

| DAY & DATE | | | STUDY STREAK # | |
|---|---|---|---|---|
| LEARNING MOOD | ☹ ☹ 😐 🙂 😀 | | # VERBS ACQUIRED | |

## PAST STUDIES IN REVIEW

| VOCABULARY FROM YESTERDAY | GOALS FROM YESTERDAY |
|---|---|
| 1 | ☐ |
| 2 | ☐ |
| 3 | ☐ |

| VOCABULARY FROM 5 DAYS AGO | VOCABULARY FROM 10 DAYS AGO |
|---|---|
| 1 | 1 |
| 2 | 2 |
| 3 | 3 |

## PRIORITIES FOR TODAY

| VOCABULARY FOR TODAY | GOALS FOR TODAY |
|---|---|
| 1 | ☐ |
| 2 | ☐ |
| 3 | ☐ |

## DESCRIBE YOUR LEARNING EXPERIENCE FOR TODAY

_____

_____

_____

_____

## SPECIAL WORDS FOR TODAY

| DAILY WORD BUILDER | VERB OF THE DAY | COGNATE OF THE DAY |
|---|---|---|
| **Ruedas Delanteras** | **Molestar** | **Vacación** |
| n. f. pl. Front wheels | To Bother, Annoy, Put Out, Upset /g: Molestando / pp: Molestado | Noun. From: Vacation (TION=CIÓN) |

## INTERESTING THINGS FROM TODAY

### FOUR SENTENCES THAT I READ, HEARD OR CREATED TODAY

**1**

**2**

**3**

**4**

## THINGS I HAVE QUESTIONS ABOUT

## DESCRIBE YOUR ACTIVITIES IN THESE TASKS FOR TODAY

| ACTIVITY | DESCRIPTION | SATISFACTION |
|---|---|---|
| READING | | ☹ ☹ 😐 🙂 😊 |
| LISTENING | | ☹ ☹ 😐 🙂 😊 |
| WRITING | | ☹ ☹ 😐 🙂 😊 |
| SPEAKING | | ☹ ☹ 😐 🙂 😊 |
| STUDYING | | ☹ ☹ 😐 🙂 😊 |
| VOCABULARY | | ☹ ☹ 😐 🙂 😊 |
| LOG YOUR STUDY TIME | | TOTAL TIME |
| EACH BOX EQUALS 5 MINS. | | : |

| DAY & DATE | | | STUDY STREAK # | |
|---|---|---|---|---|
| LEARNING MOOD | ☹ ☹ 😐 🙂 😃 | | # VERBS ACQUIRED | |

## PAST STUDIES IN REVIEW

| VOCABULARY FROM YESTERDAY | GOALS FROM YESTERDAY |
|---|---|
| 1 | ☐ |
| 2 | ☐ |
| 3 | ☐ |

| VOCABULARY FROM 5 DAYS AGO | VOCABULARY FROM 10 DAYS AGO |
|---|---|
| 1 | 1 |
| 2 | 2 |
| 3 | 3 |

## PRIORITIES FOR TODAY

| VOCABULARY FOR TODAY | GOALS FOR TODAY |
|---|---|
| 1 | ☐ |
| 2 | ☐ |
| 3 | ☐ |

## DESCRIBE YOUR LEARNING EXPERIENCE FOR TODAY

## SPECIAL WORDS FOR TODAY

| DAILY WORD BUILDER | VERB OF THE DAY | COGNATE OF THE DAY |
|---|---|---|
| **Rueda De Repuesto** | **Acordarse** | **Imperfecto** |
| n. f. Spare tire. | To Remember /g: Acordándose / pp: Acordado /Irr. | Adjective. From: Imperfect (CT=CTO) |

## INTERESTING THINGS FROM TODAY

### FOUR SENTENCES THAT I READ, HEARD OR CREATED TODAY

**1**

**2**

**3**

**4**

## THINGS I HAVE QUESTIONS ABOUT

## DESCRIBE YOUR ACTIVITIES IN THESE TASKS FOR TODAY

| ACTIVITY | DESCRIPTION | SATISFACTION |
|---|---|---|
| READING | | ☹ ☹ 😐 🙂 😊 |
| LISTENING | | ☹ ☹ 😐 🙂 😊 |
| WRITING | | ☹ ☹ 😐 🙂 😊 |
| SPEAKING | | ☹ ☹ 😐 🙂 😊 |
| STUDYING | | ☹ ☹ 😐 🙂 😊 |
| VOCABULARY | | ☹ ☹ 😐 🙂 😊 |

| LOG YOUR STUDY TIME | | | | | | | | | | | | TOTAL TIME |
|---|---|---|---|---|---|---|---|---|---|---|---|---|
| EACH BOX EQUALS 5 MINS. | | | | | | | | | | | | : |

| DAY & DATE | | STUDY STREAK # | |
|---|---|---|---|
| LEARNING MOOD | ☹ ☹ 😐 🙂 😃 | # VERBS ACQUIRED | |

## PAST STUDIES IN REVIEW

| VOCABULARY FROM YESTERDAY | GOALS FROM YESTERDAY |
|---|---|
| 1 | ☐ |
| 2 | ☐ |
| 3 | ☐ |

| VOCABULARY FROM 5 DAYS AGO | VOCABULARY FROM 10 DAYS AGO |
|---|---|
| 1 | 1 |
| 2 | 2 |
| 3 | 3 |

## PRIORITIES FOR TODAY

| VOCABULARY FOR TODAY | GOALS FOR TODAY |
|---|---|
| 1 | ☐ |
| 2 | ☐ |
| 3 | ☐ |

## DESCRIBE YOUR LEARNING EXPERIENCE FOR TODAY

## SPECIAL WORDS FOR TODAY

| DAILY WORD BUILDER | VERB OF THE DAY | COGNATE OF THE DAY |
|---|---|---|
| **Rueda De Reconocimiento** | **Caracterizar** | **Depreciar** |
| n. f. Police suspect line up, or identify parade. | To Characterize /g: Caracterizando / pp: Caracterizado /Irr. | Verb. From: Depreciate (ATE=AR) |

## INTERESTING THINGS FROM TODAY

### FOUR SENTENCES THAT I READ, HEARD OR CREATED TODAY

**1**

**2**

**3**

**4**

## THINGS I HAVE QUESTIONS ABOUT

## DESCRIBE YOUR ACTIVITIES IN THESE TASKS FOR TODAY

| ACTIVITY | DESCRIPTION | SATISFACTION |
|---|---|---|
| READING | | 😧 😦 😐 😊 😃 |
| LISTENING | | 😧 😦 😐 😊 😃 |
| WRITING | | 😧 😦 😐 😊 😃 |
| SPEAKING | | 😧 😦 😐 😊 😃 |
| STUDYING | | 😧 😦 😐 😊 😃 |
| VOCABULARY | | 😧 😦 😐 😊 😃 |

| LOG YOUR STUDY TIME | | | | | | | | | | | | TOTAL TIME |
|---|---|---|---|---|---|---|---|---|---|---|---|---|
| EACH BOX EQUALS 5 MINS. | | | | | | | | | | | | : |

**WEEK NUMBER:**

## THIS WEEK IN REVIEW

### VOCABULARY ACQUIRED

### BIGGEST ACHIEVEMENTS

☐                              ☐

☐                              ☐

☐                              ☐

### AREAS FOR IMPROVEMENT

1

2

3

4

## THINGS THAT I STILL HAVE QUESTIONS ABOUT

|  |  |
|---|---|
|  |  |
|  |  |
|  |  |

## FINAL MEASUREMENTS OF THIS WEEK

| TOTAL TIME THIS WEEK | TOTAL NEW VERBS | TOTAL NEW WORDS |
|---|---|---|
|  |  |  |

## SELF-ASSESSMENT OF MY ACTIVITIES THIS WEEK

| ACTIVITIES | SPECIFIC ASSESSMENTS | SATISFACTION |
|---|---|---|
| READING |  | ☹ ☹ 😐 🙂 😊 |
| LISTENING |  | ☹ ☹ 😐 🙂 😊 |
| WRITING |  | ☹ ☹ 😐 🙂 😊 |
| SPEAKING |  | ☹ ☹ 😐 🙂 😊 |
| STUDYING |  | ☹ ☹ 😐 🙂 😊 |
| MOTIVATION |  | ☹ ☹ 😐 🙂 😊 |

| LOG YOUR STUDY TIME | | | | | | | | | | | | | TOTAL TIME |
|---|---|---|---|---|---|---|---|---|---|---|---|---|---|
| EACH BOX EQUALS 1 HOUR | | | | | | | | | | | | | : |

| DAY & DATE | | STUDY STREAK # | |
|---|---|---|---|
| LEARNING MOOD | ☹ 😞 😐 🙂 😀 | # VERBS ACQUIRED | |

## PAST STUDIES IN REVIEW

| VOCABULARY FROM YESTERDAY | GOALS FROM YESTERDAY |
|---|---|
| **1** | ☐ |
| **2** | ☐ |
| **3** | ☐ |

| VOCABULARY FROM 5 DAYS AGO | VOCABULARY FROM 10 DAYS AGO |
|---|---|
| **1** | **1** |
| **2** | **2** |
| **3** | **3** |

## PRIORITIES FOR TODAY

| VOCABULARY FOR TODAY | GOALS FOR TODAY |
|---|---|
| **1** | ☐ |
| **2** | ☐ |
| **3** | ☐ |

## DESCRIBE YOUR LEARNING EXPERIENCE FOR TODAY

## SPECIAL WORDS FOR TODAY

| DAILY WORD BUILDER | VERB OF THE DAY | COGNATE OF THE DAY |
|---|---|---|
| **Rápido** | **Cerrar** | **Preparar** |
| adj. m. Quick. Rapid. Fast. Prompt | To Close, Shut /g: Cerrando / pp: Cerrado /Irr. | Verb. From: Prepare (E=AR OR IR) |

## INTERESTING THINGS FROM TODAY

### FOUR SENTENCES THAT I READ, HEARD OR CREATED TODAY

**1**

**2**

**3**

**4**

## THINGS I HAVE QUESTIONS ABOUT

## DESCRIBE YOUR ACTIVITIES IN THESE TASKS FOR TODAY

| ACTIVITY | DESCRIPTION | SATISFACTION |
|---|---|---|
| READING | | ☹ 😠 😐 😊 😄 |
| LISTENING | | ☹ 😠 😐 😊 😄 |
| WRITING | | ☹ 😠 😐 😊 😄 |
| SPEAKING | | ☹ 😠 😐 😊 😄 |
| STUDYING | | ☹ 😠 😐 😊 😄 |
| VOCABULARY | | ☹ 😠 😐 😊 😄 |

| LOG YOUR STUDY TIME | | | | | | | | | | | | | | TOTAL TIME |
|---|---|---|---|---|---|---|---|---|---|---|---|---|---|---|
| EACH BOX EQUALS 5 MINS. | | | | | | | | | | | | | | : |

| DAY & DATE | | STUDY STREAK # |
|---|---|---|
| LEARNING MOOD | ☹ ☹ 😐 🙂 😀 | # VERBS ACQUIRED |

## PAST STUDIES IN REVIEW

| VOCABULARY FROM YESTERDAY | GOALS FROM YESTERDAY |
|---|---|
| 1 | ☐ |
| 2 | ☐ |
| 3 | ☐ |

| VOCABULARY FROM 5 DAYS AGO | VOCABULARY FROM 10 DAYS AGO |
|---|---|
| 1 | 1 |
| 2 | 2 |
| 3 | 3 |

## PRIORITIES FOR TODAY

| VOCABULARY FOR TODAY | GOALS FOR TODAY |
|---|---|
| 1 | ☐ |
| 2 | ☐ |
| 3 | ☐ |

## DESCRIBE YOUR LEARNING EXPERIENCE FOR TODAY

## SPECIAL WORDS FOR TODAY

| DAILY WORD BUILDER | VERB OF THE DAY | COGNATE OF THE DAY |
|---|---|---|
| **Rápida Respuesta** | **Parecer** | **Etnocentrismo** |
| n. f. Quick response. Rapid response. | To Seem, Appear /g: Pareciendo / pp: Parecido /Irr. | Noun. From: Ethnocentrism (ISM=ISMO) |

## INTERESTING THINGS FROM TODAY

### FOUR SENTENCES THAT I READ, HEARD OR CREATED TODAY

**1**

**2**

**3**

**4**

## THINGS I HAVE QUESTIONS ABOUT

## DESCRIBE YOUR ACTIVITIES IN THESE TASKS FOR TODAY

| ACTIVITY | DESCRIPTION | SATISFACTION |
|---|---|---|
| READING | | 😖 😣 😐 😊 😀 |
| LISTENING | | 😖 😣 😐 😊 😀 |
| WRITING | | 😖 😣 😐 😊 😀 |
| SPEAKING | | 😖 😣 😐 😊 😀 |
| STUDYING | | 😖 😣 😐 😊 😀 |
| VOCABULARY | | 😖 😣 😐 😊 😀 |

| LOG YOUR STUDY TIME | | | | | | | | | | | | | TOTAL TIME |
|---|---|---|---|---|---|---|---|---|---|---|---|---|---|
| EACH BOX EQUALS 5 MINS. | | | | | | | | | | | | | : |

| DAY & DATE | | STUDY STREAK # | |
|---|---|---|---|
| LEARNING MOOD | ☹ ☹ 😐 🙂 😃 | # VERBS ACQUIRED | |

## PAST STUDIES IN REVIEW

| VOCABULARY FROM YESTERDAY | GOALS FROM YESTERDAY |
|---|---|
| 1 | ☐ |
| 2 | ☐ |
| 3 | ☐ |

| VOCABULARY FROM 5 DAYS AGO | VOCABULARY FROM 10 DAYS AGO |
|---|---|
| 1 | 1 |
| 2 | 2 |
| 3 | 3 |

## PRIORITIES FOR TODAY

| VOCABULARY FOR TODAY | GOALS FOR TODAY |
|---|---|
| 1 | ☐ |
| 2 | ☐ |
| 3 | ☐ |

## DESCRIBE YOUR LEARNING EXPERIENCE FOR TODAY

---

## SPECIAL WORDS FOR TODAY

| DAILY WORD BUILDER | VERB OF THE DAY | COGNATE OF THE DAY |
|---|---|---|
| **Más Rápido** | **Ver** | **Razonable** |
| adj. Faster. | To See /g: Viendo / pp: Visto /Irr. | Adjective. From: Reasonable (BLE=BLE) |

## INTERESTING THINGS FROM TODAY

### FOUR SENTENCES THAT I READ, HEARD OR CREATED TODAY

**1**

**2**

**3**

**4**

## THINGS I HAVE QUESTIONS ABOUT

## DESCRIBE YOUR ACTIVITIES IN THESE TASKS FOR TODAY

| ACTIVITY | DESCRIPTION | SATISFACTION |
|---|---|---|
| READING | | ☹ ☹ 😐 ☺ 😃 |
| LISTENING | | ☹ ☹ 😐 ☺ 😃 |
| WRITING | | ☹ ☹ 😐 ☺ 😃 |
| SPEAKING | | ☹ ☹ 😐 ☺ 😃 |
| STUDYING | | ☹ ☹ 😐 ☺ 😃 |
| VOCABULARY | | ☹ ☹ 😐 ☺ 😃 |

| LOG YOUR STUDY TIME | | | | | | | | | | | | | TOTAL TIME |
|---|---|---|---|---|---|---|---|---|---|---|---|---|---|
| EACH BOX EQUALS 5 MINS. | | | | | | | | | | | | | : |

| DAY & DATE | | STUDY STREAK # |
|---|---|---|
| LEARNING MOOD  ☹ ☹ 😐 🙂 😃 | | # VERBS ACQUIRED |

## PAST STUDIES IN REVIEW

| VOCABULARY FROM YESTERDAY | GOALS FROM YESTERDAY |
|---|---|
| 1 | ☐ |
| 2 | ☐ |
| 3 | ☐ |

| VOCABULARY FROM 5 DAYS AGO | VOCABULARY FROM 10 DAYS AGO |
|---|---|
| 1 | 1 |
| 2 | 2 |
| 3 | 3 |

## PRIORITIES FOR TODAY

| VOCABULARY FOR TODAY | GOALS FOR TODAY |
|---|---|
| 1 | ☐ |
| 2 | ☐ |
| 3 | ☐ |

## DESCRIBE YOUR LEARNING EXPERIENCE FOR TODAY

## SPECIAL WORDS FOR TODAY

| DAILY WORD BUILDER | VERB OF THE DAY | COGNATE OF THE DAY |
|---|---|---|
| **Lo Más Rápido Posible** | **Ducharse** | **Adoptar** |
| adv. As soon as possible. | To Take A Shower, Shower [Oneself] /g: Duchándose / pp: Duchado | Verb. From: Adopt (ADDING AR OR IR) |

## INTERESTING THINGS FROM TODAY

### FOUR SENTENCES THAT I READ, HEARD OR CREATED TODAY

1

2

3

4

## THINGS I HAVE QUESTIONS ABOUT

## DESCRIBE YOUR ACTIVITIES IN THESE TASKS FOR TODAY

| ACTIVITY | DESCRIPTION | SATISFACTION |
|----------|-------------|--------------|
| READING | | ☹ ☹ 😐 🙂 😊 |
| LISTENING | | ☹ ☹ 😐 🙂 😊 |
| WRITING | | ☹ ☹ 😐 🙂 😊 |
| SPEAKING | | ☹ ☹ 😐 🙂 😊 |
| STUDYING | | ☹ ☹ 😐 🙂 😊 |
| VOCABULARY | | ☹ ☹ 😐 🙂 😊 |

| LOG YOUR STUDY TIME | | | | | | | | | | | | | TOTAL TIME |
|---------------------|--|--|--|--|--|--|--|--|--|--|--|--|------------|
| EACH BOX EQUALS 5 MINS. | | | | | | | | | | | | | : |

| DAY & DATE | | STUDY STREAK # |
|---|---|---|
| LEARNING MOOD | ☹ ☹ 😐 🙂 😃 | # VERBS ACQUIRED |

## PAST STUDIES IN REVIEW

| VOCABULARY FROM YESTERDAY | GOALS FROM YESTERDAY |
|---|---|
| 1 | ☐ |
| 2 | ☐ |
| 3 | ☐ |

| VOCABULARY FROM 5 DAYS AGO | VOCABULARY FROM 10 DAYS AGO |
|---|---|
| 1 | 1 |
| 2 | 2 |
| 3 | 3 |

## PRIORITIES FOR TODAY

| VOCABULARY FOR TODAY | GOALS FOR TODAY |
|---|---|
| 1 | ☐ |
| 2 | ☐ |
| 3 | ☐ |

## DESCRIBE YOUR LEARNING EXPERIENCE FOR TODAY

## SPECIAL WORDS FOR TODAY

| DAILY WORD BUILDER | VERB OF THE DAY | COGNATE OF THE DAY |
|---|---|---|
| **Comida Rápida** | **Necesitar** | **Invitación** |
| n. f. Fast food. A quick meal. | To Need, Require /g: Necesitando / pp: Necesitado | Noun. From: Invitation (TION=CIÓN) |

## INTERESTING THINGS FROM TODAY

### FOUR SENTENCES THAT I READ, HEARD OR CREATED TODAY

**1**

**2**

**3**

**4**

## THINGS I HAVE QUESTIONS ABOUT

## DESCRIBE YOUR ACTIVITIES IN THESE TASKS FOR TODAY

| ACTIVITY | DESCRIPTION | SATISFACTION |
|---|---|---|
| READING | | ☹ 🙁 😐 🙂 😀 |
| LISTENING | | ☹ 🙁 😐 🙂 😀 |
| WRITING | | ☹ 🙁 😐 🙂 😀 |
| SPEAKING | | ☹ 🙁 😐 🙂 😀 |
| STUDYING | | ☹ 🙁 😐 🙂 😀 |
| VOCABULARY | | ☹ 🙁 😐 🙂 😀 |

| LOG YOUR STUDY TIME | | | | | | | | | | | | | TOTAL TIME |
|---|---|---|---|---|---|---|---|---|---|---|---|---|---|
| EACH BOX EQUALS 5 MINS. | | | | | | | | | | | | | : |

| DAY & DATE | | | STUDY STREAK # |
|---|---|---|---|
| LEARNING MOOD | ☹ ☹ 😐 🙂 😃 | | # VERBS ACQUIRED |

## PAST STUDIES IN REVIEW

| VOCABULARY FROM YESTERDAY | GOALS FROM YESTERDAY |
|---|---|
| 1 | ☐ |
| 2 | ☐ |
| 3 | ☐ |

| VOCABULARY FROM 5 DAYS AGO | VOCABULARY FROM 10 DAYS AGO |
|---|---|
| 1 | 1 |
| 2 | 2 |
| 3 | 3 |

## PRIORITIES FOR TODAY

| VOCABULARY FOR TODAY | GOALS FOR TODAY |
|---|---|
| 1 | ☐ |
| 2 | ☐ |
| 3 | ☐ |

## DESCRIBE YOUR LEARNING EXPERIENCE FOR TODAY

## SPECIAL WORDS FOR TODAY

| DAILY WORD BUILDER | VERB OF THE DAY | COGNATE OF THE DAY |
|---|---|---|
| **Rápido Crecimiento** | **Acostarse** | **Verificar** |
| n. m. Rapid growth. Fast growth. | To Go To Bed, Lie Down /g: Acostándose / pp: Acostado /Irr. | Verb. From: Verify (IFY=IFICAR) |

## INTERESTING THINGS FROM TODAY

### FOUR SENTENCES THAT I READ, HEARD OR CREATED TODAY

**1**

**2**

**3**

**4**

## THINGS I HAVE QUESTIONS ABOUT

## DESCRIBE YOUR ACTIVITIES IN THESE TASKS FOR TODAY

| ACTIVITY | DESCRIPTION | SATISFACTION |
|----------|-------------|--------------|
| READING | | ☹ ☹ 😐 🙂 😊 |
| LISTENING | | ☹ ☹ 😐 🙂 😊 |
| WRITING | | ☹ ☹ 😐 🙂 😊 |
| SPEAKING | | ☹ ☹ 😐 🙂 😊 |
| STUDYING | | ☹ ☹ 😐 🙂 😊 |
| VOCABULARY | | ☹ ☹ 😐 🙂 😊 |

| LOG YOUR STUDY TIME | | | | | | | | | | | | | TOTAL TIME |
|---------------------|--|--|--|--|--|--|--|--|--|--|--|--|------------|
| EACH BOX EQUALS 5 MINS. | | | | | | | | | | | | | : |

| DAY & DATE | | STUDY STREAK # | |
|---|---|---|---|
| LEARNING MOOD | 😦 😦 😐 🙂 😃 | # VERBS ACQUIRED | |

## PAST STUDIES IN REVIEW

| VOCABULARY FROM YESTERDAY | GOALS FROM YESTERDAY |
|---|---|
| 1 | ☐ |
| 2 | ☐ |
| 3 | ☐ |

| VOCABULARY FROM 5 DAYS AGO | VOCABULARY FROM 10 DAYS AGO |
|---|---|
| 1 | 1 |
| 2 | 2 |
| 3 | 3 |

## PRIORITIES FOR TODAY

| VOCABULARY FOR TODAY | GOALS FOR TODAY |
|---|---|
| 1 | ☐ |
| 2 | ☐ |
| 3 | ☐ |

## DESCRIBE YOUR LEARNING EXPERIENCE FOR TODAY

## SPECIAL WORDS FOR TODAY

| DAILY WORD BUILDER | VERB OF THE DAY | COGNATE OF THE DAY |
|---|---|---|
| **Guía Rápida** | **Cargar** | **Interferencia** |
| n. f. Quick guide. | To Load, Load Up; To Charge /g: Cargando / pp: Cargado /Irr. | Noun. From: Interference (ENCE=ENCIA) |

## INTERESTING THINGS FROM TODAY

### FOUR SENTENCES THAT I READ, HEARD OR CREATED TODAY

**1**

**2**

**3**

**4**

## THINGS I HAVE QUESTIONS ABOUT

## DESCRIBE YOUR ACTIVITIES IN THESE TASKS FOR TODAY

| ACTIVITY | DESCRIPTION | SATISFACTION |
|----------|-------------|--------------|
| READING | | ☹ ☹ 😐 🙂 😊 |
| LISTENING | | ☹ ☹ 😐 🙂 😊 |
| WRITING | | ☹ ☹ 😐 🙂 😊 |
| SPEAKING | | ☹ ☹ 😐 🙂 😊 |
| STUDYING | | ☹ ☹ 😐 🙂 😊 |
| VOCABULARY | | ☹ ☹ 😐 🙂 😊 |

| LOG YOUR STUDY TIME | | TOTAL TIME |
|---------------------|---|------------|
| EACH BOX EQUALS 5 MINS. | | : |

## THIS WEEK IN REVIEW

### VOCABULARY ACQUIRED

### BIGGEST ACHIEVEMENTS

☐ | ☐
☐ | ☐
☐ | ☐

### AREAS FOR IMPROVEMENT

1.
2.
3.
4.

## THINGS THAT I STILL HAVE QUESTIONS ABOUT

| | |
|---|---|
| | |
| | |
| | |

## FINAL MEASUREMENTS OF THIS WEEK

| TOTAL TIME THIS WEEK | TOTAL NEW VERBS | TOTAL NEW WORDS |
|---|---|---|
| | | |

## SELF-ASSESSMENT OF MY ACTIVITIES THIS WEEK

| ACTIVITIES | SPECIFIC ASSESSMENTS | SATISFACTION |
|---|---|---|
| READING | | ☹ ☹ 😐 🙂 😊 |
| LISTENING | | ☹ ☹ 😐 🙂 😊 |
| WRITING | | ☹ ☹ 😐 🙂 😊 |
| SPEAKING | | ☹ ☹ 😐 🙂 😊 |
| STUDYING | | ☹ ☹ 😐 🙂 😊 |
| MOTIVATION | | ☹ ☹ 😐 🙂 😊 |

| LOG YOUR STUDY TIME | | | | | | | | | | | | TOTAL TIME |
|---|---|---|---|---|---|---|---|---|---|---|---|---|
| EACH BOX EQUALS 1 HOUR | | | | | | | | | | | | : |

## PAST STUDIES IN REVIEW

| VOCABULARY FROM YESTERDAY | GOALS FROM YESTERDAY |
|---|---|
| 1 | ☐ |
| 2 | ☐ |
| 3 | ☐ |

| VOCABULARY FROM 5 DAYS AGO | VOCABULARY FROM 10 DAYS AGO |
|---|---|
| 1 | 1 |
| 2 | 2 |
| 3 | 3 |

## PRIORITIES FOR TODAY

| VOCABULARY FOR TODAY | GOALS FOR TODAY |
|---|---|
| 1 | ☐ |
| 2 | ☐ |
| 3 | ☐ |

## DESCRIBE YOUR LEARNING EXPERIENCE FOR TODAY

## SPECIAL WORDS FOR TODAY

| DAILY WORD BUILDER | VERB OF THE DAY | COGNATE OF THE DAY |
|---|---|---|
| **Tarde** | **Comenzar** | **Galaxia** |
| f. n. Afternoon. Evening. adv. Late | To Begin, Start, Commence /g: Comenzando / pp: Comenzado /Irr. | Noun. From: Galaxy (Y=IA OR ÍA) |

## INTERESTING THINGS FROM TODAY

### FOUR SENTENCES THAT I READ, HEARD OR CREATED TODAY

**1**

**2**

**3**

**4**

## THINGS I HAVE QUESTIONS ABOUT

## DESCRIBE YOUR ACTIVITIES IN THESE TASKS FOR TODAY

| ACTIVITY | DESCRIPTION | SATISFACTION |
|----------|-------------|--------------|
| READING | | 😩 😞 😐 😊 😃 |
| LISTENING | | 😩 😞 😐 😊 😃 |
| WRITING | | 😩 😞 😐 😊 😃 |
| SPEAKING | | 😩 😞 😐 😊 😃 |
| STUDYING | | 😩 😞 😐 😊 😃 |
| VOCABULARY | | 😩 😞 😐 😊 😃 |

| LOG YOUR STUDY TIME | | | | | | | | | | | | TOTAL TIME |
|---------------------|--|--|--|--|--|--|--|--|--|--|--|------------|
| EACH BOX EQUALS 5 MINS. | | | | | | | | | | | | : |

| DAY & DATE | | STUDY STREAK # |
|---|---|---|
| LEARNING MOOD | ☹ ☹ 😐 🙂 😀 | # VERBS ACQUIRED |

## PAST STUDIES IN REVIEW

| VOCABULARY FROM YESTERDAY | GOALS FROM YESTERDAY |
|---|---|
| 1 | ☐ |
| 2 | ☐ |
| 3 | ☐ |

| VOCABULARY FROM 5 DAYS AGO | VOCABULARY FROM 10 DAYS AGO |
|---|---|
| 1 | 1 |
| 2 | 2 |
| 3 | 3 |

## PRIORITIES FOR TODAY

| VOCABULARY FOR TODAY | GOALS FOR TODAY |
|---|---|
| 1 | ☐ |
| 2 | ☐ |
| 3 | ☐ |

## DESCRIBE YOUR LEARNING EXPERIENCE FOR TODAY

## SPECIAL WORDS FOR TODAY

| DAILY WORD BUILDER | VERB OF THE DAY | COGNATE OF THE DAY |
|---|---|---|
| **Buenas Tardes** | **Pedir** | **Sociable** |
| intj. Good afternoon. | To Request, Ask For /g: Pidiendo / pp: Pedido /Irr. | Adjective. From: Sociable (BLE=BLE) |

## INTERESTING THINGS FROM TODAY

### FOUR SENTENCES THAT I READ, HEARD OR CREATED TODAY

**1**

**2**

**3**

**4**

## THINGS I HAVE QUESTIONS ABOUT

## DESCRIBE YOUR ACTIVITIES IN THESE TASKS FOR TODAY

| ACTIVITY | DESCRIPTION | SATISFACTION |
|---|---|---|
| READING | | ☹ ☹ 😐 ☺ 😊 |
| LISTENING | | ☹ ☹ 😐 ☺ 😊 |
| WRITING | | ☹ ☹ 😐 ☺ 😊 |
| SPEAKING | | ☹ ☹ 😐 ☺ 😊 |
| STUDYING | | ☹ ☹ 😐 ☺ 😊 |
| VOCABULARY | | ☹ ☹ 😐 ☺ 😊 |
| LOG YOUR STUDY TIME | | TOTAL TIME |
| EACH BOX EQUALS 5 MINS. | | : |

| DAY & DATE | | STUDY STREAK # |
|---|---|---|
| LEARNING MOOD ☹ ☹ 😐 🙂 😃 | | # VERBS ACQUIRED |

## PAST STUDIES IN REVIEW

| VOCABULARY FROM YESTERDAY | GOALS FROM YESTERDAY |
|---|---|
| 1 | ☐ |
| 2 | ☐ |
| 3 | ☐ |

| VOCABULARY FROM 5 DAYS AGO | VOCABULARY FROM 10 DAYS AGO |
|---|---|
| 1 | 1 |
| 2 | 2 |
| 3 | 3 |

## PRIORITIES FOR TODAY

| VOCABULARY FOR TODAY | GOALS FOR TODAY |
|---|---|
| 1 | ☐ |
| 2 | ☐ |
| 3 | ☐ |

## DESCRIBE YOUR LEARNING EXPERIENCE FOR TODAY

## SPECIAL WORDS FOR TODAY

| DAILY WORD BUILDER | VERB OF THE DAY | COGNATE OF THE DAY |
|---|---|---|
| **Como Muy Tarde** | **Verificar** | **La** |
| adv. At the latest | To Verify, Check, Inspect /g: Verificando / pp: Verificado /Irr. | Verb. From: Galvanize (E=AR OR IR) |

## INTERESTING THINGS FROM TODAY

### FOUR SENTENCES THAT I READ, HEARD OR CREATED TODAY

**1**

**2**

**3**

**4**

## THINGS I HAVE QUESTIONS ABOUT

## DESCRIBE YOUR ACTIVITIES IN THESE TASKS FOR TODAY

| ACTIVITY | DESCRIPTION | SATISFACTION |
|----------|-------------|--------------|
| READING | | 😞 😟 😐 😊 😃 |
| LISTENING | | 😞 😟 😐 😊 😃 |
| WRITING | | 😞 😟 😐 😊 😃 |
| SPEAKING | | 😞 😟 😐 😊 😃 |
| STUDYING | | 😞 😟 😐 😊 😃 |
| VOCABULARY | | 😞 😟 😐 😊 😃 |

| LOG YOUR STUDY TIME | | | | | | | | | | | | | | | TOTAL TIME |
|---------------------|--|--|--|--|--|--|--|--|--|--|--|--|--|--|------------|
| EACH BOX EQUALS 5 MINS. | | | | | | | | | | | | | | | : |

| DAY & DATE | | STUDY STREAK # |
|---|---|---|
| LEARNING MOOD | ☹ ☹ 😐 🙂 😀 | # VERBS ACQUIRED |

## PAST STUDIES IN REVIEW

| VOCABULARY FROM YESTERDAY | GOALS FROM YESTERDAY |
|---|---|
| 1 | ☐ |
| 2 | ☐ |
| 3 | ☐ |

| VOCABULARY FROM 5 DAYS AGO | VOCABULARY FROM 10 DAYS AGO |
|---|---|
| 1 | 1 |
| 2 | 2 |
| 3 | 3 |

## PRIORITIES FOR TODAY

| VOCABULARY FOR TODAY | GOALS FOR TODAY |
|---|---|
| 1 | ☐ |
| 2 | ☐ |
| 3 | ☐ |

## DESCRIBE YOUR LEARNING EXPERIENCE FOR TODAY

---

---

---

---

## SPECIAL WORDS FOR TODAY

| DAILY WORD BUILDER | VERB OF THE DAY | COGNATE OF THE DAY |
|---|---|---|
| **Por La Tarde** | **Echar** | **Esotérico** |
| adv. In the afternoon. | To Throw, Cast, Fling, Hurl, Pitch, Toss /g: Echando / pp: Echado | Adjective. From: Esoteric (IC=ICO) |

## INTERESTING THINGS FROM TODAY

### FOUR SENTENCES THAT I READ, HEARD OR CREATED TODAY

**1**

**2**

**3**

**4**

## THINGS I HAVE QUESTIONS ABOUT

## DESCRIBE YOUR ACTIVITIES IN THESE TASKS FOR TODAY

| ACTIVITY | DESCRIPTION | SATISFACTION |
|----------|-------------|--------------|
| READING | | ☹ ☹ 😐 🙂 😊 |
| LISTENING | | ☹ ☹ 😐 🙂 😊 |
| WRITING | | ☹ ☹ 😐 🙂 😊 |
| SPEAKING | | ☹ ☹ 😐 🙂 😊 |
| STUDYING | | ☹ ☹ 😐 🙂 😊 |
| VOCABULARY | | ☹ ☹ 😐 🙂 😊 |
| LOG YOUR STUDY TIME | | TOTAL TIME |
| EACH BOX EQUALS 5 MINS. | | : |

| DAY & DATE | | | STUDY STREAK # | |
|---|---|---|---|---|
| LEARNING MOOD | ☹ ☹ 😐 🙂 😀 | | # VERBS ACQUIRED | |

## PAST STUDIES IN REVIEW

| VOCABULARY FROM YESTERDAY | GOALS FROM YESTERDAY |
|---|---|
| 1 | ☐ |
| 2 | ☐ |
| 3 | ☐ |

| VOCABULARY FROM 5 DAYS AGO | VOCABULARY FROM 10 DAYS AGO |
|---|---|
| 1 | 1 |
| 2 | 2 |
| 3 | 3 |

## PRIORITIES FOR TODAY

| VOCABULARY FOR TODAY | GOALS FOR TODAY |
|---|---|
| 1 | ☐ |
| 2 | ☐ |
| 3 | ☐ |

## DESCRIBE YOUR LEARNING EXPERIENCE FOR TODAY

## SPECIAL WORDS FOR TODAY

| DAILY WORD BUILDER | VERB OF THE DAY | COGNATE OF THE DAY |
|---|---|---|
| **Más Tarde** | **Olvidar** | **Acumulador** |
| adv. Later. Then. | To Forget /g: Olvidando / pp: Olvidado | Noun. From: Accumulator (OR=OR) |

## INTERESTING THINGS FROM TODAY

### FOUR SENTENCES THAT I READ, HEARD OR CREATED TODAY

**1**

**2**

**3**

**4**

## THINGS I HAVE QUESTIONS ABOUT

## DESCRIBE YOUR ACTIVITIES IN THESE TASKS FOR TODAY

| ACTIVITY | DESCRIPTION | SATISFACTION |
|---|---|---|
| READING | | ☹ ☹ 😐 🙂 😊 |
| LISTENING | | ☹ ☹ 😐 🙂 😊 |
| WRITING | | ☹ ☹ 😐 🙂 😊 |
| SPEAKING | | ☹ ☹ 😐 🙂 😊 |
| STUDYING | | ☹ ☹ 😐 🙂 😊 |
| VOCABULARY | | ☹ ☹ 😐 🙂 😊 |
| LOG YOUR STUDY TIME | | TOTAL TIME |
| EACH BOX EQUALS 5 MINS. | | : |

| DAY & DATE | | | STUDY STREAK # |
|---|---|---|---|
| LEARNING MOOD | ☹ ☹ 😐 🙂 😀 | | # VERBS ACQUIRED |

## PAST STUDIES IN REVIEW

| VOCABULARY FROM YESTERDAY | GOALS FROM YESTERDAY |
|---|---|
| 1 | ☐ |
| 2 | ☐ |
| 3 | ☐ |

| VOCABULARY FROM 5 DAYS AGO | VOCABULARY FROM 10 DAYS AGO |
|---|---|
| 1 | 1 |
| 2 | 2 |
| 3 | 3 |

## PRIORITIES FOR TODAY

| VOCABULARY FOR TODAY | GOALS FOR TODAY |
|---|---|
| 1 | ☐ |
| 2 | ☐ |
| 3 | ☐ |

## DESCRIBE YOUR LEARNING EXPERIENCE FOR TODAY

## SPECIAL WORDS FOR TODAY

| DAILY WORD BUILDER | VERB OF THE DAY | COGNATE OF THE DAY |
|---|---|---|
| **Tarde o Temprano** | **Actuar** | **Limitar** |
| adv. Sooner or later | To Act, Perform, Actuate, Operate /g: Actuando / pp: Actuado /Irr. | Verb. From: Limit (ADDING AR OR IR) |

## INTERESTING THINGS FROM TODAY

### FOUR SENTENCES THAT I READ, HEARD OR CREATED TODAY

**1**

**2**

**3**

**4**

## THINGS I HAVE QUESTIONS ABOUT

## DESCRIBE YOUR ACTIVITIES IN THESE TASKS FOR TODAY

| ACTIVITY | DESCRIPTION | SATISFACTION |
|---|---|---|
| READING | | ☹ ☹ 😐 🙂 😊 |
| LISTENING | | ☹ ☹ 😐 🙂 😊 |
| WRITING | | ☹ ☹ 😐 🙂 😊 |
| SPEAKING | | ☹ ☹ 😐 🙂 😊 |
| STUDYING | | ☹ ☹ 😐 🙂 😊 |
| VOCABULARY | | ☹ ☹ 😐 🙂 😊 |

| LOG YOUR STUDY TIME | | | | | | | | | | | | TOTAL TIME |
|---|---|---|---|---|---|---|---|---|---|---|---|---|
| EACH BOX EQUALS 5 MINS. | | | | | | | | | | | | : |

| DAY & DATE | | | STUDY STREAK # |
|---|---|---|---|
| LEARNING MOOD | ☹ ☹ ☺ ☺ ☺ | | # VERBS ACQUIRED |

## PAST STUDIES IN REVIEW

| VOCABULARY FROM YESTERDAY | GOALS FROM YESTERDAY |
|---|---|
| **1** | ☐ |
| **2** | ☐ |
| **3** | ☐ |

| VOCABULARY FROM 5 DAYS AGO | VOCABULARY FROM 10 DAYS AGO |
|---|---|
| **1** | **1** |
| **2** | **2** |
| **3** | **3** |

## PRIORITIES FOR TODAY

| VOCABULARY FOR TODAY | GOALS FOR TODAY |
|---|---|
| **1** | ☐ |
| **2** | ☐ |
| **3** | ☐ |

## DESCRIBE YOUR LEARNING EXPERIENCE FOR TODAY

---

## SPECIAL WORDS FOR TODAY

| DAILY WORD BUILDER | VERB OF THE DAY | COGNATE OF THE DAY |
|---|---|---|
| **Llegar Tarde** | **Castigar** | **Anunciar** |
| v. To be late | To Punish, Penalize, Castigate /g: Castigando / pp: Castigado /Irr. | Verb. From: Announce (E=AR OR IR) |

## INTERESTING THINGS FROM TODAY

### FOUR SENTENCES THAT I READ, HEARD OR CREATED TODAY

**1**

**2**

**3**

**4**

## THINGS I HAVE QUESTIONS ABOUT

## DESCRIBE YOUR ACTIVITIES IN THESE TASKS FOR TODAY

| ACTIVITY | DESCRIPTION | SATISFACTION |
|---|---|---|
| READING | | ☹ 😧 😐 😊 😄 |
| LISTENING | | ☹ 😧 😐 😊 😄 |
| WRITING | | ☹ 😧 😐 😊 😄 |
| SPEAKING | | ☹ 😧 😐 😊 😄 |
| STUDYING | | ☹ 😧 😐 😊 😄 |
| VOCABULARY | | ☹ 😧 😐 😊 😄 |
| LOG YOUR STUDY TIME | | TOTAL TIME |
| EACH BOX EQUALS 5 MINS. | | : |

**WEEK NUMBER:**

## THIS WEEK IN REVIEW

### VOCABULARY ACQUIRED

### BIGGEST ACHIEVEMENTS

- [ ]
- [ ]
- [ ]

- [ ]
- [ ]
- [ ]

### AREAS FOR IMPROVEMENT

1.
2.
3.
4.

## THINGS THAT I STILL HAVE QUESTIONS ABOUT

| | |
|---|---|
| | |
| | |
| | |

## FINAL MEASUREMENTS OF THIS WEEK

| TOTAL TIME THIS WEEK | TOTAL NEW VERBS | TOTAL NEW WORDS |
|---|---|---|
| | | |

## SELF-ASSESSMENT OF MY ACTIVITIES THIS WEEK

| ACTIVITIES | SPECIFIC ASSESSMENTS | SATISFACTION |
|---|---|---|
| READING | | ☹ ☹ 😐 🙂 😊 |
| LISTENING | | ☹ ☹ 😐 🙂 😊 |
| WRITING | | ☹ ☹ 😐 🙂 😊 |
| SPEAKING | | ☹ ☹ 😐 🙂 😊 |
| STUDYING | | ☹ ☹ 😐 🙂 😊 |
| MOTIVATION | | ☹ ☹ 😐 🙂 😊 |

| LOG YOUR STUDY TIME | | | | | | | | | | | | TOTAL TIME |
|---|---|---|---|---|---|---|---|---|---|---|---|---|
| EACH BOX EQUALS 1 HOUR | | | | | | | | | | | | : |

| DAY & DATE | | STUDY STREAK # |
|---|---|---|
| LEARNING MOOD  ☹ ☹ 😐 🙂 😀 | | # VERBS ACQUIRED |

## PAST STUDIES IN REVIEW

| VOCABULARY FROM YESTERDAY | GOALS FROM YESTERDAY |
|---|---|
| 1 | ☐ |
| 2 | ☐ |
| 3 | ☐ |

| VOCABULARY FROM 5 DAYS AGO | VOCABULARY FROM 10 DAYS AGO |
|---|---|
| 1 | 1 |
| 2 | 2 |
| 3 | 3 |

## PRIORITIES FOR TODAY

| VOCABULARY FOR TODAY | GOALS FOR TODAY |
|---|---|
| 1 | ☐ |
| 2 | ☐ |
| 3 | ☐ |

## DESCRIBE YOUR LEARNING EXPERIENCE FOR TODAY

## SPECIAL WORDS FOR TODAY

| DAILY WORD BUILDER | VERB OF THE DAY | COGNATE OF THE DAY |
|---|---|---|
| **Durante** | **Conocer** | **Deficiente** |
| prep. During. | To Know /g: Conociendo / pp: Conocido /Irr. | Adjective. From: Deficient (NT=NTE) |

## INTERESTING THINGS FROM TODAY

### FOUR SENTENCES THAT I READ, HEARD OR CREATED TODAY

**1**

**2**

**3**

**4**

## THINGS I HAVE QUESTIONS ABOUT

## DESCRIBE YOUR ACTIVITIES IN THESE TASKS FOR TODAY

| ACTIVITY | DESCRIPTION | SATISFACTION |
|----------|-------------|--------------|
| READING | | 😞😟😐🙂😀 |
| LISTENING | | 😞😟😐🙂😀 |
| WRITING | | 😞😟😐🙂😀 |
| SPEAKING | | 😞😟😐🙂😀 |
| STUDYING | | 😞😟😐🙂😀 |
| VOCABULARY | | 😞😟😐🙂😀 |

| LOG YOUR STUDY TIME | | | | | | | | | | | | | | TOTAL TIME |
|---|---|---|---|---|---|---|---|---|---|---|---|---|---|---|
| EACH BOX EQUALS 5 MINS. | | | | | | | | | | | | | | : |

| DAY & DATE | | STUDY STREAK # |
|---|---|---|
| LEARNING MOOD ☹ ☹ 😐 🙂 😃 | | # VERBS ACQUIRED |

## PAST STUDIES IN REVIEW

| VOCABULARY FROM YESTERDAY | GOALS FROM YESTERDAY |
|---|---|
| 1 | ☐ |
| 2 | ☐ |
| 3 | ☐ |

| VOCABULARY FROM 5 DAYS AGO | VOCABULARY FROM 10 DAYS AGO |
|---|---|
| 1 | 1 |
| 2 | 2 |
| 3 | 3 |

## PRIORITIES FOR TODAY

| VOCABULARY FOR TODAY | GOALS FOR TODAY |
|---|---|
| 1 | ☐ |
| 2 | ☐ |
| 3 | ☐ |

## DESCRIBE YOUR LEARNING EXPERIENCE FOR TODAY

## SPECIAL WORDS FOR TODAY

| DAILY WORD BUILDER | VERB OF THE DAY | COGNATE OF THE DAY |
|---|---|---|
| **Durante Mucho Tiempo** | **Poder** | **Acusar** |
| adv. For A Long Time | To Be Able, Can /g: Pudiendo / pp: Podido /Irr. | Verb. From: Accuse OR IR) |

## INTERESTING THINGS FROM TODAY

### FOUR SENTENCES THAT I READ, HEARD OR CREATED TODAY

**1**

**2**

**3**

**4**

## THINGS I HAVE QUESTIONS ABOUT

## DESCRIBE YOUR ACTIVITIES IN THESE TASKS FOR TODAY

| ACTIVITY | DESCRIPTION | SATISFACTION |
|---|---|---|
| READING | | ☹ ☹ 😐 🙂 😄 |
| LISTENING | | ☹ ☹ 😐 🙂 😄 |
| WRITING | | ☹ ☹ 😐 🙂 😄 |
| SPEAKING | | ☹ ☹ 😐 🙂 😄 |
| STUDYING | | ☹ ☹ 😐 🙂 😄 |
| VOCABULARY | | ☹ ☹ 😐 🙂 😄 |
| LOG YOUR STUDY TIME | | TOTAL TIME |
| EACH BOX EQUALS 5 MINS. | | : |

| DAY & DATE | | STUDY STREAK # | |
|---|---|---|---|
| LEARNING MOOD | ☹ ☹ 😐 🙂 😃 | # VERBS ACQUIRED | |

## PAST STUDIES IN REVIEW

| VOCABULARY FROM YESTERDAY | GOALS FROM YESTERDAY |
|---|---|
| 1 | ☐ |
| 2 | ☐ |
| 3 | ☐ |

| VOCABULARY FROM 5 DAYS AGO | VOCABULARY FROM 10 DAYS AGO |
|---|---|
| 1 | 1 |
| 2 | 2 |
| 3 | 3 |

## PRIORITIES FOR TODAY

| VOCABULARY FOR TODAY | GOALS FOR TODAY |
|---|---|
| 1 | ☐ |
| 2 | ☐ |
| 3 | ☐ |

## DESCRIBE YOUR LEARNING EXPERIENCE FOR TODAY

## SPECIAL WORDS FOR TODAY

| DAILY WORD BUILDER | VERB OF THE DAY | COGNATE OF THE DAY |
|---|---|---|
| **Durante Años** | **Volver** | **Presentar** |
| adv. For years | To Return, Go Back /g: Volviendo / pp: Vuelto /Irr. | Verb. From: Present (ADDING AR OR IR) |

## INTERESTING THINGS FROM TODAY

### FOUR SENTENCES THAT I READ, HEARD OR CREATED TODAY

**1**

**2**

**3**

**4**

## THINGS I HAVE QUESTIONS ABOUT

## DESCRIBE YOUR ACTIVITIES IN THESE TASKS FOR TODAY

| ACTIVITY | DESCRIPTION | SATISFACTION |
|---|---|---|
| READING | | 😫 😖 😐 😊 😄 |
| LISTENING | | 😫 😖 😐 😊 😄 |
| WRITING | | 😫 😖 😐 😊 😄 |
| SPEAKING | | 😫 😖 😐 😊 😄 |
| STUDYING | | 😫 😖 😐 😊 😄 |
| VOCABULARY | | 😫 😖 😐 😊 😄 |

| LOG YOUR STUDY TIME | | | | | | | | | | | | | | TOTAL TIME |
|---|---|---|---|---|---|---|---|---|---|---|---|---|---|---|
| EACH BOX EQUALS 5 MINS. | | | | | | | | | | | | | | : |

| DAY & DATE | | | STUDY STREAK # | |
|---|---|---|---|---|
| LEARNING MOOD | ☹ ☹ 😐 🙂 😃 | | # VERBS ACQUIRED | |

## PAST STUDIES IN REVIEW

| VOCABULARY FROM YESTERDAY | GOALS FROM YESTERDAY |
|---|---|
| 1 | ☐ |
| 2 | ☐ |
| 3 | ☐ |

| VOCABULARY FROM 5 DAYS AGO | VOCABULARY FROM 10 DAYS AGO |
|---|---|
| 1 | 1 |
| 2 | 2 |
| 3 | 3 |

## PRIORITIES FOR TODAY

| VOCABULARY FOR TODAY | GOALS FOR TODAY |
|---|---|
| 1 | ☐ |
| 2 | ☐ |
| 3 | ☐ |

## DESCRIBE YOUR LEARNING EXPERIENCE FOR TODAY

## SPECIAL WORDS FOR TODAY

| DAILY WORD BUILDER | VERB OF THE DAY | COGNATE OF THE DAY |
|---|---|---|
| **Durante El Día** | **Enojarse** | **Ignorar** |
| adv. During the day. | To Get Angry, Get Upset, Lose One'S Temper /g: Enojándose / pp: Enojado | Verb. From: Ignore (E=AR OR IR) |

## INTERESTING THINGS FROM TODAY

### FOUR SENTENCES THAT I READ, HEARD OR CREATED TODAY

**1**

**2**

**3**

**4**

## THINGS I HAVE QUESTIONS ABOUT

## DESCRIBE YOUR ACTIVITIES IN THESE TASKS FOR TODAY

| ACTIVITY | DESCRIPTION | SATISFACTION |
|----------|-------------|--------------|
| READING | | ☹ ☹ 😐 🙂 😊 |
| LISTENING | | ☹ ☹ 😐 🙂 😊 |
| WRITING | | ☹ ☹ 😐 🙂 😊 |
| SPEAKING | | ☹ ☹ 😐 🙂 😊 |
| STUDYING | | ☹ ☹ 😐 🙂 😊 |
| VOCABULARY | | ☹ ☹ 😐 🙂 😊 |

| LOG YOUR STUDY TIME | | | | | | | | | | | | | | TOTAL TIME |
|---------------------|--|--|--|--|--|--|--|--|--|--|--|--|--|------------|
| EACH BOX EQUALS 5 MINS. | | | | | | | | | | | | | | : |

## PAST STUDIES IN REVIEW

| VOCABULARY FROM YESTERDAY | GOALS FROM YESTERDAY |
|---|---|
| 1 | ☐ |
| 2 | ☐ |
| 3 | ☐ |

| VOCABULARY FROM 5 DAYS AGO | VOCABULARY FROM 10 DAYS AGO |
|---|---|
| 1 | 1 |
| 2 | 2 |
| 3 | 3 |

## PRIORITIES FOR TODAY

| VOCABULARY FOR TODAY | GOALS FOR TODAY |
|---|---|
| 1 | ☐ |
| 2 | ☐ |
| 3 | ☐ |

## DESCRIBE YOUR LEARNING EXPERIENCE FOR TODAY

## SPECIAL WORDS FOR TODAY

| DAILY WORD BUILDER | VERB OF THE DAY | COGNATE OF THE DAY |
|---|---|---|
| **Ayuda Durante Eventos** | **Parar** | **Consistir** |
| n. f. Event support. | To Stop, Halt /g: Parando / pp: Parado | Verb. From: Consist (V+C+T=TIR OR TAR) |

## INTERESTING THINGS FROM TODAY

### FOUR SENTENCES THAT I READ, HEARD OR CREATED TODAY

**1**

**2**

**3**

**4**

## THINGS I HAVE QUESTIONS ABOUT

## DESCRIBE YOUR ACTIVITIES IN THESE TASKS FOR TODAY

| ACTIVITY | DESCRIPTION | SATISFACTION |
|---|---|---|
| READING | | ☹ ☹ 😐 🙂 😊 |
| LISTENING | | ☹ ☹ 😐 🙂 😊 |
| WRITING | | ☹ ☹ 😐 🙂 😊 |
| SPEAKING | | ☹ ☹ 😐 🙂 😊 |
| STUDYING | | ☹ ☹ 😐 🙂 😊 |
| VOCABULARY | | ☹ ☹ 😐 🙂 😊 |
| LOG YOUR STUDY TIME | | TOTAL TIME |
| EACH BOX EQUALS 5 MINS. | | : |

| DAY & DATE | | STUDY STREAK # | |
|---|---|---|---|
| LEARNING MOOD | ☹ ☹ 😐 🙂 😃 | # VERBS ACQUIRED | |

## PAST STUDIES IN REVIEW

| VOCABULARY FROM YESTERDAY | GOALS FROM YESTERDAY |
|---|---|
| 1 | ☐ |
| 2 | ☐ |
| 3 | ☐ |

| VOCABULARY FROM 5 DAYS AGO | VOCABULARY FROM 10 DAYS AGO |
|---|---|
| 1 | 1 |
| 2 | 2 |
| 3 | 3 |

## PRIORITIES FOR TODAY

| VOCABULARY FOR TODAY | GOALS FOR TODAY |
|---|---|
| 1 | ☐ |
| 2 | ☐ |
| 3 | ☐ |

## DESCRIBE YOUR LEARNING EXPERIENCE FOR TODAY

## SPECIAL WORDS FOR TODAY

| DAILY WORD BUILDER | VERB OF THE DAY | COGNATE OF THE DAY |
|---|---|---|
| **Durante Todo** | **Advertir** | **Lamentar** |
| prep. Throughout | To Notice, Observe, Advise, Warn /g: Advirtiendo / pp: Advertido /Irr | Verb. From: Lament (ADDING AR OR IR) |

## INTERESTING THINGS FROM TODAY

### FOUR SENTENCES THAT I READ, HEARD OR CREATED TODAY

**1**

**2**

**3**

**4**

## THINGS I HAVE QUESTIONS ABOUT

## DESCRIBE YOUR ACTIVITIES IN THESE TASKS FOR TODAY

| ACTIVITY | DESCRIPTION | SATISFACTION |
|---|---|---|
| READING | | ☹️ 😟 😐 🙂 😊 |
| LISTENING | | ☹️ 😟 😐 🙂 😊 |
| WRITING | | ☹️ 😟 😐 🙂 😊 |
| SPEAKING | | ☹️ 😟 😐 🙂 😊 |
| STUDYING | | ☹️ 😟 😐 🙂 😊 |
| VOCABULARY | | ☹️ 😟 😐 🙂 😊 |

| LOG YOUR STUDY TIME | | | | | | | | | | | | | TOTAL TIME |
|---|---|---|---|---|---|---|---|---|---|---|---|---|---|
| EACH BOX EQUALS 5 MINS. | | | | | | | | | | | | | : |

| DAY & DATE | | STUDY STREAK # | |
|---|---|---|---|
| LEARNING MOOD | ☹ ☹ 😐 🙂 😃 | # VERBS ACQUIRED | |

## PAST STUDIES IN REVIEW

| VOCABULARY FROM YESTERDAY | GOALS FROM YESTERDAY |
|---|---|
| 1 | ☐ |
| 2 | ☐ |
| 3 | ☐ |

| VOCABULARY FROM 5 DAYS AGO | VOCABULARY FROM 10 DAYS AGO |
|---|---|
| 1 | 1 |
| 2 | 2 |
| 3 | 3 |

## PRIORITIES FOR TODAY

| VOCABULARY FOR TODAY | GOALS FOR TODAY |
|---|---|
| 1 | ☐ |
| 2 | ☐ |
| 3 | ☐ |

## DESCRIBE YOUR LEARNING EXPERIENCE FOR TODAY

_____

_____

_____

_____

## SPECIAL WORDS FOR TODAY

| DAILY WORD BUILDER | VERB OF THE DAY | COGNATE OF THE DAY |
|---|---|---|
| **Durante Largo Tiempo** | **Cazar** | **Lúcido** |
| adv. For a long time. | To Hunt, Represent, Stand For /g: Cazando / pp: Cazado /Irr. | Adjective. From: Lucid (ID=IDO) |

## INTERESTING THINGS FROM TODAY

### FOUR SENTENCES THAT I READ, HEARD OR CREATED TODAY

**1**

**2**

**3**

**4**

## THINGS I HAVE QUESTIONS ABOUT

## DESCRIBE YOUR ACTIVITIES IN THESE TASKS FOR TODAY

| ACTIVITY | DESCRIPTION | SATISFACTION |
|----------|-------------|--------------|
| READING | | 😣😟😐😊😄 |
| LISTENING | | 😣😟😐😊😄 |
| WRITING | | 😣😟😐😊😄 |
| SPEAKING | | 😣😟😐😊😄 |
| STUDYING | | 😣😟😐😊😄 |
| VOCABULARY | | 😣😟😐😊😄 |

| LOG YOUR STUDY TIME | | | | | | | | | | | | | | TOTAL TIME |
|---------------------|--|--|--|--|--|--|--|--|--|--|--|--|--|------------|
| EACH BOX EQUALS 5 MINS. | | | | | | | | | | | | | | : |

## THIS WEEK IN REVIEW

### VOCABULARY ACQUIRED

### BIGGEST ACHIEVEMENTS

☐            ☐

☐            ☐

☐            ☐

### AREAS FOR IMPROVEMENT

1

2

3

4

## THINGS THAT I STILL HAVE QUESTIONS ABOUT

|  |  |
|---|---|
|  |  |
|  |  |
|  |  |

## FINAL MEASUREMENTS OF THIS WEEK

| TOTAL TIME THIS WEEK | TOTAL NEW VERBS | TOTAL NEW WORDS |
|---|---|---|
|  |  |  |

## SELF-ASSESSMENT OF MY ACTIVITIES THIS WEEK

| ACTIVITIES | SPECIFIC ASSESSMENTS | SATISFACTION |
|---|---|---|
| READING | | ☹ ☹ 😐 🙂 😊 |
| LISTENING | | ☹ ☹ 😐 🙂 😊 |
| WRITING | | ☹ ☹ 😐 🙂 😊 |
| SPEAKING | | ☹ ☹ 😐 🙂 😊 |
| STUDYING | | ☹ ☹ 😐 🙂 😊 |
| MOTIVATION | | ☹ ☹ 😐 🙂 😊 |
| LOG YOUR STUDY TIME | | TOTAL TIME |
| EACH BOX EQUALS 1 HOUR | | : |

| DAY & DATE | | STUDY STREAK # |
|---|---|---|
| LEARNING MOOD ☹ ☹ 😐 🙂 😀 | | # VERBS ACQUIRED |

## PAST STUDIES IN REVIEW

| VOCABULARY FROM YESTERDAY | GOALS FROM YESTERDAY |
|---|---|
| 1 | ☐ |
| 2 | ☐ |
| 3 | ☐ |

| VOCABULARY FROM 5 DAYS AGO | VOCABULARY FROM 10 DAYS AGO |
|---|---|
| 1 | 1 |
| 2 | 2 |
| 3 | 3 |

## PRIORITIES FOR TODAY

| VOCABULARY FOR TODAY | GOALS FOR TODAY |
|---|---|
| 1 | ☐ |
| 2 | ☐ |
| 3 | ☐ |

## DESCRIBE YOUR LEARNING EXPERIENCE FOR TODAY

## SPECIAL WORDS FOR TODAY

| DAILY WORD BUILDER | VERB OF THE DAY | COGNATE OF THE DAY |
|---|---|---|
| **Aviso** | **Contar** | **Existencialismo** |
| n. m. Notice. Notification. Nudge. | To Count, Relate, Tell /g: Contando / pp: Contado /Irr. | Noun. From: Existentialism (ISM=ISMO) |

## INTERESTING THINGS FROM TODAY

### FOUR SENTENCES THAT I READ, HEARD OR CREATED TODAY

**1**

**2**

**3**

**4**

## THINGS I HAVE QUESTIONS ABOUT

## DESCRIBE YOUR ACTIVITIES IN THESE TASKS FOR TODAY

| ACTIVITY | DESCRIPTION | SATISFACTION |
|---|---|---|
| READING | | ☹ ☹ 😐 🙂 😊 |
| LISTENING | | ☹ ☹ 😐 🙂 😊 |
| WRITING | | ☹ ☹ 😐 🙂 😊 |
| SPEAKING | | ☹ ☹ 😐 🙂 😊 |
| STUDYING | | ☹ ☹ 😐 🙂 😊 |
| VOCABULARY | | ☹ ☹ 😐 🙂 😊 |

| LOG YOUR STUDY TIME | | | | | | | | | | | | | | TOTAL TIME |
|---|---|---|---|---|---|---|---|---|---|---|---|---|---|---|
| EACH BOX EQUALS 5 MINS. | | | | | | | | | | | | | | : |

| DAY & DATE | | STUDY STREAK # | |
|---|---|---|---|
| LEARNING MOOD | ☹ ☹ 😐 🙂 😄 | # VERBS ACQUIRED | |

## PAST STUDIES IN REVIEW

| VOCABULARY FROM YESTERDAY | GOALS FROM YESTERDAY |
|---|---|
| 1 | ☐ |
| 2 | ☐ |
| 3 | ☐ |

| VOCABULARY FROM 5 DAYS AGO | VOCABULARY FROM 10 DAYS AGO |
|---|---|
| 1 | 1 |
| 2 | 2 |
| 3 | 3 |

## PRIORITIES FOR TODAY

| VOCABULARY FOR TODAY | GOALS FOR TODAY |
|---|---|
| 1 | ☐ |
| 2 | ☐ |
| 3 | ☐ |

## DESCRIBE YOUR LEARNING EXPERIENCE FOR TODAY

## SPECIAL WORDS FOR TODAY

| DAILY WORD BUILDER | VERB OF THE DAY | COGNATE OF THE DAY |
|---|---|---|
| **Aviso Legal** | **Poner** | **Gloria** |
| n. m. Legal notice. Legal warning | To Put, Place, Set /g: Poniendo / pp: Puesto /Irr. | Noun. From: Glory (Y=IA OR ÍA) |

### FOUR SENTENCES THAT I READ, HEARD OR CREATED TODAY

**1**

**2**

**3**

**4**

## THINGS I HAVE QUESTIONS ABOUT

## DESCRIBE YOUR ACTIVITIES IN THESE TASKS FOR TODAY

| ACTIVITY | DESCRIPTION | SATISFACTION |
|---|---|---|
| READING | | ☹ ☹ 😐 ☺ 😃 |
| LISTENING | | ☹ ☹ 😐 ☺ 😃 |
| WRITING | | ☹ ☹ 😐 ☺ 😃 |
| SPEAKING | | ☹ ☹ 😐 ☺ 😃 |
| STUDYING | | ☹ ☹ 😐 ☺ 😃 |
| VOCABULARY | | ☹ ☹ 😐 ☺ 😃 |

| LOG YOUR STUDY TIME | | | | | | | | | | | | | TOTAL TIME |
|---|---|---|---|---|---|---|---|---|---|---|---|---|---|
| EACH BOX EQUALS 5 MINS. | | | | | | | | | | | | | : |

| DAY & DATE | | STUDY STREAK # | |
|---|---|---|---|
| LEARNING MOOD | ☹ ☹ 😐 🙂 😃 | # VERBS ACQUIRED | |

## PAST STUDIES IN REVIEW

| VOCABULARY FROM YESTERDAY | GOALS FROM YESTERDAY |
|---|---|
| 1 | ☐ |
| 2 | ☐ |
| 3 | ☐ |

| VOCABULARY FROM 5 DAYS AGO | VOCABULARY FROM 10 DAYS AGO |
|---|---|
| 1 | 1 |
| 2 | 2 |
| 3 | 3 |

## PRIORITIES FOR TODAY

| VOCABULARY FOR TODAY | GOALS FOR TODAY |
|---|---|
| 1 | ☐ |
| 2 | ☐ |
| 3 | ☐ |

## DESCRIBE YOUR LEARNING EXPERIENCE FOR TODAY

## SPECIAL WORDS FOR TODAY

| DAILY WORD BUILDER | VERB OF THE DAY | COGNATE OF THE DAY |
|---|---|---|
| **Sin Previo Aviso** | **Abandonar** | **Fantástico** |
| adv. Without notice. adj. Unannounced. Sudden | To Abandon, Leave Behind, Desert; To Quit, Give Up /g: Abandonando /pp: Abandonado | Adjective. From: Fantastic (IC=ICO) |

## INTERESTING THINGS FROM TODAY

### FOUR SENTENCES THAT I READ, HEARD OR CREATED TODAY

**1**

**2**

**3**

**4**

## THINGS I HAVE QUESTIONS ABOUT

## DESCRIBE YOUR ACTIVITIES IN THESE TASKS FOR TODAY

| ACTIVITY | DESCRIPTION | SATISFACTION |
|---|---|---|
| READING | | 😧 😣 😐 🙂 😄 |
| LISTENING | | 😧 😣 😐 🙂 😄 |
| WRITING | | 😧 😣 😐 🙂 😄 |
| SPEAKING | | 😧 😣 😐 🙂 😄 |
| STUDYING | | 😧 😣 😐 🙂 😄 |
| VOCABULARY | | 😧 😣 😐 🙂 😄 |

| LOG YOUR STUDY TIME | | TOTAL TIME |
|---|---|---|
| EACH BOX EQUALS 5 MINS. | | : |

| DAY & DATE | | | STUDY STREAK # |
|---|---|---|---|
| LEARNING MOOD | ☹ ☹ 😐 🙂 😃 | | # VERBS ACQUIRED |

## PAST STUDIES IN REVIEW

| VOCABULARY FROM YESTERDAY | GOALS FROM YESTERDAY |
|---|---|
| **1** | ☐ |
| **2** | ☐ |
| **3** | ☐ |

| VOCABULARY FROM 5 DAYS AGO | VOCABULARY FROM 10 DAYS AGO |
|---|---|
| **1** | **1** |
| **2** | **2** |
| **3** | **3** |

## PRIORITIES FOR TODAY

| VOCABULARY FOR TODAY | GOALS FOR TODAY |
|---|---|
| **1** | ☐ |
| **2** | ☐ |
| **3** | ☐ |

## DESCRIBE YOUR LEARNING EXPERIENCE FOR TODAY

## SPECIAL WORDS FOR TODAY

| DAILY WORD BUILDER | VERB OF THE DAY | COGNATE OF THE DAY |
|---|---|---|
| **Hasta Nuevo Aviso** | **Escoger** | **Discriminante** |
| adv. Until further notice. | To Choose, Select, Pick /g: Escogiendo / pp: Escogido | Adjective. From: Discriminant (NT=NTE) |

## INTERESTING THINGS FROM TODAY

### FOUR SENTENCES THAT I READ, HEARD OR CREATED TODAY

**1**

**2**

**3**

**4**

## THINGS I HAVE QUESTIONS ABOUT

## DESCRIBE YOUR ACTIVITIES IN THESE TASKS FOR TODAY

| ACTIVITY | DESCRIPTION | SATISFACTION |
|---|---|---|
| READING | | 😞😟😐🙂😃 |
| LISTENING | | 😞😟😐🙂😃 |
| WRITING | | 😞😟😐🙂😃 |
| SPEAKING | | 😞😟😐🙂😃 |
| STUDYING | | 😞😟😐🙂😃 |
| VOCABULARY | | 😞😟😐🙂😃 |

| LOG YOUR STUDY TIME | | | | | | | | | | | | | TOTAL TIME |
|---|---|---|---|---|---|---|---|---|---|---|---|---|---|
| EACH BOX EQUALS 5 MINS. | | | | | | | | | | | | | : |

| DAY & DATE | | | STUDY STREAK # | |
|---|---|---|---|---|
| LEARNING MOOD | ☹ ☹ 😐 🙂 😄 | | # VERBS ACQUIRED | |

## PAST STUDIES IN REVIEW

| VOCABULARY FROM YESTERDAY | GOALS FROM YESTERDAY |
|---|---|
| 1 | ☐ |
| 2 | ☐ |
| 3 | ☐ |

| VOCABULARY FROM 5 DAYS AGO | VOCABULARY FROM 10 DAYS AGO |
|---|---|
| 1 | 1 |
| 2 | 2 |
| 3 | 3 |

## PRIORITIES FOR TODAY

| VOCABULARY FOR TODAY | GOALS FOR TODAY |
|---|---|
| 1 | ☐ |
| 2 | ☐ |
| 3 | ☐ |

## DESCRIBE YOUR LEARNING EXPERIENCE FOR TODAY

_____

_____

_____

_____

## SPECIAL WORDS FOR TODAY

| DAILY WORD BUILDER | VERB OF THE DAY | COGNATE OF THE DAY |
|---|---|---|
| **Previo Aviso** | **Pasar** | **Directamente** |
| n. m. Prior notice. | To Pass, Pass By; To Pass On; To Spend [Time]; To Happen /g: Pasando / pp: Pasado | Adverb. From: Directly (LY=MENTE) |

## INTERESTING THINGS FROM TODAY

### FOUR SENTENCES THAT I READ, HEARD OR CREATED TODAY

**1**

**2**

**3**

**4**

## THINGS I HAVE QUESTIONS ABOUT

## DESCRIBE YOUR ACTIVITIES IN THESE TASKS FOR TODAY

| ACTIVITY | DESCRIPTION | SATISFACTION |
|----------|-------------|--------------|
| READING | | ☹ ☹ 😐 🙂 😀 |
| LISTENING | | ☹ ☹ 😐 🙂 😀 |
| WRITING | | ☹ ☹ 😐 🙂 😀 |
| SPEAKING | | ☹ ☹ 😐 🙂 😀 |
| STUDYING | | ☹ ☹ 😐 🙂 😀 |
| VOCABULARY | | ☹ ☹ 😐 🙂 😀 |

| LOG YOUR STUDY TIME | | | | | | | | | | | | TOTAL TIME |
|---------------------|--|--|--|--|--|--|--|--|--|--|--|------------|
| EACH BOX EQUALS 5 MINS. | | | | | | | | | | | | : |

| DAY & DATE | | STUDY STREAK # |
|---|---|---|
| LEARNING MOOD  ☹ ☹ 😐 🙂 😄 | | # VERBS ACQUIRED |

## PAST STUDIES IN REVIEW

| VOCABULARY FROM YESTERDAY | GOALS FROM YESTERDAY |
|---|---|
| 1 | ☐ |
| 2 | ☐ |
| 3 | ☐ |

| VOCABULARY FROM 5 DAYS AGO | VOCABULARY FROM 10 DAYS AGO |
|---|---|
| 1 | 1 |
| 2 | 2 |
| 3 | 3 |

## PRIORITIES FOR TODAY

| VOCABULARY FOR TODAY | GOALS FOR TODAY |
|---|---|
| 1 | ☐ |
| 2 | ☐ |
| 3 | ☐ |

## DESCRIBE YOUR LEARNING EXPERIENCE FOR TODAY

## SPECIAL WORDS FOR TODAY

| DAILY WORD BUILDER | VERB OF THE DAY | COGNATE OF THE DAY |
|---|---|---|
| **Aviso Importante** | **Afligir** | **Recesión** |
| n. m. Important notice | To Afflict, To Grieve, To Pain, To Distress /g: Afligiendo / pp: Afligido /Irr. | Noun. From: Recession (SION=SIÓN) |

## INTERESTING THINGS FROM TODAY

### FOUR SENTENCES THAT I READ, HEARD OR CREATED TODAY

**1**

**2**

**3**

**4**

## THINGS I HAVE QUESTIONS ABOUT

## DESCRIBE YOUR ACTIVITIES IN THESE TASKS FOR TODAY

| ACTIVITY | DESCRIPTION | SATISFACTION |
|----------|-------------|--------------|
| READING | | ☹ ☹ 😐 🙂 😀 |
| LISTENING | | ☹ ☹ 😐 🙂 😀 |
| WRITING | | ☹ ☹ 😐 🙂 😀 |
| SPEAKING | | ☹ ☹ 😐 🙂 😀 |
| STUDYING | | ☹ ☹ 😐 🙂 😀 |
| VOCABULARY | | ☹ ☹ 😐 🙂 😀 |
| LOG YOUR STUDY TIME | | TOTAL TIME |
| EACH BOX EQUALS 5 MINS. | | : |

## PAST STUDIES IN REVIEW

| VOCABULARY FROM YESTERDAY | GOALS FROM YESTERDAY |
|---|---|
| **1** | ☐ |
| **2** | ☐ |
| **3** | ☐ |

| VOCABULARY FROM 5 DAYS AGO | VOCABULARY FROM 10 DAYS AGO |
|---|---|
| **1** | **1** |
| **2** | **2** |
| **3** | **3** |

## PRIORITIES FOR TODAY

| VOCABULARY FOR TODAY | GOALS FOR TODAY |
|---|---|
| **1** | ☐ |
| **2** | ☐ |
| **3** | ☐ |

## DESCRIBE YOUR LEARNING EXPERIENCE FOR TODAY

## SPECIAL WORDS FOR TODAY

| DAILY WORD BUILDER | VERB OF THE DAY | COGNATE OF THE DAY |
|---|---|---|
| **Aviso de Privacidad** | **Chocar** | **Sesión** |
| n. m. Privacy notice. | To Shock; To Startle; To Be Suprising; To Collide, Crash /g: Chocando / pp: Chocado /Irr. | Noun. From: Session (SION=SIÓN) |

## INTERESTING THINGS FROM TODAY

### FOUR SENTENCES THAT I READ, HEARD OR CREATED TODAY

**1**

**2**

**3**

**4**

## THINGS I HAVE QUESTIONS ABOUT

## DESCRIBE YOUR ACTIVITIES IN THESE TASKS FOR TODAY

| ACTIVITY | DESCRIPTION | SATISFACTION |
|---|---|---|
| READING | | ☹ 😫 😐 🙂 😊 |
| LISTENING | | ☹ 😫 😐 🙂 😊 |
| WRITING | | ☹ 😫 😐 🙂 😊 |
| SPEAKING | | ☹ 😫 😐 🙂 😊 |
| STUDYING | | ☹ 😫 😐 🙂 😊 |
| VOCABULARY | | ☹ 😫 😐 🙂 😊 |

| LOG YOUR STUDY TIME | | | | | | | | | | | | | | TOTAL TIME |
|---|---|---|---|---|---|---|---|---|---|---|---|---|---|---|
| EACH BOX EQUALS 5 MINS. | | | | | | | | | | | | | | : |

## THIS WEEK IN REVIEW

### VOCABULARY ACQUIRED

### BIGGEST ACHIEVEMENTS

☐ ☐

☐ ☐

☐ ☐

### AREAS FOR IMPROVEMENT

**1**

**2**

**3**

**4**

## THINGS THAT I STILL HAVE QUESTIONS ABOUT

| | |
|---|---|
| | |
| | |
| | |

## FINAL MEASUREMENTS OF THIS WEEK

| TOTAL TIME THIS WEEK | TOTAL NEW VERBS | TOTAL NEW WORDS |
|---|---|---|
| | | |

## SELF-ASSESSMENT OF MY ACTIVITIES THIS WEEK

| ACTIVITIES | SPECIFIC ASSESSMENTS | SATISFACTION |
|---|---|---|
| READING | | 😞😟😐😊😄 |
| LISTENING | | 😞😟😐😊😄 |
| WRITING | | 😞😟😐😊😄 |
| SPEAKING | | 😞😟😐😊😄 |
| STUDYING | | 😞😟😐😊😄 |
| MOTIVATION | | 😞😟😐😊😄 |

| LOG YOUR STUDY TIME | | | | | | | | | | | | TOTAL TIME |
|---|---|---|---|---|---|---|---|---|---|---|---|---|
| EACH BOX EQUALS 1 HOUR | | | | | | | | | | | | : |

| DAY & DATE | | STUDY STREAK # | |
| --- | --- | --- | --- |
| LEARNING MOOD | ☹ ☹ 😐 🙂 😀 | # VERBS ACQUIRED | |

## PAST STUDIES IN REVIEW

| VOCABULARY FROM YESTERDAY | GOALS FROM YESTERDAY |
| --- | --- |
| 1 | ☐ |
| 2 | ☐ |
| 3 | ☐ |

| VOCABULARY FROM 5 DAYS AGO | VOCABULARY FROM 10 DAYS AGO |
| --- | --- |
| 1 | 1 |
| 2 | 2 |
| 3 | 3 |

## PRIORITIES FOR TODAY

| VOCABULARY FOR TODAY | GOALS FOR TODAY |
| --- | --- |
| 1 | ☐ |
| 2 | ☐ |
| 3 | ☐ |

## DESCRIBE YOUR LEARNING EXPERIENCE FOR TODAY

## SPECIAL WORDS FOR TODAY

| DAILY WORD BUILDER | VERB OF THE DAY | COGNATE OF THE DAY |
| --- | --- | --- |
| **Vida** | **Continuar** | **Automóvil** |
| n. m. Life. Living. | To Continue /g: Continuando / pp: Continuado /Irr. | Noun. From: Automobile (ILE=IL) |

## INTERESTING THINGS FROM TODAY
### FOUR SENTENCES THAT I READ, HEARD OR CREATED TODAY

**1**

**2**

**3**

**4**

## THINGS I HAVE QUESTIONS ABOUT

## DESCRIBE YOUR ACTIVITIES IN THESE TASKS FOR TODAY

| ACTIVITY | DESCRIPTION | SATISFACTION |
|---|---|---|
| READING | | ☹ ☹ 😐 🙂 😊 |
| LISTENING | | ☹ ☹ 😐 🙂 😊 |
| WRITING | | ☹ ☹ 😐 🙂 😊 |
| SPEAKING | | ☹ ☹ 😐 🙂 😊 |
| STUDYING | | ☹ ☹ 😐 🙂 😊 |
| VOCABULARY | | ☹ ☹ 😐 🙂 😊 |
| LOG YOUR STUDY TIME | | TOTAL TIME |
| EACH BOX EQUALS 5 MINS. | | : |

| LEARNING MOOD  ☹ ☹ 😐 🙂 😀 | # VERBS ACQUIRED |

## PAST STUDIES IN REVIEW

| VOCABULARY FROM YESTERDAY | GOALS FROM YESTERDAY |
|---|---|
| 1 | ☐ |
| 2 | ☐ |
| 3 | ☐ |

| VOCABULARY FROM 5 DAYS AGO | VOCABULARY FROM 10 DAYS AGO |
|---|---|
| 1 | 1 |
| 2 | 2 |
| 3 | 3 |

## PRIORITIES FOR TODAY

| VOCABULARY FOR TODAY | GOALS FOR TODAY |
|---|---|
| 1 | ☐ |
| 2 | ☐ |
| 3 | ☐ |

## DESCRIBE YOUR LEARNING EXPERIENCE FOR TODAY

## SPECIAL WORDS FOR TODAY

| DAILY WORD BUILDER | VERB OF THE DAY | COGNATE OF THE DAY |
|---|---|---|
| **Calidad de Vida** | **Ponerse** | **Alcohólico** |
| n. f. Quality of life | To Put On [Clothing]; To Put/Place [Oneself]; /g: Poniéndose / pp: Puesto /Irr. | Adjective. From: Alcoholic (IC=ICO) |

## INTERESTING THINGS FROM TODAY

### FOUR SENTENCES THAT I READ, HEARD OR CREATED TODAY

**1**

**2**

**3**

**4**

## THINGS I HAVE QUESTIONS ABOUT

## DESCRIBE YOUR ACTIVITIES IN THESE TASKS FOR TODAY

| ACTIVITY | DESCRIPTION | SATISFACTION |
|---|---|---|
| READING | | ☹ ☹ 😐 🙂 😊 |
| LISTENING | | ☹ ☹ 😐 🙂 😊 |
| WRITING | | ☹ ☹ 😐 🙂 😊 |
| SPEAKING | | ☹ ☹ 😐 🙂 😊 |
| STUDYING | | ☹ ☹ 😐 🙂 😊 |
| VOCABULARY | | ☹ ☹ 😐 🙂 😊 |
| LOG YOUR STUDY TIME | | TOTAL TIME |
| EACH BOX EQUALS 5 MINS. | | : |

| DAY & DATE | | STUDY STREAK # |
|---|---|---|
| LEARNING MOOD | ☹ ☹ 😐 🙂 😀 | # VERBS ACQUIRED |

## PAST STUDIES IN REVIEW

| VOCABULARY FROM YESTERDAY | GOALS FROM YESTERDAY |
|---|---|
| 1 | ☐ |
| 2 | ☐ |
| 3 | ☐ |

| VOCABULARY FROM 5 DAYS AGO | VOCABULARY FROM 10 DAYS AGO |
|---|---|
| 1 | 1 |
| 2 | 2 |
| 3 | 3 |

## PRIORITIES FOR TODAY

| VOCABULARY FOR TODAY | GOALS FOR TODAY |
|---|---|
| 1 | ☐ |
| 2 | ☐ |
| 3 | ☐ |

## DESCRIBE YOUR LEARNING EXPERIENCE FOR TODAY

## SPECIAL WORDS FOR TODAY

| DAILY WORD BUILDER | VERB OF THE DAY | COGNATE OF THE DAY |
|---|---|---|
| **Vida Útil** | **Aburrirse** | **División** |
| n. f. Useful life. Service life. | To Get Bored, Become Bored, Be Bored /g: Aburriéndose / pp: Aburrido | Noun. From: Division (SION=SIÓN) |

## INTERESTING THINGS FROM TODAY

### FOUR SENTENCES THAT I READ, HEARD OR CREATED TODAY

**1**

**2**

**3**

**4**

## THINGS I HAVE QUESTIONS ABOUT

## DESCRIBE YOUR ACTIVITIES IN THESE TASKS FOR TODAY

| ACTIVITY | DESCRIPTION | SATISFACTION |
|---|---|---|
| READING | | ☹ 😦 😐 🙂 😃 |
| LISTENING | | ☹ 😦 😐 🙂 😃 |
| WRITING | | ☹ 😦 😐 🙂 😃 |
| SPEAKING | | ☹ 😦 😐 🙂 😃 |
| STUDYING | | ☹ 😦 😐 🙂 😃 |
| VOCABULARY | | ☹ 😦 😐 🙂 😃 |

| LOG YOUR STUDY TIME | | | | | | | | | | | | TOTAL TIME |
|---|---|---|---|---|---|---|---|---|---|---|---|---|
| EACH BOX EQUALS 5 MINS. | | | | | | | | | | | | : |

## PAST STUDIES IN REVIEW

| VOCABULARY FROM YESTERDAY | GOALS FROM YESTERDAY |
|---|---|
| 1 | ☐ |
| 2 | ☐ |
| 3 | ☐ |

| VOCABULARY FROM 5 DAYS AGO | VOCABULARY FROM 10 DAYS AGO |
|---|---|
| 1 | 1 |
| 2 | 2 |
| 3 | 3 |

## PRIORITIES FOR TODAY

| VOCABULARY FOR TODAY | GOALS FOR TODAY |
|---|---|
| 1 | ☐ |
| 2 | ☐ |
| 3 | ☐ |

## DESCRIBE YOUR LEARNING EXPERIENCE FOR TODAY

## SPECIAL WORDS FOR TODAY

| DAILY WORD BUILDER | VERB OF THE DAY | COGNATE OF THE DAY |
|---|---|---|
| **Vida Laboral** | **Escribir** | **Discriminación** |
| n. f. Work life. Working life. | To Write /g: Escribiendo / pp: Escrito | Noun. From: Discrimination (TION=CIÓN) |

## INTERESTING THINGS FROM TODAY

### FOUR SENTENCES THAT I READ, HEARD OR CREATED TODAY

**1**

**2**

**3**

**4**

## THINGS I HAVE QUESTIONS ABOUT

## DESCRIBE YOUR ACTIVITIES IN THESE TASKS FOR TODAY

| ACTIVITY | DESCRIPTION | SATISFACTION |
|---|---|---|
| READING | | ☹ ☹ 😐 🙂 😊 |
| LISTENING | | ☹ ☹ 😐 🙂 😊 |
| WRITING | | ☹ ☹ 😐 🙂 😊 |
| SPEAKING | | ☹ ☹ 😐 🙂 😊 |
| STUDYING | | ☹ ☹ 😐 🙂 😊 |
| VOCABULARY | | ☹ ☹ 😐 🙂 😊 |

| LOG YOUR STUDY TIME | | | | | | | | | | | | | TOTAL TIME |
|---|---|---|---|---|---|---|---|---|---|---|---|---|---|
| EACH BOX EQUALS 5 MINS. | | | | | | | | | | | | | : |

| DAY & DATE | | STUDY STREAK # |
|---|---|---|
| LEARNING MOOD | ☹ ☹ 😐 🙂 😃 | # VERBS ACQUIRED |

## PAST STUDIES IN REVIEW

| VOCABULARY FROM YESTERDAY | GOALS FROM YESTERDAY |
|---|---|
| 1 | ☐ |
| 2 | ☐ |
| 3 | ☐ |

| VOCABULARY FROM 5 DAYS AGO | VOCABULARY FROM 10 DAYS AGO |
|---|---|
| 1 | 1 |
| 2 | 2 |
| 3 | 3 |

## PRIORITIES FOR TODAY

| VOCABULARY FOR TODAY | GOALS FOR TODAY |
|---|---|
| 1 | ☐ |
| 2 | ☐ |
| 3 | ☐ |

## DESCRIBE YOUR LEARNING EXPERIENCE FOR TODAY

## SPECIAL WORDS FOR TODAY

| DAILY WORD BUILDER | VERB OF THE DAY | COGNATE OF THE DAY |
|---|---|---|
| **Vida Cotidiana** | **Preguntar** | **Fabricar** |
| n. f. Daily life. Everday life. | To Ask, Inquire /g: Preguntando / pp: Preguntado | Verb. From: Fabricate (ATE=AR) |

## INTERESTING THINGS FROM TODAY

### FOUR SENTENCES THAT I READ, HEARD OR CREATED TODAY

**1**

**2**

**3**

**4**

## THINGS I HAVE QUESTIONS ABOUT

## DESCRIBE YOUR ACTIVITIES IN THESE TASKS FOR TODAY

| ACTIVITY | DESCRIPTION | SATISFACTION |
|---|---|---|
| READING | | ☹ ☹ 😐 🙂 😃 |
| LISTENING | | ☹ ☹ 😐 🙂 😃 |
| WRITING | | ☹ ☹ 😐 🙂 😃 |
| SPEAKING | | ☹ ☹ 😐 🙂 😃 |
| STUDYING | | ☹ ☹ 😐 🙂 😃 |
| VOCABULARY | | ☹ ☹ 😐 🙂 😃 |

| LOG YOUR STUDY TIME | | | | | | | | | | | | | TOTAL TIME |
|---|---|---|---|---|---|---|---|---|---|---|---|---|---|
| EACH BOX EQUALS 5 MINS. | | | | | | | | | | | | | : |

| DAY & DATE | | STUDY STREAK # |
|---|---|---|
| LEARNING MOOD | ☹ ☹ 😐 🙂 😃 | # VERBS ACQUIRED |

## PAST STUDIES IN REVIEW

| VOCABULARY FROM YESTERDAY | GOALS FROM YESTERDAY |
|---|---|
| 1 | ☐ |
| 2 | ☐ |
| 3 | ☐ |

| VOCABULARY FROM 5 DAYS AGO | VOCABULARY FROM 10 DAYS AGO |
|---|---|
| 1 | 1 |
| 2 | 2 |
| 3 | 3 |

## PRIORITIES FOR TODAY

| VOCABULARY FOR TODAY | GOALS FOR TODAY |
|---|---|
| 1 | ☐ |
| 2 | ☐ |
| 3 | ☐ |

## DESCRIBE YOUR LEARNING EXPERIENCE FOR TODAY

## SPECIAL WORDS FOR TODAY

| DAILY WORD BUILDER | VERB OF THE DAY | COGNATE OF THE DAY |
|---|---|---|
| **Nivel de Vida** | **Agorar** | **Eligible** |
| n. m. Standard of living | To Predict, Prophesy /g: Agorando / pp: Agorado /Irr. | Adjective. From: Eligible (BLE=BLE) |

## INTERESTING THINGS FROM TODAY

### FOUR SENTENCES THAT I READ, HEARD OR CREATED TODAY

**1**

**2**

**3**

**4**

## THINGS I HAVE QUESTIONS ABOUT

## DESCRIBE YOUR ACTIVITIES IN THESE TASKS FOR TODAY

| ACTIVITY | DESCRIPTION | SATISFACTION |
|---|---|---|
| READING | | ☹ 😦 😐 🙂 😀 |
| LISTENING | | ☹ 😦 😐 🙂 😀 |
| WRITING | | ☹ 😦 😐 🙂 😀 |
| SPEAKING | | ☹ 😦 😐 🙂 😀 |
| STUDYING | | ☹ 😦 😐 🙂 😀 |
| VOCABULARY | | ☹ 😦 😐 🙂 😀 |
| LOG YOUR STUDY TIME | | TOTAL TIME |
| EACH BOX EQUALS 5 MINS. | | : |

| DAY & DATE | | | STUDY STREAK # | |
|---|---|---|---|---|
| LEARNING MOOD | ☹ ☹ ☺ ☺ ☺ | | # VERBS ACQUIRED | |

## PAST STUDIES IN REVIEW

| VOCABULARY FROM YESTERDAY | GOALS FROM YESTERDAY |
|---|---|
| 1 | ☐ |
| 2 | ☐ |
| 3 | ☐ |

| VOCABULARY FROM 5 DAYS AGO | VOCABULARY FROM 10 DAYS AGO |
|---|---|
| 1 | 1 |
| 2 | 2 |
| 3 | 3 |

## PRIORITIES FOR TODAY

| VOCABULARY FOR TODAY | GOALS FOR TODAY |
|---|---|
| 1 | ☐ |
| 2 | ☐ |
| 3 | ☐ |

## DESCRIBE YOUR LEARNING EXPERIENCE FOR TODAY

## SPECIAL WORDS FOR TODAY

| DAILY WORD BUILDER | VERB OF THE DAY | COGNATE OF THE DAY |
|---|---|---|
| **Estilo De Vida** | **Civilizar** | **Primario** |
| n. m. Lifestyle. Way of life. | To Civilize /g: Civilizando / pp: Civilizado /Irr. | Adjective. From: Primary (ARY=ARIO) |

## INTERESTING THINGS FROM TODAY

### FOUR SENTENCES THAT I READ, HEARD OR CREATED TODAY

**1**

**2**

**3**

**4**

## THINGS I HAVE QUESTIONS ABOUT

## DESCRIBE YOUR ACTIVITIES IN THESE TASKS FOR TODAY

| ACTIVITY | DESCRIPTION | SATISFACTION |
|----------|-------------|--------------|
| READING | | ☹️ ☹️ 😐 🙂 😊 |
| LISTENING | | ☹️ ☹️ 😐 🙂 😊 |
| WRITING | | ☹️ ☹️ 😐 🙂 😊 |
| SPEAKING | | ☹️ ☹️ 😐 🙂 😊 |
| STUDYING | | ☹️ ☹️ 😐 🙂 😊 |
| VOCABULARY | | ☹️ ☹️ 😐 🙂 😊 |

| LOG YOUR STUDY TIME | | | | | | | | | | | | | TOTAL TIME |
|---------------------|--|--|--|--|--|--|--|--|--|--|--|--|------------|
| EACH BOX EQUALS 5 MINS. | | | | | | | | | | | | | : |

**WEEK NUMBER:**

## THIS WEEK IN REVIEW

### VOCABULARY ACQUIRED

### BIGGEST ACHIEVEMENTS

- [ ]
- [ ]
- [ ]

- [ ]
- [ ]
- [ ]

### AREAS FOR IMPROVEMENT

1
2
3
4

## THINGS THAT I STILL HAVE QUESTIONS ABOUT

## FINAL MEASUREMENTS OF THIS WEEK

| TOTAL TIME THIS WEEK | TOTAL NEW VERBS | TOTAL NEW WORDS |
|---|---|---|
| | | |

## SELF-ASSESSMENT OF MY ACTIVITIES THIS WEEK

| ACTIVITIES | SPECIFIC ASSESSMENTS | SATISFACTION |
|---|---|---|
| READING | | ☹️☹️😐🙂😄 |
| LISTENING | | ☹️☹️😐🙂😄 |
| WRITING | | ☹️☹️😐🙂😄 |
| SPEAKING | | ☹️☹️😐🙂😄 |
| STUDYING | | ☹️☹️😐🙂😄 |
| MOTIVATION | | ☹️☹️😐🙂😄 |

| LOG YOUR STUDY TIME | | | | | | | | | | | TOTAL TIME |
|---|---|---|---|---|---|---|---|---|---|---|---|
| EACH BOX EQUALS 1 HOUR | | | | | | | | | | | : |

| DAY & DATE | | STUDY STREAK # | |
|---|---|---|---|
| LEARNING MOOD | ☹ ☹ 😐 🙂 😀 | # VERBS ACQUIRED | |

## PAST STUDIES IN REVIEW

| VOCABULARY FROM YESTERDAY | GOALS FROM YESTERDAY |
|---|---|
| 1 | ☐ |
| 2 | ☐ |
| 3 | ☐ |

| VOCABULARY FROM 5 DAYS AGO | VOCABULARY FROM 10 DAYS AGO |
|---|---|
| 1 | 1 |
| 2 | 2 |
| 3 | 3 |

## PRIORITIES FOR TODAY

| VOCABULARY FOR TODAY | GOALS FOR TODAY |
|---|---|
| 1 | ☐ |
| 2 | ☐ |
| 3 | ☐ |

## DESCRIBE YOUR LEARNING EXPERIENCE FOR TODAY

## SPECIAL WORDS FOR TODAY

| DAILY WORD BUILDER | VERB OF THE DAY | COGNATE OF THE DAY |
|---|---|---|
| **Tomar** | **Creer** | **Abdicar** |
| v. Take. Drink. | To Believe /g: Creyendo / pp: Creído /Irr. | Verb. From: Abdicate (ATE=AR) |

## INTERESTING THINGS FROM TODAY

### FOUR SENTENCES THAT I READ, HEARD OR CREATED TODAY

**1**

**2**

**3**

**4**

## THINGS I HAVE QUESTIONS ABOUT

## DESCRIBE YOUR ACTIVITIES IN THESE TASKS FOR TODAY

| ACTIVITY | DESCRIPTION | SATISFACTION |
|---|---|---|
| READING | | ☹️ 🙁 😐 🙂 😃 |
| LISTENING | | ☹️ 🙁 😐 🙂 😃 |
| WRITING | | ☹️ 🙁 😐 🙂 😃 |
| SPEAKING | | ☹️ 🙁 😐 🙂 😃 |
| STUDYING | | ☹️ 🙁 😐 🙂 😃 |
| VOCABULARY | | ☹️ 🙁 😐 🙂 😃 |
| LOG YOUR STUDY TIME | | TOTAL TIME |
| EACH BOX EQUALS 5 MINS. | | : |

## PAST STUDIES IN REVIEW

| VOCABULARY FROM YESTERDAY | GOALS FROM YESTERDAY |
|---|---|
| 1 | ☐ |
| 2 | ☐ |
| 3 | ☐ |

| VOCABULARY FROM 5 DAYS AGO | VOCABULARY FROM 10 DAYS AGO |
|---|---|
| 1 | 1 |
| 2 | 2 |
| 3 | 3 |

## PRIORITIES FOR TODAY

| VOCABULARY FOR TODAY | GOALS FOR TODAY |
|---|---|
| 1 | ☐ |
| 2 | ☐ |
| 3 | ☐ |

## DESCRIBE YOUR LEARNING EXPERIENCE FOR TODAY

## SPECIAL WORDS FOR TODAY

| DAILY WORD BUILDER | VERB OF THE DAY | COGNATE OF THE DAY |
|---|---|---|
| **Tomar Medidas** | **Practicar** | **Diario** |
| v. Take steps. Take action. | To Practice /g: Practicando / pp: Practicado /Irr. | Adverb. From: Diary (ARY=ARIO) |

## INTERESTING THINGS FROM TODAY

### FOUR SENTENCES THAT I READ, HEARD OR CREATED TODAY

**1**

**2**

**3**

**4**

## THINGS I HAVE QUESTIONS ABOUT

## DESCRIBE YOUR ACTIVITIES IN THESE TASKS FOR TODAY

| ACTIVITY | DESCRIPTION | SATISFACTION |
|---|---|---|
| READING | | ☹ ☹ 😐 🙂 😄 |
| LISTENING | | ☹ ☹ 😐 🙂 😄 |
| WRITING | | ☹ ☹ 😐 🙂 😄 |
| SPEAKING | | ☹ ☹ 😐 🙂 😄 |
| STUDYING | | ☹ ☹ 😐 🙂 😄 |
| VOCABULARY | | ☹ ☹ 😐 🙂 😄 |

| LOG YOUR STUDY TIME | | | | | | | | | | | | | | TOTAL TIME |
|---|---|---|---|---|---|---|---|---|---|---|---|---|---|---|
| EACH BOX EQUALS 5 MINS. | | | | | | | | | | | | | | : |

## PAST STUDIES IN REVIEW

| VOCABULARY FROM YESTERDAY | GOALS FROM YESTERDAY |
|---|---|
| 1 | ☐ |
| 2 | ☐ |
| 3 | ☐ |

| VOCABULARY FROM 5 DAYS AGO | VOCABULARY FROM 10 DAYS AGO |
|---|---|
| 1 | 1 |
| 2 | 2 |
| 3 | 3 |

## PRIORITIES FOR TODAY

| VOCABULARY FOR TODAY | GOALS FOR TODAY |
|---|---|
| 1 | ☐ |
| 2 | ☐ |
| 3 | ☐ |

## DESCRIBE YOUR LEARNING EXPERIENCE FOR TODAY

## SPECIAL WORDS FOR TODAY

| DAILY WORD BUILDER | VERB OF THE DAY | COGNATE OF THE DAY |
|---|---|---|
| **Tomar En Cuenta** | **Acostumbrarse** | **Estuario** |
| v. Take into account. | To Get Used To (accustomed) /g: Acostumbrándose / pp: Acostumbrado | Noun. From: Estuary (ARY=ARIO) |

### FOUR SENTENCES THAT I READ, HEARD OR CREATED TODAY

**1**

**2**

**3**

**4**

## THINGS I HAVE QUESTIONS ABOUT

## DESCRIBE YOUR ACTIVITIES IN THESE TASKS FOR TODAY

| ACTIVITY | DESCRIPTION | SATISFACTION |
|---|---|---|
| READING | | 😟 😦 😐 🙂 😊 |
| LISTENING | | 😟 😦 😐 🙂 😊 |
| WRITING | | 😟 😦 😐 🙂 😊 |
| SPEAKING | | 😟 😦 😐 🙂 😊 |
| STUDYING | | 😟 😦 😐 🙂 😊 |
| VOCABULARY | | 😟 😦 😐 🙂 😊 |

| LOG YOUR STUDY TIME | | | | | | | | | | | | TOTAL TIME |
|---|---|---|---|---|---|---|---|---|---|---|---|---|
| EACH BOX EQUALS 5 MINS. | | | | | | | | | | | | : |

| DAY & DATE | | | STUDY STREAK # | |
|---|---|---|---|---|
| LEARNING MOOD | ☹ ☹ ☺ ☺ ☺ | | # VERBS ACQUIRED | |

## PAST STUDIES IN REVIEW

| VOCABULARY FROM YESTERDAY | GOALS FROM YESTERDAY |
|---|---|
| 1 | ☐ |
| 2 | ☐ |
| 3 | ☐ |

| VOCABULARY FROM 5 DAYS AGO | VOCABULARY FROM 10 DAYS AGO |
|---|---|
| 1 | 1 |
| 2 | 2 |
| 3 | 3 |

## PRIORITIES FOR TODAY

| VOCABULARY FOR TODAY | GOALS FOR TODAY |
|---|---|
| 1 | ☐ |
| 2 | ☐ |
| 3 | ☐ |

## DESCRIBE YOUR LEARNING EXPERIENCE FOR TODAY

## SPECIAL WORDS FOR TODAY

| DAILY WORD BUILDER | VERB OF THE DAY | COGNATE OF THE DAY |
|---|---|---|
| **Tomar Una Decisión** | **Escuchar** | **Revulsión** |
| v. Take a decision. | To Listen To, Hear /g: Escuchando / pp: Escuchado | Noun. From: Revulsion (SION=SIÓN) |

## INTERESTING THINGS FROM TODAY

### FOUR SENTENCES THAT I READ, HEARD OR CREATED TODAY

**1**

**2**

**3**

**4**

## THINGS I HAVE QUESTIONS ABOUT

## DESCRIBE YOUR ACTIVITIES IN THESE TASKS FOR TODAY

| ACTIVITY | DESCRIPTION | SATISFACTION |
|---|---|---|
| READING | | ☹ ☹ 😐 🙂 😄 |
| LISTENING | | ☹ ☹ 😐 🙂 😄 |
| WRITING | | ☹ ☹ 😐 🙂 😄 |
| SPEAKING | | ☹ ☹ 😐 🙂 😄 |
| STUDYING | | ☹ ☹ 😐 🙂 😄 |
| VOCABULARY | | ☹ ☹ 😐 🙂 😄 |

| LOG YOUR STUDY TIME | | | | | | | | | | | | | TOTAL TIME |
|---|---|---|---|---|---|---|---|---|---|---|---|---|---|
| EACH BOX EQUALS 5 MINS. | | | | | | | | | | | | | : |

| DAY & DATE | | STUDY STREAK # | |
|---|---|---|---|
| LEARNING MOOD | ☹ ☹ 😐 🙂 😃 | # VERBS ACQUIRED | |

## PAST STUDIES IN REVIEW

| VOCABULARY FROM YESTERDAY | GOALS FROM YESTERDAY |
|---|---|
| 1 | ☐ |
| 2 | ☐ |
| 3 | ☐ |

| VOCABULARY FROM 5 DAYS AGO | VOCABULARY FROM 10 DAYS AGO |
|---|---|
| 1 | 1 |
| 2 | 2 |
| 3 | 3 |

## PRIORITIES FOR TODAY

| VOCABULARY FOR TODAY | GOALS FOR TODAY |
|---|---|
| 1 | ☐ |
| 2 | ☐ |
| 3 | ☐ |

## DESCRIBE YOUR LEARNING EXPERIENCE FOR TODAY

## SPECIAL WORDS FOR TODAY

| DAILY WORD BUILDER | VERB OF THE DAY | COGNATE OF THE DAY |
|---|---|---|
| **Tomar El Sol** | **Quedar** | **Divergencia** |
| v. Sunbathe. | To Stay, Remain, Be Left; To Be [Indicating Location] /g: Quedando / pp: Quedado | Noun. From: Divergence (ENCE=ENCIA) |

## INTERESTING THINGS FROM TODAY

### FOUR SENTENCES THAT I READ, HEARD OR CREATED TODAY

**1**

**2**

**3**

**4**

## THINGS I HAVE QUESTIONS ABOUT

## DESCRIBE YOUR ACTIVITIES IN THESE TASKS FOR TODAY

| ACTIVITY | DESCRIPTION | SATISFACTION |
|----------|-------------|--------------|
| READING | | ☹️😟😐🙂😃 |
| LISTENING | | ☹️😟😐🙂😃 |
| WRITING | | ☹️😟😐🙂😃 |
| SPEAKING | | ☹️😟😐🙂😃 |
| STUDYING | | ☹️😟😐🙂😃 |
| VOCABULARY | | ☹️😟😐🙂😃 |

| LOG YOUR STUDY TIME | | | | | | | | | | | | | TOTAL TIME |
|---------------------|--|--|--|--|--|--|--|--|--|--|--|--|------------|
| EACH BOX EQUALS 5 MINS. | | | | | | | | | | | | | : |

| DAY & DATE | | STUDY STREAK # |
| --- | --- | --- |
| LEARNING MOOD ☹ ☹ 😐 🙂 😃 | | # VERBS ACQUIRED |

## PAST STUDIES IN REVIEW

| VOCABULARY FROM YESTERDAY | GOALS FROM YESTERDAY |
| --- | --- |
| 1 | ☐ |
| 2 | ☐ |
| 3 | ☐ |

| VOCABULARY FROM 5 DAYS AGO | VOCABULARY FROM 10 DAYS AGO |
| --- | --- |
| 1 | 1 |
| 2 | 2 |
| 3 | 3 |

## PRIORITIES FOR TODAY

| VOCABULARY FOR TODAY | GOALS FOR TODAY |
| --- | --- |
| 1 | ☐ |
| 2 | ☐ |
| 3 | ☐ |

## DESCRIBE YOUR LEARNING EXPERIENCE FOR TODAY

## SPECIAL WORDS FOR TODAY

| DAILY WORD BUILDER | VERB OF THE DAY | COGNATE OF THE DAY |
| --- | --- | --- |
| **Tomar Nota** | **Agradecer** | **Profusión** |
| v. Note down. To take a note of something. | To Be Thankful For /g: Agradeciendo / pp: Agradecido /Irr. | Noun. From: Profusion (SION=SIÓN) |

# INTERESTING THINGS FROM TODAY

## FOUR SENTENCES THAT I READ, HEARD OR CREATED TODAY

**1**

**2**

**3**

**4**

# THINGS I HAVE QUESTIONS ABOUT

# DESCRIBE YOUR ACTIVITIES IN THESE TASKS FOR TODAY

| ACTIVITY | DESCRIPTION | SATISFACTION |
|----------|-------------|--------------|
| READING | | 😟 😞 😐 🙂 😊 |
| LISTENING | | 😟 😞 😐 🙂 😊 |
| WRITING | | 😟 😞 😐 🙂 😊 |
| SPEAKING | | 😟 😞 😐 🙂 😊 |
| STUDYING | | 😟 😞 😐 🙂 😊 |
| VOCABULARY | | 😟 😞 😐 🙂 😊 |

| LOG YOUR STUDY TIME | | | | | | | | | | | | TOTAL TIME |
|---|---|---|---|---|---|---|---|---|---|---|---|---|
| EACH BOX EQUALS 5 MINS. | | | | | | | | | | | | : |

| DAY & DATE | | | STUDY STREAK # | |
|---|---|---|---|---|
| LEARNING MOOD | ☹ ☹ 😐 🙂 😃 | | # VERBS ACQUIRED | |

## PAST STUDIES IN REVIEW

| VOCABULARY FROM YESTERDAY | GOALS FROM YESTERDAY |
|---|---|
| 1 | ☐ |
| 2 | ☐ |
| 3 | ☐ |

| VOCABULARY FROM 5 DAYS AGO | VOCABULARY FROM 10 DAYS AGO |
|---|---|
| 1 | 1 |
| 2 | 2 |
| 3 | 3 |

## PRIORITIES FOR TODAY

| VOCABULARY FOR TODAY | GOALS FOR TODAY |
|---|---|
| 1 | ☐ |
| 2 | ☐ |
| 3 | ☐ |

## DESCRIBE YOUR LEARNING EXPERIENCE FOR TODAY

## SPECIAL WORDS FOR TODAY

| DAILY WORD BUILDER | VERB OF THE DAY | COGNATE OF THE DAY |
|---|---|---|
| **Tomar Parte** | **Clarificar** | **Puntuación** |
| v. Partake. Participate. | To Clarify, Illuminate, Light [Up], Brighten /g: Clarificando / pp: Clarificado /Irr. | Noun. From: Punctuation (TION=CIÓN) |

## INTERESTING THINGS FROM TODAY

### FOUR SENTENCES THAT I READ, HEARD OR CREATED TODAY

**1**

**2**

**3**

**4**

## THINGS I HAVE QUESTIONS ABOUT

## DESCRIBE YOUR ACTIVITIES IN THESE TASKS FOR TODAY

| ACTIVITY | DESCRIPTION | SATISFACTION |
|---|---|---|
| READING | | ☹ ☹ 😐 🙂 😊 |
| LISTENING | | ☹ ☹ 😐 🙂 😊 |
| WRITING | | ☹ ☹ 😐 🙂 😊 |
| SPEAKING | | ☹ ☹ 😐 🙂 😊 |
| STUDYING | | ☹ ☹ 😐 🙂 😊 |
| VOCABULARY | | ☹ ☹ 😐 🙂 😊 |

| LOG YOUR STUDY TIME | | TOTAL TIME |
|---|---|---|
| EACH BOX EQUALS 5 MINS. | | : |

**WEEK NUMBER:**

## THIS WEEK IN REVIEW

### VOCABULARY ACQUIRED

### BIGGEST ACHIEVEMENTS

☐     ☐

☐     ☐

☐     ☐

### AREAS FOR IMPROVEMENT

1

2

3

4

## THINGS THAT I STILL HAVE QUESTIONS ABOUT

## FINAL MEASUREMENTS OF THIS WEEK

| TOTAL TIME THIS WEEK | TOTAL NEW VERBS | TOTAL NEW WORDS |
|---|---|---|
| | | |

## SELF-ASSESSMENT OF MY ACTIVITIES THIS WEEK

| ACTIVITIES | SPECIFIC ASSESSMENTS | SATISFACTION |
|---|---|---|
| READING | | ☹☹😐☺😄 |
| LISTENING | | ☹☹😐☺😄 |
| WRITING | | ☹☹😐☺😄 |
| SPEAKING | | ☹☹😐☺😄 |
| STUDYING | | ☹☹😐☺😄 |
| MOTIVATION | | ☹☹😐☺😄 |
| LOG YOUR STUDY TIME | | TOTAL TIME |
| EACH BOX EQUALS 1 HOUR | | : |

| DAY & DATE | | STUDY STREAK # |
|---|---|---|
| LEARNING MOOD | ☹ ☹ 😐 🙂 😀 | # VERBS ACQUIRED |

## PAST STUDIES IN REVIEW

| VOCABULARY FROM YESTERDAY | GOALS FROM YESTERDAY |
|---|---|
| 1 | ☐ |
| 2 | ☐ |
| 3 | ☐ |

| VOCABULARY FROM 5 DAYS AGO | VOCABULARY FROM 10 DAYS AGO |
|---|---|
| 1 | 1 |
| 2 | 2 |
| 3 | 3 |

## PRIORITIES FOR TODAY

| VOCABULARY FOR TODAY | GOALS FOR TODAY |
|---|---|
| 1 | ☐ |
| 2 | ☐ |
| 3 | ☐ |

## DESCRIBE YOUR LEARNING EXPERIENCE FOR TODAY

## SPECIAL WORDS FOR TODAY

| DAILY WORD BUILDER | VERB OF THE DAY | COGNATE OF THE DAY |
|---|---|---|
| **Correcta** | **Dar** | **Académico** |
| adj. f. Correct. m. Correcto. Right. Accurate. Polite. | To Give /g: Dando / pp: Dado /Irr. | Adjective. From: Academic (IC=ICO) |

## INTERESTING THINGS FROM TODAY

### FOUR SENTENCES THAT I READ, HEARD OR CREATED TODAY

**1**

**2**

**3**

**4**

## THINGS I HAVE QUESTIONS ABOUT

## DESCRIBE YOUR ACTIVITIES IN THESE TASKS FOR TODAY

| ACTIVITY | DESCRIPTION | SATISFACTION |
|----------|-------------|--------------|
| READING | | 😖 😞 😐 🙂 😊 |
| LISTENING | | 😖 😞 😐 🙂 😊 |
| WRITING | | 😖 😞 😐 🙂 😊 |
| SPEAKING | | 😖 😞 😐 🙂 😊 |
| STUDYING | | 😖 😞 😐 🙂 😊 |
| VOCABULARY | | 😖 😞 😐 🙂 😊 |
| LOG YOUR STUDY TIME | | TOTAL TIME |
| EACH BOX EQUALS 5 MINS. | | : |

## PAST STUDIES IN REVIEW

| VOCABULARY FROM YESTERDAY | GOALS FROM YESTERDAY |
|---|---|
| 1 | ☐ |
| 2 | ☐ |
| 3 | ☐ |

| VOCABULARY FROM 5 DAYS AGO | VOCABULARY FROM 10 DAYS AGO |
|---|---|
| 1 | 1 |
| 2 | 2 |
| 3 | 3 |

## PRIORITIES FOR TODAY

| VOCABULARY FOR TODAY | GOALS FOR TODAY |
|---|---|
| 1 | ☐ |
| 2 | ☐ |
| 3 | ☐ |

## DESCRIBE YOUR LEARNING EXPERIENCE FOR TODAY

## SPECIAL WORDS FOR TODAY

| DAILY WORD BUILDER | VERB OF THE DAY | COGNATE OF THE DAY |
|---|---|---|
| **Persona Correcta** | **Probar** | **Integrar** |
| n. f. Right Person | To Taste, Try, Test /g: Probando / pp: Probado /Irr. | Verb. From: Integrate (ATE=AR) |

## INTERESTING THINGS FROM TODAY

### FOUR SENTENCES THAT I READ, HEARD OR CREATED TODAY

1

2

3

4

## THINGS I HAVE QUESTIONS ABOUT

## DESCRIBE YOUR ACTIVITIES IN THESE TASKS FOR TODAY

| ACTIVITY | DESCRIPTION | SATISFACTION |
|---|---|---|
| READING | | 😞 😟 😐 🙂 😊 |
| LISTENING | | 😞 😟 😐 🙂 😊 |
| WRITING | | 😞 😟 😐 🙂 😊 |
| SPEAKING | | 😞 😟 😐 🙂 😊 |
| STUDYING | | 😞 😟 😐 🙂 😊 |
| VOCABULARY | | 😞 😟 😐 🙂 😊 |

| LOG YOUR STUDY TIME | | | | | | | | | | | | | TOTAL TIME |
|---|---|---|---|---|---|---|---|---|---|---|---|---|---|
| EACH BOX EQUALS 5 MINS. | | | | | | | | | | | | | : |

| DAY & DATE | | STUDY STREAK # |
| LEARNING MOOD | 😧 😟 😐 😊 😃 | # VERBS ACQUIRED |

## PAST STUDIES IN REVIEW

| VOCABULARY FROM YESTERDAY | GOALS FROM YESTERDAY |
|---|---|
| 1 | ☐ |
| 2 | ☐ |
| 3 | ☐ |

| VOCABULARY FROM 5 DAYS AGO | VOCABULARY FROM 10 DAYS AGO |
|---|---|
| 1 | 1 |
| 2 | 2 |
| 3 | 3 |

## PRIORITIES FOR TODAY

| VOCABULARY FOR TODAY | GOALS FOR TODAY |
|---|---|
| 1 | ☐ |
| 2 | ☐ |
| 3 | ☐ |

## DESCRIBE YOUR LEARNING EXPERIENCE FOR TODAY

## SPECIAL WORDS FOR TODAY

| DAILY WORD BUILDER | VERB OF THE DAY | COGNATE OF THE DAY |
|---|---|---|
| **Forma Correcta** | **Alquilar** | **Explotación** |
| n. f. Right way. Correct Form. | To Rent; To Rent Out, Let /g: Alquilando / pp: Alquilado | Noun. From: Exploitation (TION=CIÓN) |

## INTERESTING THINGS FROM TODAY

### FOUR SENTENCES THAT I READ, HEARD OR CREATED TODAY

**1**

**2**

**3**

**4**

## THINGS I HAVE QUESTIONS ABOUT

## DESCRIBE YOUR ACTIVITIES IN THESE TASKS FOR TODAY

| ACTIVITY | DESCRIPTION | SATISFACTION |
|---|---|---|
| READING | | ☹ ☹ 😐 🙂 😄 |
| LISTENING | | ☹ ☹ 😐 🙂 😄 |
| WRITING | | ☹ ☹ 😐 🙂 😄 |
| SPEAKING | | ☹ ☹ 😐 🙂 😄 |
| STUDYING | | ☹ ☹ 😐 🙂 😄 |
| VOCABULARY | | ☹ ☹ 😐 🙂 😄 |

| LOG YOUR STUDY TIME | | TOTAL TIME |
|---|---|---|
| EACH BOX EQUALS 5 MINS. | | : |

| DAY & DATE | | STUDY STREAK # | |
|---|---|---|---|
| LEARNING MOOD | ☹ ☹ 😐 🙂 😃 | # VERBS ACQUIRED | |

## PAST STUDIES IN REVIEW

| VOCABULARY FROM YESTERDAY | GOALS FROM YESTERDAY |
|---|---|
| **1** | ☐ |
| **2** | ☐ |
| **3** | ☐ |

| VOCABULARY FROM 5 DAYS AGO | VOCABULARY FROM 10 DAYS AGO |
|---|---|
| **1** | **1** |
| **2** | **2** |
| **3** | **3** |

## PRIORITIES FOR TODAY

| VOCABULARY FOR TODAY | GOALS FOR TODAY |
|---|---|
| **1** | ☐ |
| **2** | ☐ |
| **3** | ☐ |

## DESCRIBE YOUR LEARNING EXPERIENCE FOR TODAY

## SPECIAL WORDS FOR TODAY

| DAILY WORD BUILDER | VERB OF THE DAY | COGNATE OF THE DAY |
|---|---|---|
| **Manera Correcta** | **Esperar** | **Localidad** |
| n. f. Right way. Proper way. | To Hope /g: Esperando / pp: Esperado | Noun. From: Locality (TY=IDAD) |

## INTERESTING THINGS FROM TODAY

### FOUR SENTENCES THAT I READ, HEARD OR CREATED TODAY

1

2

3

4

## THINGS I HAVE QUESTIONS ABOUT

## DESCRIBE YOUR ACTIVITIES IN THESE TASKS FOR TODAY

| ACTIVITY | DESCRIPTION | SATISFACTION |
|---|---|---|
| READING | | ☹️ 🙁 😐 🙂 😀 |
| LISTENING | | ☹️ 🙁 😐 🙂 😀 |
| WRITING | | ☹️ 🙁 😐 🙂 😀 |
| SPEAKING | | ☹️ 🙁 😐 🙂 😀 |
| STUDYING | | ☹️ 🙁 😐 🙂 😀 |
| VOCABULARY | | ☹️ 🙁 😐 🙂 😀 |

| LOG YOUR STUDY TIME | | TOTAL TIME |
|---|---|---|
| EACH BOX EQUALS 5 MINS. | | : |

| DAY & DATE | | STUDY STREAK # | |
|---|---|---|---|
| LEARNING MOOD | ☹ ☹ 😐 🙂 😀 | # VERBS ACQUIRED | |

## PAST STUDIES IN REVIEW

| VOCABULARY FROM YESTERDAY | GOALS FROM YESTERDAY |
|---|---|
| 1 | ☐ |
| 2 | ☐ |
| 3 | ☐ |

| VOCABULARY FROM 5 DAYS AGO | VOCABULARY FROM 10 DAYS AGO |
|---|---|
| 1 | 1 |
| 2 | 2 |
| 3 | 3 |

## PRIORITIES FOR TODAY

| VOCABULARY FOR TODAY | GOALS FOR TODAY |
|---|---|
| 1 | ☐ |
| 2 | ☐ |
| 3 | ☐ |

## DESCRIBE YOUR LEARNING EXPERIENCE FOR TODAY

## SPECIAL WORDS FOR TODAY

| DAILY WORD BUILDER | VERB OF THE DAY | COGNATE OF THE DAY |
|---|---|---|
| **Correcta Aplicación** | **Quedarse** | **Decidir** |
| n. f. Correct application. | To Stay [Behind], Remain [Behind] /g: Quedándose / pp: Quedado | Verb. From: Decide (E=AR OR IR) |

## INTERESTING THINGS FROM TODAY

### FOUR SENTENCES THAT I READ, HEARD OR CREATED TODAY

**1**

**2**

**3**

**4**

## THINGS I HAVE QUESTIONS ABOUT

## DESCRIBE YOUR ACTIVITIES IN THESE TASKS FOR TODAY

| ACTIVITY | DESCRIPTION | SATISFACTION |
|----------|-------------|--------------|
| READING | | 😞 😟 😐 🙂 😊 |
| LISTENING | | 😞 😟 😐 🙂 😊 |
| WRITING | | 😞 😟 😐 🙂 😊 |
| SPEAKING | | 😞 😟 😐 🙂 😊 |
| STUDYING | | 😞 😟 😐 🙂 😊 |
| VOCABULARY | | 😞 😟 😐 🙂 😊 |
| LOG YOUR STUDY TIME | | TOTAL TIME |
| EACH BOX EQUALS 5 MINS. | | : |

| DAY & DATE | | STUDY STREAK # | |
|---|---|---|---|
| LEARNING MOOD | 😧 😦 😐 🙂 😀 | # VERBS ACQUIRED | |

## PAST STUDIES IN REVIEW

| VOCABULARY FROM YESTERDAY | GOALS FROM YESTERDAY |
|---|---|
| 1 | ☐ |
| 2 | ☐ |
| 3 | ☐ |

| VOCABULARY FROM 5 DAYS AGO | VOCABULARY FROM 10 DAYS AGO |
|---|---|
| 1 | 1 |
| 2 | 2 |
| 3 | 3 |

## PRIORITIES FOR TODAY

| VOCABULARY FOR TODAY | GOALS FOR TODAY |
|---|---|
| 1 | ☐ |
| 2 | ☐ |
| 3 | ☐ |

## DESCRIBE YOUR LEARNING EXPERIENCE FOR TODAY

## SPECIAL WORDS FOR TODAY

| DAILY WORD BUILDER | VERB OF THE DAY | COGNATE OF THE DAY |
|---|---|---|
| **Respusta Correcta** | **Ahorcar** | **Conmutar** |
| n. f. Correct answer. | To Hang /g: Ahorcando / pp: Ahorcado /Irr. | Verb. From: Commute (E=AR OR IR) |

## INTERESTING THINGS FROM TODAY
### FOUR SENTENCES THAT I READ, HEARD OR CREATED TODAY

1

2

3

4

## THINGS I HAVE QUESTIONS ABOUT

## DESCRIBE YOUR ACTIVITIES IN THESE TASKS FOR TODAY

| ACTIVITY | DESCRIPTION | SATISFACTION |
|---|---|---|
| READING | | 😟😞😐🙂😃 |
| LISTENING | | 😟😞😐🙂😃 |
| WRITING | | 😟😞😐🙂😃 |
| SPEAKING | | 😟😞😐🙂😃 |
| STUDYING | | 😟😞😐🙂😃 |
| VOCABULARY | | 😟😞😐🙂😃 |

| LOG YOUR STUDY TIME | | | | | | | | | | | | TOTAL TIME |
|---|---|---|---|---|---|---|---|---|---|---|---|---|
| EACH BOX EQUALS 5 MINS. | | | | | | | | | | | | : |

| DAY & DATE | | STUDY STREAK # | |
|---|---|---|---|
| LEARNING MOOD | 😖 😞 😐 🙂 😄 | # VERBS ACQUIRED | |

## PAST STUDIES IN REVIEW

| VOCABULARY FROM YESTERDAY | GOALS FROM YESTERDAY |
|---|---|
| 1 | ☐ |
| 2 | ☐ |
| 3 | ☐ |

| VOCABULARY FROM 5 DAYS AGO | VOCABULARY FROM 10 DAYS AGO |
|---|---|
| 1 | 1 |
| 2 | 2 |
| 3 | 3 |

## PRIORITIES FOR TODAY

| VOCABULARY FOR TODAY | GOALS FOR TODAY |
|---|---|
| 1 | ☐ |
| 2 | ☐ |
| 3 | ☐ |

## DESCRIBE YOUR LEARNING EXPERIENCE FOR TODAY

## SPECIAL WORDS FOR TODAY

| DAILY WORD BUILDER | VERB OF THE DAY | COGNATE OF THE DAY |
|---|---|---|
| **Dirección Correcta** | **Clasificar** | **Consolidar** |
| n. f. Right Direction | To Classify, Grade, Rate, Sort /g: Clasificando / pp: Clasificado /Irr. | Verb. From: Consolidate (ATE=AR) |

## INTERESTING THINGS FROM TODAY

### FOUR SENTENCES THAT I READ, HEARD OR CREATED TODAY

**1**

**2**

**3**

**4**

## THINGS I HAVE QUESTIONS ABOUT

## DESCRIBE YOUR ACTIVITIES IN THESE TASKS FOR TODAY

| ACTIVITY | DESCRIPTION | SATISFACTION |
|---|---|---|
| READING | | ☹ ☹ 😐 🙂 😊 |
| LISTENING | | ☹ ☹ 😐 🙂 😊 |
| WRITING | | ☹ ☹ 😐 🙂 😊 |
| SPEAKING | | ☹ ☹ 😐 🙂 😊 |
| STUDYING | | ☹ ☹ 😐 🙂 😊 |
| VOCABULARY | | ☹ ☹ 😐 🙂 😊 |

| LOG YOUR STUDY TIME | | | | | | | | | | | | | | | TOTAL TIME |
|---|---|---|---|---|---|---|---|---|---|---|---|---|---|---|---|
| EACH BOX EQUALS 5 MINS. | | | | | | | | | | | | | | | : |

## THIS WEEK IN REVIEW

### VOCABULARY ACQUIRED

### BIGGEST ACHIEVEMENTS

☐      ☐

☐      ☐

☐      ☐

### AREAS FOR IMPROVEMENT

**1**

**2**

**3**

**4**

## THINGS THAT I STILL HAVE QUESTIONS ABOUT

|  |  |
|---|---|
|  |  |
|  |  |
|  |  |

## FINAL MEASUREMENTS OF THIS WEEK

| TOTAL TIME THIS WEEK | TOTAL NEW VERBS | TOTAL NEW WORDS |
|---|---|---|
|  |  |  |

## SELF-ASSESSMENT OF MY ACTIVITIES THIS WEEK

| ACTIVITIES | SPECIFIC ASSESSMENTS | SATISFACTION |
|---|---|---|
| READING |  | ☹ ☹ 😐 🙂 😄 |
| LISTENING |  | ☹ ☹ 😐 🙂 😄 |
| WRITING |  | ☹ ☹ 😐 🙂 😄 |
| SPEAKING |  | ☹ ☹ 😐 🙂 😄 |
| STUDYING |  | ☹ ☹ 😐 🙂 😄 |
| MOTIVATION |  | ☹ ☹ 😐 🙂 😄 |
| LOG YOUR STUDY TIME |  | TOTAL TIME |
| EACH BOX EQUALS 1 HOUR |  | : |

| DAY & DATE | | STUDY STREAK # |
|---|---|---|
| LEARNING MOOD  ☹ ☹ 😐 🙂 😀 | | # VERBS ACQUIRED |

## PAST STUDIES IN REVIEW

| VOCABULARY FROM YESTERDAY | GOALS FROM YESTERDAY |
|---|---|
| **1** | ☐ |
| **2** | ☐ |
| **3** | ☐ |

| VOCABULARY FROM 5 DAYS AGO | VOCABULARY FROM 10 DAYS AGO |
|---|---|
| **1** | **1** |
| **2** | **2** |
| **3** | **3** |

## PRIORITIES FOR TODAY

| VOCABULARY FOR TODAY | GOALS FOR TODAY |
|---|---|
| **1** | ☐ |
| **2** | ☐ |
| **3** | ☐ |

## DESCRIBE YOUR LEARNING EXPERIENCE FOR TODAY

## SPECIAL WORDS FOR TODAY

| DAILY WORD BUILDER | VERB OF THE DAY | COGNATE OF THE DAY |
|---|---|---|
| **Ultimo** | **Decir** | **Misterioso** |
| adj. Last. Final. Latter. | To Say, Tell /g: Diciendo / pp: Dicho /Irr. | Adjective. From: Mysterious (OUS=OSO) |

## INTERESTING THINGS FROM TODAY

### FOUR SENTENCES THAT I READ, HEARD OR CREATED TODAY

**1**

**2**

**3**

**4**

## THINGS I HAVE QUESTIONS ABOUT

## DESCRIBE YOUR ACTIVITIES IN THESE TASKS FOR TODAY

| ACTIVITY | DESCRIPTION | SATISFACTION |
|---|---|---|
| READING | | 😞 😟 😐 🙂 😊 |
| LISTENING | | 😞 😟 😐 🙂 😊 |
| WRITING | | 😞 😟 😐 🙂 😊 |
| SPEAKING | | 😞 😟 😐 🙂 😊 |
| STUDYING | | 😞 😟 😐 🙂 😊 |
| VOCABULARY | | 😞 😟 😐 🙂 😊 |

| LOG YOUR STUDY TIME | | | | | | | | | | | | | | | TOTAL TIME |
|---|---|---|---|---|---|---|---|---|---|---|---|---|---|---|---|
| EACH BOX EQUALS 5 MINS. | | | | | | | | | | | | | | | : |

| DAY & DATE | | STUDY STREAK # |
|---|---|---|
| LEARNING MOOD | ☹ ☹ 😐 🙂 😀 | # VERBS ACQUIRED |

## PAST STUDIES IN REVIEW

| VOCABULARY FROM YESTERDAY | GOALS FROM YESTERDAY |
|---|---|
| 1 | ☐ |
| 2 | ☐ |
| 3 | ☐ |

| VOCABULARY FROM 5 DAYS AGO | VOCABULARY FROM 10 DAYS AGO |
|---|---|
| 1 | 1 |
| 2 | 2 |
| 3 | 3 |

## PRIORITIES FOR TODAY

| VOCABULARY FOR TODAY | GOALS FOR TODAY |
|---|---|
| 1 | ☐ |
| 2 | ☐ |
| 3 | ☐ |

## DESCRIBE YOUR LEARNING EXPERIENCE FOR TODAY

## SPECIAL WORDS FOR TODAY

| DAILY WORD BUILDER | VERB OF THE DAY | COGNATE OF THE DAY |
|---|---|---|
| **Por Último** | **Querer** | **Horizontalmente** |
| adv. Finally. In the end. | To Want, Love /g: Queriendo / pp: Querido /Irr. | Adverb. From: Horizontally (LY=MENTE) |

## INTERESTING THINGS FROM TODAY

### FOUR SENTENCES THAT I READ, HEARD OR CREATED TODAY

**1**

**2**

**3**

**4**

## THINGS I HAVE QUESTIONS ABOUT

## DESCRIBE YOUR ACTIVITIES IN THESE TASKS FOR TODAY

| ACTIVITY | DESCRIPTION | SATISFACTION |
|---|---|---|
| READING | | ☹ 😟 😐 🙂 😀 |
| LISTENING | | ☹ 😟 😐 🙂 😀 |
| WRITING | | ☹ 😟 😐 🙂 😀 |
| SPEAKING | | ☹ 😟 😐 🙂 😀 |
| STUDYING | | ☹ 😟 😐 🙂 😀 |
| VOCABULARY | | ☹ 😟 😐 🙂 😀 |
| LOG YOUR STUDY TIME | | TOTAL TIME |
| EACH BOX EQUALS 5 MINS. | | : |

| DAY & DATE | | | | | STUDY STREAK # | |
|---|---|---|---|---|---|---|
| LEARNING MOOD | ☹ ☹ 😐 🙂 😃 | | | | # VERBS ACQUIRED | |

## PAST STUDIES IN REVIEW

| VOCABULARY FROM YESTERDAY | GOALS FROM YESTERDAY |
|---|---|
| 1 | ☐ |
| 2 | ☐ |
| 3 | ☐ |

| VOCABULARY FROM 5 DAYS AGO | VOCABULARY FROM 10 DAYS AGO |
|---|---|
| 1 | 1 |
| 2 | 2 |
| 3 | 3 |

## PRIORITIES FOR TODAY

| VOCABULARY FOR TODAY | GOALS FOR TODAY |
|---|---|
| 1 | ☐ |
| 2 | ☐ |
| 3 | ☐ |

## DESCRIBE YOUR LEARNING EXPERIENCE FOR TODAY

## SPECIAL WORDS FOR TODAY

| DAILY WORD BUILDER | VERB OF THE DAY | COGNATE OF THE DAY |
|---|---|---|
| **En El Último Momento** | **Amar** | **Biología** |
| adv. At the eleventh hour | To Love /g: Amando / pp: Amado | Noun. From: Biology (Y=IA OR ÍA) |

### FOUR SENTENCES THAT I READ, HEARD OR CREATED TODAY

**1**

**2**

**3**

**4**

## THINGS I HAVE QUESTIONS ABOUT

## DESCRIBE YOUR ACTIVITIES IN THESE TASKS FOR TODAY

| ACTIVITY | DESCRIPTION | SATISFACTION |
|---|---|---|
| READING | | ☹ ☹ 😐 🙂 😊 |
| LISTENING | | ☹ ☹ 😐 🙂 😊 |
| WRITING | | ☹ ☹ 😐 🙂 😊 |
| SPEAKING | | ☹ ☹ 😐 🙂 😊 |
| STUDYING | | ☹ ☹ 😐 🙂 😊 |
| VOCABULARY | | ☹ ☹ 😐 🙂 😊 |

| LOG YOUR STUDY TIME | | | | | | | | | | | | | TOTAL TIME |
|---|---|---|---|---|---|---|---|---|---|---|---|---|---|
| EACH BOX EQUALS 5 MINS. | | | | | | | | | | | | | : |

| DAY & DATE | | | STUDY STREAK # | |
|---|---|---|---|---|
| LEARNING MOOD | ☹ ☹ 😐 🙂 😃 | | # VERBS ACQUIRED | |

## PAST STUDIES IN REVIEW

| VOCABULARY FROM YESTERDAY | GOALS FROM YESTERDAY |
|---|---|
| 1 | ☐ |
| 2 | ☐ |
| 3 | ☐ |

| VOCABULARY FROM 5 DAYS AGO | VOCABULARY FROM 10 DAYS AGO |
|---|---|
| 1 | 1 |
| 2 | 2 |
| 3 | 3 |

## PRIORITIES FOR TODAY

| VOCABULARY FOR TODAY | GOALS FOR TODAY |
|---|---|
| 1 | ☐ |
| 2 | ☐ |
| 3 | ☐ |

## DESCRIBE YOUR LEARNING EXPERIENCE FOR TODAY

## SPECIAL WORDS FOR TODAY

| DAILY WORD BUILDER | VERB OF THE DAY | COGNATE OF THE DAY |
|---|---|---|
| **Último Recurso** | **Faltar** | **Tolerante** |
| n. m. Last resort. Last resource | To Lack, Be Lacking, Be Missing, Be Absent /g: Faltando / pp: Faltado | Adjective. From: Tolerant (NT=NTE) |

## INTERESTING THINGS FROM TODAY

### FOUR SENTENCES THAT I READ, HEARD OR CREATED TODAY

**1**

**2**

**3**

**4**

## THINGS I HAVE QUESTIONS ABOUT

## DESCRIBE YOUR ACTIVITIES IN THESE TASKS FOR TODAY

| ACTIVITY | DESCRIPTION | SATISFACTION |
|----------|-------------|--------------|
| READING | | ☹ ☹ 😐 🙂 😄 |
| LISTENING | | ☹ ☹ 😐 🙂 😄 |
| WRITING | | ☹ ☹ 😐 🙂 😄 |
| SPEAKING | | ☹ ☹ 😐 🙂 😄 |
| STUDYING | | ☹ ☹ 😐 🙂 😄 |
| VOCABULARY | | ☹ ☹ 😐 🙂 😄 |

| LOG YOUR STUDY TIME | | | | | | | | | | | | | TOTAL TIME |
|---------------------|--|--|--|--|--|--|--|--|--|--|--|--|------------|
| EACH BOX EQUALS 5 MINS. | | | | | | | | | | | | | : |

| DAY & DATE | | STUDY STREAK # | |
|---|---|---|---|
| LEARNING MOOD | 😟 😣 😐 🙂 😃 | # VERBS ACQUIRED | |

## PAST STUDIES IN REVIEW

| VOCABULARY FROM YESTERDAY | GOALS FROM YESTERDAY |
|---|---|
| 1 | ☐ |
| 2 | ☐ |
| 3 | ☐ |

| VOCABULARY FROM 5 DAYS AGO | VOCABULARY FROM 10 DAYS AGO |
|---|---|
| 1 | 1 |
| 2 | 2 |
| 3 | 3 |

## PRIORITIES FOR TODAY

| VOCABULARY FOR TODAY | GOALS FOR TODAY |
|---|---|
| 1 | ☐ |
| 2 | ☐ |
| 3 | ☐ |

## DESCRIBE YOUR LEARNING EXPERIENCE FOR TODAY

---

## SPECIAL WORDS FOR TODAY

| DAILY WORD BUILDER | VERB OF THE DAY | COGNATE OF THE DAY |
|---|---|---|
| **Último Años** | **Quemar** | **Médico** |
| n. m, pl. Recent years. Last few years | To Burn [Up], Set On Fire, Scald; To Be Burning Hot /g: Quemando / pp: Quemado | Noun. From: Medic (IC=ICO) |

## INTERESTING THINGS FROM TODAY

### FOUR SENTENCES THAT I READ, HEARD OR CREATED TODAY

**1**

**2**

**3**

**4**

## THINGS I HAVE QUESTIONS ABOUT

## DESCRIBE YOUR ACTIVITIES IN THESE TASKS FOR TODAY

| ACTIVITY | DESCRIPTION | SATISFACTION |
|---|---|---|
| READING | | ☹ ☹ 😐 ☺ 😊 |
| LISTENING | | ☹ ☹ 😐 ☺ 😊 |
| WRITING | | ☹ ☹ 😐 ☺ 😊 |
| SPEAKING | | ☹ ☹ 😐 ☺ 😊 |
| STUDYING | | ☹ ☹ 😐 ☺ 😊 |
| VOCABULARY | | ☹ ☹ 😐 ☺ 😊 |
| LOG YOUR STUDY TIME | | TOTAL TIME |
| EACH BOX EQUALS 5 MINS. | | : |

| DAY & DATE | | STUDY STREAK # | |
|---|---|---|---|
| LEARNING MOOD | ☹ ☹ ☺ ☺ ☺ | # VERBS ACQUIRED | |

## PAST STUDIES IN REVIEW

| VOCABULARY FROM YESTERDAY | GOALS FROM YESTERDAY |
|---|---|
| 1 | ☐ |
| 2 | ☐ |
| 3 | ☐ |

| VOCABULARY FROM 5 DAYS AGO | VOCABULARY FROM 10 DAYS AGO |
|---|---|
| 1 | 1 |
| 2 | 2 |
| 3 | 3 |

## PRIORITIES FOR TODAY

| VOCABULARY FOR TODAY | GOALS FOR TODAY |
|---|---|
| 1 | ☐ |
| 2 | ☐ |
| 3 | ☐ |

## DESCRIBE YOUR LEARNING EXPERIENCE FOR TODAY

## SPECIAL WORDS FOR TODAY

| DAILY WORD BUILDER | VERB OF THE DAY | COGNATE OF THE DAY |
|---|---|---|
| **Fin Último** | **Alcanzar** | **Excursión** |
| n. m. Ultimate aim. | To Reach, Catch, Catch Up To, Catch Up With /g: Alcanzando / pp: Alcanzado | Noun. From: Excursion (SION=SIÓN) |

## INTERESTING THINGS FROM TODAY

### FOUR SENTENCES THAT I READ, HEARD OR CREATED TODAY

**1**

**2**

**3**

**4**

## THINGS I HAVE QUESTIONS ABOUT

## DESCRIBE YOUR ACTIVITIES IN THESE TASKS FOR TODAY

| ACTIVITY | DESCRIPTION | SATISFACTION |
|---|---|---|
| READING | | ☹ ☹ 😐 🙂 😃 |
| LISTENING | | ☹ ☹ 😐 🙂 😃 |
| WRITING | | ☹ ☹ 😐 🙂 😃 |
| SPEAKING | | ☹ ☹ 😐 🙂 😃 |
| STUDYING | | ☹ ☹ 😐 🙂 😃 |
| VOCABULARY | | ☹ ☹ 😐 🙂 😃 |

| LOG YOUR STUDY TIME | | | | | | | | | | | | | | TOTAL TIME |
|---|---|---|---|---|---|---|---|---|---|---|---|---|---|---|
| EACH BOX EQUALS 5 MINS. | | | | | | | | | | | | | | : |

| DAY & DATE | | STUDY STREAK # |
|---|---|---|
| LEARNING MOOD ☹ ☹ 😐 🙂 😃 | | # VERBS ACQUIRED |

## PAST STUDIES IN REVIEW

| VOCABULARY FROM YESTERDAY | GOALS FROM YESTERDAY |
|---|---|
| 1 | ☐ |
| 2 | ☐ |
| 3 | ☐ |

| VOCABULARY FROM 5 DAYS AGO | VOCABULARY FROM 10 DAYS AGO |
|---|---|
| 1 | 1 |
| 2 | 2 |
| 3 | 3 |

## PRIORITIES FOR TODAY

| VOCABULARY FOR TODAY | GOALS FOR TODAY |
|---|---|
| 1 | ☐ |
| 2 | ☐ |
| 3 | ☐ |

## DESCRIBE YOUR LEARNING EXPERIENCE FOR TODAY

## SPECIAL WORDS FOR TODAY

| DAILY WORD BUILDER | VERB OF THE DAY | COGNATE OF THE DAY |
|---|---|---|
| **Últimos Avances** | **Colgar** | **Perpendicular** |
| n. m, pl. Latest advances | To Hang, Hang Up, Be Hanging, Be Suspended /g: Colgando / pp: Colgado /Irr. | Adjective. From: Perpendicular (AR=AR) |

## INTERESTING THINGS FROM TODAY

### FOUR SENTENCES THAT I READ, HEARD OR CREATED TODAY

**1**

**2**

**3**

**4**

## THINGS I HAVE QUESTIONS ABOUT

## DESCRIBE YOUR ACTIVITIES IN THESE TASKS FOR TODAY

| ACTIVITY | DESCRIPTION | SATISFACTION |
|----------|-------------|--------------|
| READING | | ☹ ☹ 😐 🙂 😊 |
| LISTENING | | ☹ ☹ 😐 🙂 😊 |
| WRITING | | ☹ ☹ 😐 🙂 😊 |
| SPEAKING | | ☹ ☹ 😐 🙂 😊 |
| STUDYING | | ☹ ☹ 😐 🙂 😊 |
| VOCABULARY | | ☹ ☹ 😐 🙂 😊 |

| LOG YOUR STUDY TIME | | | | | | | | | | | | TOTAL TIME |
|---------------------|--|--|--|--|--|--|--|--|--|--|--|------------|
| EACH BOX EQUALS 5 MINS. | | | | | | | | | | | | : |

## THIS WEEK IN REVIEW

### VOCABULARY ACQUIRED

### BIGGEST ACHIEVEMENTS

☐         ☐

☐         ☐

☐         ☐

### AREAS FOR IMPROVEMENT

1

2

3

4

## THINGS THAT I STILL HAVE QUESTIONS ABOUT

| | |
|---|---|
| | |
| | |
| | |

## FINAL MEASUREMENTS OF THIS WEEK

| TOTAL TIME THIS WEEK | TOTAL NEW VERBS | TOTAL NEW WORDS |
|---|---|---|
| | | |

## SELF-ASSESSMENT OF MY ACTIVITIES THIS WEEK

| ACTIVITIES | SPECIFIC ASSESSMENTS | SATISFACTION |
|---|---|---|
| READING | | ☹️😟😐🙂😄 |
| LISTENING | | ☹️😟😐🙂😄 |
| WRITING | | ☹️😟😐🙂😄 |
| SPEAKING | | ☹️😟😐🙂😄 |
| STUDYING | | ☹️😟😐🙂😄 |
| MOTIVATION | | ☹️😟😐🙂😄 |
| LOG YOUR STUDY TIME | | TOTAL TIME |
| EACH BOX EQUALS 1 HOUR | | : |

| DAY & DATE | | STUDY STREAK # |
|---|---|---|
| LEARNING MOOD ☹ ☹ 😐 🙂 😀 | | # VERBS ACQUIRED |

## PAST STUDIES IN REVIEW

| VOCABULARY FROM YESTERDAY | GOALS FROM YESTERDAY |
|---|---|
| 1 | ☐ |
| 2 | ☐ |
| 3 | ☐ |

| VOCABULARY FROM 5 DAYS AGO | VOCABULARY FROM 10 DAYS AGO |
|---|---|
| 1 | 1 |
| 2 | 2 |
| 3 | 3 |

## PRIORITIES FOR TODAY

| VOCABULARY FOR TODAY | GOALS FOR TODAY |
|---|---|
| 1 | ☐ |
| 2 | ☐ |
| 3 | ☐ |

## DESCRIBE YOUR LEARNING EXPERIENCE FOR TODAY

## SPECIAL WORDS FOR TODAY

| DAILY WORD BUILDER | VERB OF THE DAY | COGNATE OF THE DAY |
|---|---|---|
| **Noche** | **Deshacer** | **Actor** |
| n. f. Night. Evening. | To Undo, Unmake, Ruin, Spoil, Take Apart /g: Deshaciendo / pp: Deshecho /Irr. | Noun. From: Actor (OR=OR) |

## INTERESTING THINGS FROM TODAY

### FOUR SENTENCES THAT I READ, HEARD OR CREATED TODAY

**1**

**2**

**3**

**4**

## THINGS I HAVE QUESTIONS ABOUT

## DESCRIBE YOUR ACTIVITIES IN THESE TASKS FOR TODAY

| ACTIVITY | DESCRIPTION | SATISFACTION |
|----------|-------------|--------------|
| READING | | ☹️☹️😐🙂😄 |
| LISTENING | | ☹️☹️😐🙂😄 |
| WRITING | | ☹️☹️😐🙂😄 |
| SPEAKING | | ☹️☹️😐🙂😄 |
| STUDYING | | ☹️☹️😐🙂😄 |
| VOCABULARY | | ☹️☹️😐🙂😄 |

| LOG YOUR STUDY TIME | | TOTAL TIME |
|---------------------|--|------------|
| EACH BOX EQUALS 5 MINS. | | : |

| DAY & DATE | | STUDY STREAK # |
|---|---|---|
| LEARNING MOOD  ☹ ☹ 😐 🙂 😃 | | # VERBS ACQUIRED |

## PAST STUDIES IN REVIEW

| VOCABULARY FROM YESTERDAY | GOALS FROM YESTERDAY |
|---|---|
| 1 | ☐ |
| 2 | ☐ |
| 3 | ☐ |

| VOCABULARY FROM 5 DAYS AGO | VOCABULARY FROM 10 DAYS AGO |
|---|---|
| 1 | 1 |
| 2 | 2 |
| 3 | 3 |

## PRIORITIES FOR TODAY

| VOCABULARY FOR TODAY | GOALS FOR TODAY |
|---|---|
| 1 | ☐ |
| 2 | ☐ |
| 3 | ☐ |

## DESCRIBE YOUR LEARNING EXPERIENCE FOR TODAY

## SPECIAL WORDS FOR TODAY

| DAILY WORD BUILDER | VERB OF THE DAY | COGNATE OF THE DAY |
|---|---|---|
| **Buenas Noches** | **Reír** | **Fermentar** |
| intj. Good night. | To Laugh /g: Riendo / pp: Reído /Irr. | Verb. From: Ferment (ADDING AR OR IR) |

## INTERESTING THINGS FROM TODAY

### FOUR SENTENCES THAT I READ, HEARD OR CREATED TODAY

**1**

**2**

**3**

**4**

## THINGS I HAVE QUESTIONS ABOUT

## DESCRIBE YOUR ACTIVITIES IN THESE TASKS FOR TODAY

| ACTIVITY | DESCRIPTION | SATISFACTION |
|----------|-------------|--------------|
| READING | | ☹ ☹ ☺ ☺ ☺ |
| LISTENING | | ☹ ☹ ☺ ☺ ☺ |
| WRITING | | ☹ ☹ ☺ ☺ ☺ |
| SPEAKING | | ☹ ☹ ☺ ☺ ☺ |
| STUDYING | | ☹ ☹ ☺ ☺ ☺ |
| VOCABULARY | | ☹ ☹ ☺ ☺ ☺ |

| LOG YOUR STUDY TIME | | TOTAL TIME |
|---------------------|--|------------|
| EACH BOX EQUALS 5 MINS. | | : |

| DAY & DATE | | | STUDY STREAK # |
|---|---|---|---|
| LEARNING MOOD | ☹ ☹ 😐 🙂 😃 | | # VERBS ACQUIRED |

## PAST STUDIES IN REVIEW

| VOCABULARY FROM YESTERDAY | GOALS FROM YESTERDAY |
|---|---|
| **1** | ☐ |
| **2** | ☐ |
| **3** | ☐ |

| VOCABULARY FROM 5 DAYS AGO | VOCABULARY FROM 10 DAYS AGO |
|---|---|
| **1** | **1** |
| **2** | **2** |
| **3** | **3** |

## PRIORITIES FOR TODAY

| VOCABULARY FOR TODAY | GOALS FOR TODAY |
|---|---|
| **1** | ☐ |
| **2** | ☐ |
| **3** | ☐ |

## DESCRIBE YOUR LEARNING EXPERIENCE FOR TODAY

_____

_____

_____

_____

## SPECIAL WORDS FOR TODAY

| DAILY WORD BUILDER | VERB OF THE DAY | COGNATE OF THE DAY |
|---|---|---|
| **Por La Noche** | **Arreglar** | **Comparar** |
| adv. At night. Overnight. | To Arrange, Settle, Fix Up, Repair, Tidy Up /g: Arreglando / pp: Arreglado | Verb. From: Compare (E=AR OR IR) |

## INTERESTING THINGS FROM TODAY

### FOUR SENTENCES THAT I READ, HEARD OR CREATED TODAY

**1**

**2**

**3**

**4**

## THINGS I HAVE QUESTIONS ABOUT

## DESCRIBE YOUR ACTIVITIES IN THESE TASKS FOR TODAY

| ACTIVITY | DESCRIPTION | SATISFACTION |
|---|---|---|
| READING | | ☹ ☹ 😐 🙂 😄 |
| LISTENING | | ☹ ☹ 😐 🙂 😄 |
| WRITING | | ☹ ☹ 😐 🙂 😄 |
| SPEAKING | | ☹ ☹ 😐 🙂 😄 |
| STUDYING | | ☹ ☹ 😐 🙂 😄 |
| VOCABULARY | | ☹ ☹ 😐 🙂 😄 |

| LOG YOUR STUDY TIME | | | | | | | | | | | | | TOTAL TIME |
|---|---|---|---|---|---|---|---|---|---|---|---|---|---|
| EACH BOX EQUALS 5 MINS. | | | | | | | | | | | | | : |

| DAY & DATE | | STUDY STREAK # |
| --- | --- | --- |
| LEARNING MOOD  ☹ ☹ 😐 🙂 😃 | | # VERBS ACQUIRED |

## PAST STUDIES IN REVIEW

| VOCABULARY FROM YESTERDAY | GOALS FROM YESTERDAY |
| --- | --- |
| 1 | ☐ |
| 2 | ☐ |
| 3 | ☐ |

| VOCABULARY FROM 5 DAYS AGO | VOCABULARY FROM 10 DAYS AGO |
| --- | --- |
| 1 | 1 |
| 2 | 2 |
| 3 | 3 |

## PRIORITIES FOR TODAY

| VOCABULARY FOR TODAY | GOALS FOR TODAY |
| --- | --- |
| 1 | ☐ |
| 2 | ☐ |
| 3 | ☐ |

## DESCRIBE YOUR LEARNING EXPERIENCE FOR TODAY

## SPECIAL WORDS FOR TODAY

| DAILY WORD BUILDER | VERB OF THE DAY | COGNATE OF THE DAY |
| --- | --- | --- |
| **Pasar La Noche** | **Ganar** | **Concesión** |
| v. To spend the night. | To Win, Gain, Earn, Get, Acquire /g: Ganando / pp: Ganado | Noun. From: Concession (SION=SIÓN) |

## INTERESTING THINGS FROM TODAY

### FOUR SENTENCES THAT I READ, HEARD OR CREATED TODAY

**1**

**2**

**3**

**4**

## THINGS I HAVE QUESTIONS ABOUT

## DESCRIBE YOUR ACTIVITIES IN THESE TASKS FOR TODAY

| ACTIVITY | DESCRIPTION | SATISFACTION |
|---|---|---|
| READING | | ☹ ☹ 😐 🙂 😃 |
| LISTENING | | ☹ ☹ 😐 🙂 😃 |
| WRITING | | ☹ ☹ 😐 🙂 😃 |
| SPEAKING | | ☹ ☹ 😐 🙂 😃 |
| STUDYING | | ☹ ☹ 😐 🙂 😃 |
| VOCABULARY | | ☹ ☹ 😐 🙂 😃 |

| LOG YOUR STUDY TIME | | | | | | | | | | | | | TOTAL TIME |
|---|---|---|---|---|---|---|---|---|---|---|---|---|---|
| EACH BOX EQUALS 5 MINS. | | | | | | | | | | | | | : |

| DAY & DATE | | STUDY STREAK # |
|---|---|---|
| LEARNING MOOD  ☹ ☹ 😐 🙂 😃 | | # VERBS ACQUIRED |

## PAST STUDIES IN REVIEW

| VOCABULARY FROM YESTERDAY | GOALS FROM YESTERDAY |
|---|---|
| 1 | ☐ |
| 2 | ☐ |
| 3 | ☐ |

| VOCABULARY FROM 5 DAYS AGO | VOCABULARY FROM 10 DAYS AGO |
|---|---|
| 1 | 1 |
| 2 | 2 |
| 3 | 3 |

## PRIORITIES FOR TODAY

| VOCABULARY FOR TODAY | GOALS FOR TODAY |
|---|---|
| 1 | ☐ |
| 2 | ☐ |
| 3 | ☐ |

## DESCRIBE YOUR LEARNING EXPERIENCE FOR TODAY

## SPECIAL WORDS FOR TODAY

| DAILY WORD BUILDER | VERB OF THE DAY | COGNATE OF THE DAY |
|---|---|---|
| **Mesita de Noche** | **Recoger** | **Escapar** |
| n. f. Bedside table. Nightstand. | To Pick Up /g: Recogiendo / pp: Recogido | Verb. From: Escape (E=AR OR IR) |

# INTERESTING THINGS FROM TODAY

## FOUR SENTENCES THAT I READ, HEARD OR CREATED TODAY

**1**

**2**

**3**

**4**

# THINGS I HAVE QUESTIONS ABOUT

# DESCRIBE YOUR ACTIVITIES IN THESE TASKS FOR TODAY

| ACTIVITY | DESCRIPTION | SATISFACTION |
|---|---|---|
| READING | | 😞 😦 😐 🙂 😄 |
| LISTENING | | 😞 😦 😐 🙂 😄 |
| WRITING | | 😞 😦 😐 🙂 😄 |
| SPEAKING | | 😞 😦 😐 🙂 😄 |
| STUDYING | | 😞 😦 😐 🙂 😄 |
| VOCABULARY | | 😞 😦 😐 🙂 😄 |

| LOG YOUR STUDY TIME | | TOTAL TIME |
|---|---|---|
| EACH BOX EQUALS 5 MINS. | | : |

| DAY & DATE | | STUDY STREAK # | |
|---|---|---|---|
| LEARNING MOOD | ☹ ☹ 😐 ☺ 😃 | # VERBS ACQUIRED | |

## PAST STUDIES IN REVIEW

| VOCABULARY FROM YESTERDAY | GOALS FROM YESTERDAY |
|---|---|
| 1 | ☐ |
| 2 | ☐ |
| 3 | ☐ |

| VOCABULARY FROM 5 DAYS AGO | VOCABULARY FROM 10 DAYS AGO |
|---|---|
| 1 | 1 |
| 2 | 2 |
| 3 | 3 |

## PRIORITIES FOR TODAY

| VOCABULARY FOR TODAY | GOALS FOR TODAY |
|---|---|
| 1 | ☐ |
| 2 | ☐ |
| 3 | ☐ |

## DESCRIBE YOUR LEARNING EXPERIENCE FOR TODAY

## SPECIAL WORDS FOR TODAY

| DAILY WORD BUILDER | VERB OF THE DAY | COGNATE OF THE DAY |
|---|---|---|
| **De La Noche A La Mañana** | **Alentar** | **Lamentable** |
| adv. Overnight. | To Encourage, Cheer, Inspire, Bolster Up /g: Alentando /pp: Alentado /Irr. | Adjective. From: Lamentable (BLE=BLE) |

## INTERESTING THINGS FROM TODAY

### FOUR SENTENCES THAT I READ, HEARD OR CREATED TODAY

**1**

**2**

**3**

**4**

## THINGS I HAVE QUESTIONS ABOUT

## DESCRIBE YOUR ACTIVITIES IN THESE TASKS FOR TODAY

| ACTIVITY | DESCRIPTION | SATISFACTION |
|----------|-------------|--------------|
| READING | | ☹ ☹ 😐 🙂 😀 |
| LISTENING | | ☹ ☹ 😐 🙂 😀 |
| WRITING | | ☹ ☹ 😐 🙂 😀 |
| SPEAKING | | ☹ ☹ 😐 🙂 😀 |
| STUDYING | | ☹ ☹ 😐 🙂 😀 |
| VOCABULARY | | ☹ ☹ 😐 🙂 😀 |
| LOG YOUR STUDY TIME | | TOTAL TIME |
| EACH BOX EQUALS 5 MINS. | | : |

| DAY & DATE | | | | | | STUDY STREAK # |
|---|---|---|---|---|---|---|
| LEARNING MOOD | ☹ | ☹ | 😐 | 🙂 | 😃 | # VERBS ACQUIRED |

## PAST STUDIES IN REVIEW

| VOCABULARY FROM YESTERDAY | GOALS FROM YESTERDAY |
|---|---|
| **1** | ☐ |
| **2** | ☐ |
| **3** | ☐ |

| VOCABULARY FROM 5 DAYS AGO | VOCABULARY FROM 10 DAYS AGO |
|---|---|
| **1** | **1** |
| **2** | **2** |
| **3** | **3** |

## PRIORITIES FOR TODAY

| VOCABULARY FOR TODAY | GOALS FOR TODAY |
|---|---|
| **1** | ☐ |
| **2** | ☐ |
| **3** | ☐ |

## DESCRIBE YOUR LEARNING EXPERIENCE FOR TODAY

## SPECIAL WORDS FOR TODAY

| DAILY WORD BUILDER | VERB OF THE DAY | COGNATE OF THE DAY |
|---|---|---|
| **Toda la Noche** | **Colocar** | **Esencia** |
| adv. Overnight. | To Locate, Place /g: Colocando / pp: Colocado /Irr. | Noun. From: Essence (ENCE=ENCIA) |

## INTERESTING THINGS FROM TODAY

### FOUR SENTENCES THAT I READ, HEARD OR CREATED TODAY

**1**

**2**

**3**

**4**

## THINGS I HAVE QUESTIONS ABOUT

## DESCRIBE YOUR ACTIVITIES IN THESE TASKS FOR TODAY

| ACTIVITY | DESCRIPTION | SATISFACTION |
|---|---|---|
| READING | | ☹ ☹ 😐 🙂 😄 |
| LISTENING | | ☹ ☹ 😐 🙂 😄 |
| WRITING | | ☹ ☹ 😐 🙂 😄 |
| SPEAKING | | ☹ ☹ 😐 🙂 😄 |
| STUDYING | | ☹ ☹ 😐 🙂 😄 |
| VOCABULARY | | ☹ ☹ 😐 🙂 😄 |

| LOG YOUR STUDY TIME | | | | | | | | | | | | | TOTAL TIME |
|---|---|---|---|---|---|---|---|---|---|---|---|---|---|
| EACH BOX EQUALS 5 MINS. | | | | | | | | | | | | | : |

## THIS WEEK IN REVIEW

### VOCABULARY ACQUIRED

### BIGGEST ACHIEVEMENTS

- ☐
- ☐
- ☐

- ☐
- ☐
- ☐

### AREAS FOR IMPROVEMENT

1.
2.
3.
4.

## THINGS THAT I STILL HAVE QUESTIONS ABOUT

| | |
|---|---|
| | |
| | |
| | |

## FINAL MEASUREMENTS OF THIS WEEK

| TOTAL TIME THIS WEEK | TOTAL NEW VERBS | TOTAL NEW WORDS |
|---|---|---|
| | | |

## SELF-ASSESSMENT OF MY ACTIVITIES THIS WEEK

| ACTIVITIES | SPECIFIC ASSESSMENTS | SATISFACTION |
|---|---|---|
| READING | | 😞😟😐🙂😄 |
| LISTENING | | 😞😟😐🙂😄 |
| WRITING | | 😞😟😐🙂😄 |
| SPEAKING | | 😞😟😐🙂😄 |
| STUDYING | | 😞😟😐🙂😄 |
| MOTIVATION | | 😞😟😐🙂😄 |
| LOG YOUR STUDY TIME | | TOTAL TIME |
| EACH BOX EQUALS 1 HOUR | | : |

| DAY & DATE | | STUDY STREAK # |
|---|---|---|
| LEARNING MOOD  ☹ ☹ 😐 🙂 😀 | | # VERBS ACQUIRED |

## PAST STUDIES IN REVIEW

| VOCABULARY FROM YESTERDAY | GOALS FROM YESTERDAY |
|---|---|
| 1 | ☐ |
| 2 | ☐ |
| 3 | ☐ |

| VOCABULARY FROM 5 DAYS AGO | VOCABULARY FROM 10 DAYS AGO |
|---|---|
| 1 | 1 |
| 2 | 2 |
| 3 | 3 |

## PRIORITIES FOR TODAY

| VOCABULARY FOR TODAY | GOALS FOR TODAY |
|---|---|
| 1 | ☐ |
| 2 | ☐ |
| 3 | ☐ |

## DESCRIBE YOUR LEARNING EXPERIENCE FOR TODAY

## SPECIAL WORDS FOR TODAY

| DAILY WORD BUILDER | VERB OF THE DAY | COGNATE OF THE DAY |
|---|---|---|
| **Ocupado** | **Dormir** | **Emisión** |
| adj. Past Participle. m. Ocupada, f. | To Sleep /g: Durmiendo / pp: Dormido /Irr. | Noun. From: Emission (SION=SIÓN) |

## INTERESTING THINGS FROM TODAY

### FOUR SENTENCES THAT I READ, HEARD OR CREATED TODAY

**1**

**2**

**3**

**4**

## THINGS I HAVE QUESTIONS ABOUT

## DESCRIBE YOUR ACTIVITIES IN THESE TASKS FOR TODAY

| ACTIVITY | DESCRIPTION | SATISFACTION |
|----------|-------------|--------------|
| READING | | ☹ ☹ 😐 🙂 😊 |
| LISTENING | | ☹ ☹ 😐 🙂 😊 |
| WRITING | | ☹ ☹ 😐 🙂 😊 |
| SPEAKING | | ☹ ☹ 😐 🙂 😊 |
| STUDYING | | ☹ ☹ 😐 🙂 😊 |
| VOCABULARY | | ☹ ☹ 😐 🙂 😊 |

| LOG YOUR STUDY TIME | | | | | | | | | | | | | TOTAL TIME |
|---|---|---|---|---|---|---|---|---|---|---|---|---|---|
| EACH BOX EQUALS 5 MINS. | | | | | | | | | | | | | : |

| DAY & DATE | | STUDY STREAK # |
|---|---|---|
| LEARNING MOOD  ☹ ☹ 😐 🙂 😀 | | # VERBS ACQUIRED |

## PAST STUDIES IN REVIEW

| VOCABULARY FROM YESTERDAY | GOALS FROM YESTERDAY |
|---|---|
| **1** | ☐ |
| **2** | ☐ |
| **3** | ☐ |

| VOCABULARY FROM 5 DAYS AGO | VOCABULARY FROM 10 DAYS AGO |
|---|---|
| **1** | **1** |
| **2** | **2** |
| **3** | **3** |

## PRIORITIES FOR TODAY

| VOCABULARY FOR TODAY | GOALS FOR TODAY |
|---|---|
| **1** | ☐ |
| **2** | ☐ |
| **3** | ☐ |

## DESCRIBE YOUR LEARNING EXPERIENCE FOR TODAY

## SPECIAL WORDS FOR TODAY

| DAILY WORD BUILDER | VERB OF THE DAY | COGNATE OF THE DAY |
|---|---|---|
| **Muy Ocupado** | **Repetir** | **Interferir** |
| adj. Very busy. | To Repeat /g: Repitiendo / pp: Repetido /Irr. | Verb. From: Interfere (E=AR OR IR) |

## INTERESTING THINGS FROM TODAY

### FOUR SENTENCES THAT I READ, HEARD OR CREATED TODAY

**1**

**2**

**3**

**4**

## THINGS I HAVE QUESTIONS ABOUT

## DESCRIBE YOUR ACTIVITIES IN THESE TASKS FOR TODAY

| ACTIVITY | DESCRIPTION | SATISFACTION |
|---|---|---|
| READING | | 😦 😣 😐 🙂 😀 |
| LISTENING | | 😦 😣 😐 🙂 😀 |
| WRITING | | 😦 😣 😐 🙂 😀 |
| SPEAKING | | 😦 😣 😐 🙂 😀 |
| STUDYING | | 😦 😣 😐 🙂 😀 |
| VOCABULARY | | 😦 😣 😐 🙂 😀 |

| LOG YOUR STUDY TIME | | | | | | | | | | | | TOTAL TIME |
|---|---|---|---|---|---|---|---|---|---|---|---|---|
| EACH BOX EQUALS 5 MINS. | | | | | | | | | | | | : |

| DAY & DATE | | STUDY STREAK # | |
|---|---|---|---|
| LEARNING MOOD | ☹ ☹ 😐 🙂 😀 | # VERBS ACQUIRED | |

## PAST STUDIES IN REVIEW

| VOCABULARY FROM YESTERDAY | GOALS FROM YESTERDAY |
|---|---|
| 1 | ☐ |
| 2 | ☐ |
| 3 | ☐ |

| VOCABULARY FROM 5 DAYS AGO | VOCABULARY FROM 10 DAYS AGO |
|---|---|
| 1 | 1 |
| 2 | 2 |
| 3 | 3 |

## PRIORITIES FOR TODAY

| VOCABULARY FOR TODAY | GOALS FOR TODAY |
|---|---|
| 1 | ☐ |
| 2 | ☐ |
| 3 | ☐ |

## DESCRIBE YOUR LEARNING EXPERIENCE FOR TODAY

## SPECIAL WORDS FOR TODAY

| DAILY WORD BUILDER | VERB OF THE DAY | COGNATE OF THE DAY |
|---|---|---|
| **Puesto Ocupado** | **Ayudar** | **Manipular** |
| n. m. Position held. | To Help /g: Ayudando / pp: Ayudado | Verb. From: Manipulate (E=AR OR IR) |

## INTERESTING THINGS FROM TODAY

### FOUR SENTENCES THAT I READ, HEARD OR CREATED TODAY

**1**

**2**

**3**

**4**

## THINGS I HAVE QUESTIONS ABOUT

## DESCRIBE YOUR ACTIVITIES IN THESE TASKS FOR TODAY

| ACTIVITY | DESCRIPTION | SATISFACTION |
|----------|-------------|--------------|
| READING | | ☹ ☹ 😐 🙂 😀 |
| LISTENING | | ☹ ☹ 😐 🙂 😀 |
| WRITING | | ☹ ☹ 😐 🙂 😀 |
| SPEAKING | | ☹ ☹ 😐 🙂 😀 |
| STUDYING | | ☹ ☹ 😐 🙂 😀 |
| VOCABULARY | | ☹ ☹ 😐 🙂 😀 |

| LOG YOUR STUDY TIME | | | | | | | | | | | | | | TOTAL TIME |
|---------------------|--|--|--|--|--|--|--|--|--|--|--|--|--|------------|
| EACH BOX EQUALS 5 MINS. | | | | | | | | | | | | | | : |

| DAY & DATE | | STUDY STREAK # | |
|---|---|---|---|
| LEARNING MOOD | ☹ ☹ 😐 🙂 😀 | # VERBS ACQUIRED | |

## PAST STUDIES IN REVIEW

| VOCABULARY FROM YESTERDAY | GOALS FROM YESTERDAY |
|---|---|
| 1 | ☐ |
| 2 | ☐ |
| 3 | ☐ |

| VOCABULARY FROM 5 DAYS AGO | VOCABULARY FROM 10 DAYS AGO |
|---|---|
| 1 | 1 |
| 2 | 2 |
| 3 | 3 |

## PRIORITIES FOR TODAY

| VOCABULARY FOR TODAY | GOALS FOR TODAY |
|---|---|
| 1 | ☐ |
| 2 | ☐ |
| 3 | ☐ |

## DESCRIBE YOUR LEARNING EXPERIENCE FOR TODAY

## SPECIAL WORDS FOR TODAY

| DAILY WORD BUILDER | VERB OF THE DAY | COGNATE OF THE DAY |
|---|---|---|
| **Persona Ocupada** | **Gastar** | **Exponente** |
| n. f. Employed person. | To Spend; To Use Up, Consume; To Wear Away /g: Gastando / pp: Gastado | Verb. From: Exponent (NT=NTE) |

## INTERESTING THINGS FROM TODAY

### FOUR SENTENCES THAT I READ, HEARD OR CREATED TODAY

**1**

**2**

**3**

**4**

## THINGS I HAVE QUESTIONS ABOUT

## DESCRIBE YOUR ACTIVITIES IN THESE TASKS FOR TODAY

| ACTIVITY | DESCRIPTION | SATISFACTION |
|----------|-------------|--------------|
| READING | | ☹ 😦 😐 🙂 😄 |
| LISTENING | | ☹ 😦 😐 🙂 😄 |
| WRITING | | ☹ 😦 😐 🙂 😄 |
| SPEAKING | | ☹ 😦 😐 🙂 😄 |
| STUDYING | | ☹ 😦 😐 🙂 😄 |
| VOCABULARY | | ☹ 😦 😐 🙂 😄 |

| LOG YOUR STUDY TIME | | | | | | | | | | | | | | TOTAL TIME |
|---------------------|--|--|--|--|--|--|--|--|--|--|--|--|--|------------|
| EACH BOX EQUALS 5 MINS. | | | | | | | | | | | | | | : |

| DAY & DATE | | STUDY STREAK # |
|---|---|---|
| LEARNING MOOD ☹ ☹ 😐 🙂 😃 | | # VERBS ACQUIRED |

## PAST STUDIES IN REVIEW

| VOCABULARY FROM YESTERDAY | GOALS FROM YESTERDAY |
|---|---|
| 1 | ☐ |
| 2 | ☐ |
| 3 | ☐ |

| VOCABULARY FROM 5 DAYS AGO | VOCABULARY FROM 10 DAYS AGO |
|---|---|
| 1 | 1 |
| 2 | 2 |
| 3 | 3 |

## PRIORITIES FOR TODAY

| VOCABULARY FOR TODAY | GOALS FOR TODAY |
|---|---|
| 1 | ☐ |
| 2 | ☐ |
| 3 | ☐ |

## DESCRIBE YOUR LEARNING EXPERIENCE FOR TODAY

_____

_____

_____

_____

## SPECIAL WORDS FOR TODAY

| DAILY WORD BUILDER | VERB OF THE DAY | COGNATE OF THE DAY |
|---|---|---|
| **Agenda Ocupada** | **Regalar** | **Decente** |
| n. f. Busy agenda | To Give [As A Gift]; To Present; Give Away; Pamper /g: Regalando / pp: Regalado | Adjective. From: Decent (NT=NTE) |

## INTERESTING THINGS FROM TODAY

### FOUR SENTENCES THAT I READ, HEARD OR CREATED TODAY

**1**

**2**

**3**

**4**

## THINGS I HAVE QUESTIONS ABOUT

## DESCRIBE YOUR ACTIVITIES IN THESE TASKS FOR TODAY

| ACTIVITY | DESCRIPTION | SATISFACTION |
|----------|-------------|--------------|
| READING | | ☹️☹️😐🙂😀 |
| LISTENING | | ☹️☹️😐🙂😀 |
| WRITING | | ☹️☹️😐🙂😀 |
| SPEAKING | | ☹️☹️😐🙂😀 |
| STUDYING | | ☹️☹️😐🙂😀 |
| VOCABULARY | | ☹️☹️😐🙂😀 |

| LOG YOUR STUDY TIME | | | | | | | | | | | | | | | TOTAL TIME |
|---------------------|--|--|--|--|--|--|--|--|--|--|--|--|--|--|------------|
| EACH BOX EQUALS 5 MINS. | | | | | | | | | | | | | | | : |

| DAY & DATE | | STUDY STREAK # |
|---|---|---|
| LEARNING MOOD  ☹ ☹ 😐 🙂 😃 | | # VERBS ACQUIRED |

## PAST STUDIES IN REVIEW

| VOCABULARY FROM YESTERDAY | GOALS FROM YESTERDAY |
|---|---|
| 1 | ☐ |
| 2 | ☐ |
| 3 | ☐ |

| VOCABULARY FROM 5 DAYS AGO | VOCABULARY FROM 10 DAYS AGO |
|---|---|
| 1 | 1 |
| 2 | 2 |
| 3 | 3 |

## PRIORITIES FOR TODAY

| VOCABULARY FOR TODAY | GOALS FOR TODAY |
|---|---|
| 1 | ☐ |
| 2 | ☐ |
| 3 | ☐ |

## DESCRIBE YOUR LEARNING EXPERIENCE FOR TODAY

## SPECIAL WORDS FOR TODAY

| DAILY WORD BUILDER | VERB OF THE DAY | COGNATE OF THE DAY |
|---|---|---|
| **Tono de Ocupado** | **Amanecer** | **Gigante** |
| n. Busy tone. | To Dawn /g: Amaneciendo / pp: Amanecido /Irr. | Adjective. From: Giant (NT=NTE) |

## INTERESTING THINGS FROM TODAY

### FOUR SENTENCES THAT I READ, HEARD OR CREATED TODAY

**1**

**2**

**3**

**4**

## THINGS I HAVE QUESTIONS ABOUT

## DESCRIBE YOUR ACTIVITIES IN THESE TASKS FOR TODAY

| ACTIVITY | DESCRIPTION | SATISFACTION |
|---|---|---|
| READING | | ☹ 😣 😐 🙂 😀 |
| LISTENING | | ☹ 😣 😐 🙂 😀 |
| WRITING | | ☹ 😣 😐 🙂 😀 |
| SPEAKING | | ☹ 😣 😐 🙂 😀 |
| STUDYING | | ☹ 😣 😐 🙂 😀 |
| VOCABULARY | | ☹ 😣 😐 🙂 😀 |
| LOG YOUR STUDY TIME | | TOTAL TIME |
| EACH BOX EQUALS 5 MINS. | | : |

| DAY & DATE | | STUDY STREAK # | |
|---|---|---|---|
| LEARNING MOOD | ☹ ☹ 😐 🙂 😃 | # VERBS ACQUIRED | |

## PAST STUDIES IN REVIEW

| VOCABULARY FROM YESTERDAY | GOALS FROM YESTERDAY |
|---|---|
| 1 | ☐ |
| 2 | ☐ |
| 3 | ☐ |

| VOCABULARY FROM 5 DAYS AGO | VOCABULARY FROM 10 DAYS AGO |
|---|---|
| 1 | 1 |
| 2 | 2 |
| 3 | 3 |

## PRIORITIES FOR TODAY

| VOCABULARY FOR TODAY | GOALS FOR TODAY |
|---|---|
| 1 | ☐ |
| 2 | ☐ |
| 3 | ☐ |

## DESCRIBE YOUR LEARNING EXPERIENCE FOR TODAY

## SPECIAL WORDS FOR TODAY

| DAILY WORD BUILDER | VERB OF THE DAY | COGNATE OF THE DAY |
|---|---|---|
| **Semana Ocupada** | **Colonizar** | **Furioso** |
| n. f. Busy week. | To Colonize, Settle /g: Colonizando / pp: Colonizado /Irr. | Adjective. From: Furious (OUS=OSO) |

## INTERESTING THINGS FROM TODAY

### FOUR SENTENCES THAT I READ, HEARD OR CREATED TODAY

**1**

**2**

**3**

**4**

## THINGS I HAVE QUESTIONS ABOUT

## DESCRIBE YOUR ACTIVITIES IN THESE TASKS FOR TODAY

| ACTIVITY | DESCRIPTION | SATISFACTION |
|---|---|---|
| READING | | ☹ ☹ 😐 🙂 😃 |
| LISTENING | | ☹ ☹ 😐 🙂 😃 |
| WRITING | | ☹ ☹ 😐 🙂 😃 |
| SPEAKING | | ☹ ☹ 😐 🙂 😃 |
| STUDYING | | ☹ ☹ 😐 🙂 😃 |
| VOCABULARY | | ☹ ☹ 😐 🙂 😃 |

| LOG YOUR STUDY TIME | | TOTAL TIME |
|---|---|---|
| EACH BOX EQUALS 5 MINS. | | : |

## WEEK NUMBER:

## THIS WEEK IN REVIEW

### VOCABULARY ACQUIRED

### BIGGEST ACHIEVEMENTS

☐     ☐

☐     ☐

☐     ☐

### AREAS FOR IMPROVEMENT

1

2

3

4

## THINGS THAT I STILL HAVE QUESTIONS ABOUT

| | |
|---|---|
| | |
| | |
| | |

## FINAL MEASUREMENTS OF THIS WEEK

| TOTAL TIME THIS WEEK | TOTAL NEW VERBS | TOTAL NEW WORDS |
|---|---|---|
| | | |

## SELF-ASSESSMENT OF MY ACTIVITIES THIS WEEK

| ACTIVITIES | SPECIFIC ASSESSMENTS | SATISFACTION |
|---|---|---|
| READING | | 😞😟😐😊😄 |
| LISTENING | | 😞😟😐😊😄 |
| WRITING | | 😞😟😐😊😄 |
| SPEAKING | | 😞😟😐😊😄 |
| STUDYING | | 😞😟😐😊😄 |
| MOTIVATION | | 😞😟😐😊😄 |

| LOG YOUR STUDY TIME | | | | | | | | | | TOTAL TIME |
|---|---|---|---|---|---|---|---|---|---|---|
| EACH BOX EQUALS 1 HOUR | | | | | | | | | | : |

| DAY & DATE | | STUDY STREAK # |
|---|---|---|
| LEARNING MOOD ☹ ☹ 😐 🙂 😀 | | # VERBS ACQUIRED |

## PAST STUDIES IN REVIEW

| VOCABULARY FROM YESTERDAY | GOALS FROM YESTERDAY |
|---|---|
| 1 | ☐ |
| 2 | ☐ |
| 3 | ☐ |

| VOCABULARY FROM 5 DAYS AGO | VOCABULARY FROM 10 DAYS AGO |
|---|---|
| 1 | 1 |
| 2 | 2 |
| 3 | 3 |

## PRIORITIES FOR TODAY

| VOCABULARY FOR TODAY | GOALS FOR TODAY |
|---|---|
| 1 | ☐ |
| 2 | ☐ |
| 3 | ☐ |

## DESCRIBE YOUR LEARNING EXPERIENCE FOR TODAY

## SPECIAL WORDS FOR TODAY

| DAILY WORD BUILDER | VERB OF THE DAY | COGNATE OF THE DAY |
|---|---|---|
| **Problemas** | **Empezar** | **Audacia** |
| n. m. pl. Problems. Challenges. Issues | To Begin, Start /g: Empezando / pp: Empezado /Irr. | Adjective. From: Audacity (Y=IA OR ÍA) |

## INTERESTING THINGS FROM TODAY

### FOUR SENTENCES THAT I READ, HEARD OR CREATED TODAY

**1**

**2**

**3**

**4**

## THINGS I HAVE QUESTIONS ABOUT

## DESCRIBE YOUR ACTIVITIES IN THESE TASKS FOR TODAY

| ACTIVITY | DESCRIPTION | SATISFACTION |
|----------|-------------|--------------|
| READING | | ☹ ☹ 😐 🙂 😊 |
| LISTENING | | ☹ ☹ 😐 🙂 😊 |
| WRITING | | ☹ ☹ 😐 🙂 😊 |
| SPEAKING | | ☹ ☹ 😐 🙂 😊 |
| STUDYING | | ☹ ☹ 😐 🙂 😊 |
| VOCABULARY | | ☹ ☹ 😐 🙂 😊 |

| LOG YOUR STUDY TIME | | | | | | | | | | | TOTAL TIME |
|---------------------|--|--|--|--|--|--|--|--|--|--|------------|
| EACH BOX EQUALS 5 MINS. | | | | | | | | | | | : |

| DAY & DATE | | STUDY STREAK # |
|---|---|---|
| LEARNING MOOD | ☹ 🙁 😐 🙂 😃 | # VERBS ACQUIRED |

## PAST STUDIES IN REVIEW

| VOCABULARY FROM YESTERDAY | GOALS FROM YESTERDAY |
|---|---|
| 1 | ☐ |
| 2 | ☐ |
| 3 | ☐ |

| VOCABULARY FROM 5 DAYS AGO | VOCABULARY FROM 10 DAYS AGO |
|---|---|
| 1 | 1 |
| 2 | 2 |
| 3 | 3 |

## PRIORITIES FOR TODAY

| VOCABULARY FOR TODAY | GOALS FOR TODAY |
|---|---|
| 1 | ☐ |
| 2 | ☐ |
| 3 | ☐ |

## DESCRIBE YOUR LEARNING EXPERIENCE FOR TODAY

## SPECIAL WORDS FOR TODAY

| DAILY WORD BUILDER | VERB OF THE DAY | COGNATE OF THE DAY |
|---|---|---|
| **Sin Problemas** | **Saber** | **Continuar** |
| adv. Smoothly. Seamlessly. adj. Trouble-free. | To Know /g: Sabiendo / pp: Sabido /Irr. | Verb. From: Continue (E=AR OR IR) |

## INTERESTING THINGS FROM TODAY

### FOUR SENTENCES THAT I READ, HEARD OR CREATED TODAY

**1**

**2**

**3**

**4**

## THINGS I HAVE QUESTIONS ABOUT

## DESCRIBE YOUR ACTIVITIES IN THESE TASKS FOR TODAY

| ACTIVITY | DESCRIPTION | SATISFACTION |
|---|---|---|
| READING | | ☹ ☹ 😐 ☺ 😃 |
| LISTENING | | ☹ ☹ 😐 ☺ 😃 |
| WRITING | | ☹ ☹ 😐 ☺ 😃 |
| SPEAKING | | ☹ ☹ 😐 ☺ 😃 |
| STUDYING | | ☹ ☹ 😐 ☺ 😃 |
| VOCABULARY | | ☹ ☹ 😐 ☺ 😃 |

| LOG YOUR STUDY TIME | | | | | | | | | | | | | | | TOTAL TIME |
|---|---|---|---|---|---|---|---|---|---|---|---|---|---|---|---|
| EACH BOX EQUALS 5 MINS. | | | | | | | | | | | | | | | : |

| DAY & DATE | | STUDY STREAK # | |
|---|---|---|---|
| LEARNING MOOD | ☹ ☹ 😐 🙂 😀 | # VERBS ACQUIRED | |

## PAST STUDIES IN REVIEW

| VOCABULARY FROM YESTERDAY | GOALS FROM YESTERDAY |
|---|---|
| 1 | ☐ |
| 2 | ☐ |
| 3 | ☐ |

| VOCABULARY FROM 5 DAYS AGO | VOCABULARY FROM 10 DAYS AGO |
|---|---|
| 1 | 1 |
| 2 | 2 |
| 3 | 3 |

## PRIORITIES FOR TODAY

| VOCABULARY FOR TODAY | GOALS FOR TODAY |
|---|---|
| 1 | ☐ |
| 2 | ☐ |
| 3 | ☐ |

## DESCRIBE YOUR LEARNING EXPERIENCE FOR TODAY

_____

_____

_____

_____

## SPECIAL WORDS FOR TODAY

| DAILY WORD BUILDER | VERB OF THE DAY | COGNATE OF THE DAY |
|---|---|---|
| **Problemas de Salud** | **Bailar** | **Odioso** |
| n. m. Pls. Health problems. Health issues. | To Dance /g: Bailando / pp: Bailado | Adjective. From: Odious (OUS=OSO) |

## INTERESTING THINGS FROM TODAY

### FOUR SENTENCES THAT I READ, HEARD OR CREATED TODAY

**1**

**2**

**3**

**4**

## THINGS I HAVE QUESTIONS ABOUT

## DESCRIBE YOUR ACTIVITIES IN THESE TASKS FOR TODAY

| ACTIVITY | DESCRIPTION | SATISFACTION |
|---|---|---|
| READING | | 😞 😟 😐 🙂 😊 |
| LISTENING | | 😞 😟 😐 🙂 😊 |
| WRITING | | 😞 😟 😐 🙂 😊 |
| SPEAKING | | 😞 😟 😐 🙂 😊 |
| STUDYING | | 😞 😟 😐 🙂 😊 |
| VOCABULARY | | 😞 😟 😐 🙂 😊 |

| LOG YOUR STUDY TIME | | | | | | | | | | | TOTAL TIME |
|---|---|---|---|---|---|---|---|---|---|---|---|
| EACH BOX EQUALS 5 MINS. | | | | | | | | | | | : |

| DAY & DATE | | STUDY STREAK # | |
|---|---|---|---|
| LEARNING MOOD | ☹ ☹ ☺ ☺ 😄 | # VERBS ACQUIRED | |

## PAST STUDIES IN REVIEW

| VOCABULARY FROM YESTERDAY | GOALS FROM YESTERDAY |
|---|---|
| **1** | ☐ |
| **2** | ☐ |
| **3** | ☐ |

| VOCABULARY FROM 5 DAYS AGO | VOCABULARY FROM 10 DAYS AGO |
|---|---|
| **1** | **1** |
| **2** | **2** |
| **3** | **3** |

## PRIORITIES FOR TODAY

| VOCABULARY FOR TODAY | GOALS FOR TODAY |
|---|---|
| **1** | ☐ |
| **2** | ☐ |
| **3** | ☐ |

## DESCRIBE YOUR LEARNING EXPERIENCE FOR TODAY

## SPECIAL WORDS FOR TODAY

| DAILY WORD BUILDER | VERB OF THE DAY | COGNATE OF THE DAY |
|---|---|---|
| **Solución de Problemas** | **Gritar** | **Narcótico** |
| n. f. Troubleshooting. | To Shout, Yell, Scream, Cry Out /g: Gritando / pp: Gritado | Adjective. From: Narcotic (IC=ICO) |

## INTERESTING THINGS FROM TODAY

### FOUR SENTENCES THAT I READ, HEARD OR CREATED TODAY

**1**

**2**

**3**

**4**

## THINGS I HAVE QUESTIONS ABOUT

## DESCRIBE YOUR ACTIVITIES IN THESE TASKS FOR TODAY

| ACTIVITY | DESCRIPTION | SATISFACTION |
|---|---|---|
| READING | | 😠 😟 😐 😊 😃 |
| LISTENING | | 😠 😟 😐 😊 😃 |
| WRITING | | 😠 😟 😐 😊 😃 |
| SPEAKING | | 😠 😟 😐 😊 😃 |
| STUDYING | | 😠 😟 😐 😊 😃 |
| VOCABULARY | | 😠 😟 😐 😊 😃 |

| LOG YOUR STUDY TIME | | | | | | | | | | | | TOTAL TIME |
|---|---|---|---|---|---|---|---|---|---|---|---|---|
| EACH BOX EQUALS 5 MINS. | | | | | | | | | | | | : |

| DAY & DATE | | STUDY STREAK # | |
|---|---|---|---|
| LEARNING MOOD | ☹ ☹ 😐 🙂 😀 | # VERBS ACQUIRED | |

## PAST STUDIES IN REVIEW

| VOCABULARY FROM YESTERDAY | GOALS FROM YESTERDAY |
|---|---|
| 1 | ☐ |
| 2 | ☐ |
| 3 | ☐ |

| VOCABULARY FROM 5 DAYS AGO | VOCABULARY FROM 10 DAYS AGO |
|---|---|
| 1 | 1 |
| 2 | 2 |
| 3 | 3 |

## PRIORITIES FOR TODAY

| VOCABULARY FOR TODAY | GOALS FOR TODAY |
|---|---|
| 1 | ☐ |
| 2 | ☐ |
| 3 | ☐ |

## DESCRIBE YOUR LEARNING EXPERIENCE FOR TODAY

## SPECIAL WORDS FOR TODAY

| DAILY WORD BUILDER | VERB OF THE DAY | COGNATE OF THE DAY |
|---|---|---|
| **Problemas Familiares** | **Regresar** | **Estandarización** |
| n. m. pl. Family problems. | To Return, Go Back /g: Regresando / pp: Regresado | Noun. From: Standardization (TION=CIÓN) |

## INTERESTING THINGS FROM TODAY

### FOUR SENTENCES THAT I READ, HEARD OR CREATED TODAY

**1**

**2**

**3**

**4**

## THINGS I HAVE QUESTIONS ABOUT

## DESCRIBE YOUR ACTIVITIES IN THESE TASKS FOR TODAY

| ACTIVITY | DESCRIPTION | SATISFACTION |
|---|---|---|
| READING | | ☹ ☹ 😐 🙂 😊 |
| LISTENING | | ☹ ☹ 😐 🙂 😊 |
| WRITING | | ☹ ☹ 😐 🙂 😊 |
| SPEAKING | | ☹ ☹ 😐 🙂 😊 |
| STUDYING | | ☹ ☹ 😐 🙂 😊 |
| VOCABULARY | | ☹ ☹ 😐 🙂 😊 |

| LOG YOUR STUDY TIME | | | | | | | | | | | | | TOTAL TIME |
|---|---|---|---|---|---|---|---|---|---|---|---|---|---|
| EACH BOX EQUALS 5 MINS. | | | | | | | | | | | | | : |

| DAY & DATE | | STUDY STREAK # | |
|---|---|---|---|
| LEARNING MOOD | ☹ ☹ 😐 🙂 😄 | # VERBS ACQUIRED | |

## PAST STUDIES IN REVIEW

| VOCABULARY FROM YESTERDAY | GOALS FROM YESTERDAY |
|---|---|
| 1 | ☐ |
| 2 | ☐ |
| 3 | ☐ |

| VOCABULARY FROM 5 DAYS AGO | VOCABULARY FROM 10 DAYS AGO |
|---|---|
| 1 | 1 |
| 2 | 2 |
| 3 | 3 |

## PRIORITIES FOR TODAY

| VOCABULARY FOR TODAY | GOALS FOR TODAY |
|---|---|
| 1 | ☐ |
| 2 | ☐ |
| 3 | ☐ |

## DESCRIBE YOUR LEARNING EXPERIENCE FOR TODAY

## SPECIAL WORDS FOR TODAY

| DAILY WORD BUILDER | VERB OF THE DAY | COGNATE OF THE DAY |
|---|---|---|
| **Problemas Económicos** | **Amenazar** | **Excluir** |
| n. m. pl. Financial problems. | To Threaten, Menace /g: Amenazando / pp: Amenazado /Irr. | Verb. From: Exclude (E=AR OR IR) |

## INTERESTING THINGS FROM TODAY

### FOUR SENTENCES THAT I READ, HEARD OR CREATED TODAY

1

2

3

4

## THINGS I HAVE QUESTIONS ABOUT

## DESCRIBE YOUR ACTIVITIES IN THESE TASKS FOR TODAY

| ACTIVITY | DESCRIPTION | SATISFACTION |
|---|---|---|
| READING | | ☹️ ☹️ 😐 🙂 😊 |
| LISTENING | | ☹️ ☹️ 😐 🙂 😊 |
| WRITING | | ☹️ ☹️ 😐 🙂 😊 |
| SPEAKING | | ☹️ ☹️ 😐 🙂 😊 |
| STUDYING | | ☹️ ☹️ 😐 🙂 😊 |
| VOCABULARY | | ☹️ ☹️ 😐 🙂 😊 |
| LOG YOUR STUDY TIME | | TOTAL TIME |
| EACH BOX EQUALS 5 MINS. | | : |

| DAY & DATE | | STUDY STREAK # |
| --- | --- | --- |
| LEARNING MOOD | ☹ ☹ 😐 🙂 😃 | # VERBS ACQUIRED |

## PAST STUDIES IN REVIEW

| VOCABULARY FROM YESTERDAY | GOALS FROM YESTERDAY |
| --- | --- |
| 1 | ☐ |
| 2 | ☐ |
| 3 | ☐ |

| VOCABULARY FROM 5 DAYS AGO | VOCABULARY FROM 10 DAYS AGO |
| --- | --- |
| 1 | 1 |
| 2 | 2 |
| 3 | 3 |

## PRIORITIES FOR TODAY

| VOCABULARY FOR TODAY | GOALS FOR TODAY |
| --- | --- |
| 1 | ☐ |
| 2 | ☐ |
| 3 | ☐ |

## DESCRIBE YOUR LEARNING EXPERIENCE FOR TODAY

## SPECIAL WORDS FOR TODAY

| DAILY WORD BUILDER | VERB OF THE DAY | COGNATE OF THE DAY |
| --- | --- | --- |
| **Problemas Ambientales** | **Competir** | **Toxicología** |
| n. pl. Environmental Problems | To Compete /g: Compitiendo / pp: Competido /Irr. | Noun. From: Toxicology (Y=IA OR ÍA) |

## INTERESTING THINGS FROM TODAY

### FOUR SENTENCES THAT I READ, HEARD OR CREATED TODAY

**1**

**2**

**3**

**4**

## THINGS I HAVE QUESTIONS ABOUT

## DESCRIBE YOUR ACTIVITIES IN THESE TASKS FOR TODAY

| ACTIVITY | DESCRIPTION | SATISFACTION |
|---|---|---|
| READING | | ☹️ ☹️ 😐 🙂 😄 |
| LISTENING | | ☹️ ☹️ 😐 🙂 😄 |
| WRITING | | ☹️ ☹️ 😐 🙂 😄 |
| SPEAKING | | ☹️ ☹️ 😐 🙂 😄 |
| STUDYING | | ☹️ ☹️ 😐 🙂 😄 |
| VOCABULARY | | ☹️ ☹️ 😐 🙂 😄 |
| LOG YOUR STUDY TIME | | TOTAL TIME |
| EACH BOX EQUALS 5 MINS. | | : |

## THIS WEEK IN REVIEW

### VOCABULARY ACQUIRED

### BIGGEST ACHIEVEMENTS

☐              ☐

☐              ☐

☐              ☐

### AREAS FOR IMPROVEMENT

1

2

3

4

## THINGS THAT I STILL HAVE QUESTIONS ABOUT

|  |  |
|---|---|
|  |  |
|  |  |
|  |  |

## FINAL MEASUREMENTS OF THIS WEEK

| TOTAL TIME THIS WEEK | TOTAL NEW VERBS | TOTAL NEW WORDS |
|---|---|---|
|  |  |  |

## SELF-ASSESSMENT OF MY ACTIVITIES THIS WEEK

| ACTIVITIES | SPECIFIC ASSESSMENTS | SATISFACTION |
|---|---|---|
| READING |  | ☹ ☹ 😐 🙂 😃 |
| LISTENING |  | ☹ ☹ 😐 🙂 😃 |
| WRITING |  | ☹ ☹ 😐 🙂 😃 |
| SPEAKING |  | ☹ ☹ 😐 🙂 😃 |
| STUDYING |  | ☹ ☹ 😐 🙂 😃 |
| MOTIVATION |  | ☹ ☹ 😐 🙂 😃 |

| LOG YOUR STUDY TIME |  |  |  |  |  |  |  |  |  |  |  | TOTAL TIME |
|---|---|---|---|---|---|---|---|---|---|---|---|---|
| EACH BOX EQUALS 1 HOUR |  |  |  |  |  |  |  |  |  |  |  | : |

| DAY & DATE | | STUDY STREAK # |
|---|---|---|
| LEARNING MOOD ☹ ☹ 😐 🙂 😀 | | # VERBS ACQUIRED |

## PAST STUDIES IN REVIEW

| VOCABULARY FROM YESTERDAY | GOALS FROM YESTERDAY |
|---|---|
| 1 | ☐ |
| 2 | ☐ |
| 3 | ☐ |

| VOCABULARY FROM 5 DAYS AGO | VOCABULARY FROM 10 DAYS AGO |
|---|---|
| 1 | 1 |
| 2 | 2 |
| 3 | 3 |

## PRIORITIES FOR TODAY

| VOCABULARY FOR TODAY | GOALS FOR TODAY |
|---|---|
| 1 | ☐ |
| 2 | ☐ |
| 3 | ☐ |

## DESCRIBE YOUR LEARNING EXPERIENCE FOR TODAY

## SPECIAL WORDS FOR TODAY

| DAILY WORD BUILDER | VERB OF THE DAY | COGNATE OF THE DAY |
|---|---|---|
| **Verdadero** | **Encontrar** | **Iluminar** |
| adj. Real. True. | To Find, Encounter /g: Encontrando / pp: Encontrado /Irr. | Verb. From: Illuminate (ATE=AR) |

# INTERESTING THINGS FROM TODAY

## FOUR SENTENCES THAT I READ, HEARD OR CREATED TODAY

**1**

**2**

**3**

**4**

## THINGS I HAVE QUESTIONS ABOUT

## DESCRIBE YOUR ACTIVITIES IN THESE TASKS FOR TODAY

| ACTIVITY | DESCRIPTION | SATISFACTION |
|---|---|---|
| READING | | 😟😦😐😊😄 |
| LISTENING | | 😟😦😐😊😄 |
| WRITING | | 😟😦😐😊😄 |
| SPEAKING | | 😟😦😐😊😄 |
| STUDYING | | 😟😦😐😊😄 |
| VOCABULARY | | 😟😦😐😊😄 |

| LOG YOUR STUDY TIME | | TOTAL TIME |
|---|---|---|
| EACH BOX EQUALS 5 MINS. | | : |

| LEARNING MOOD | ☹ ☹ 😐 🙂 😀 | # VERBS ACQUIRED |

## PAST STUDIES IN REVIEW

| VOCABULARY FROM YESTERDAY | GOALS FROM YESTERDAY |
|---|---|
| 1 | ☐ |
| 2 | ☐ |
| 3 | ☐ |

| VOCABULARY FROM 5 DAYS AGO | VOCABULARY FROM 10 DAYS AGO |
|---|---|
| 1 | 1 |
| 2 | 2 |
| 3 | 3 |

## PRIORITIES FOR TODAY

| VOCABULARY FOR TODAY | GOALS FOR TODAY |
|---|---|
| 1 | ☐ |
| 2 | ☐ |
| 3 | ☐ |

## DESCRIBE YOUR LEARNING EXPERIENCE FOR TODAY

## SPECIAL WORDS FOR TODAY

| DAILY WORD BUILDER | VERB OF THE DAY | COGNATE OF THE DAY |
|---|---|---|
| **Amor Verdadero** | **Sacar** | **Distribuir** |
| n. m. True love. Real love. | To Take Out, Stick Out /g: Sacando / pp: Sacado /Irr. | Verb. From: Distribute (E=AR OR IR) |

## INTERESTING THINGS FROM TODAY

### FOUR SENTENCES THAT I READ, HEARD OR CREATED TODAY

**1**

**2**

**3**

**4**

## THINGS I HAVE QUESTIONS ABOUT

## DESCRIBE YOUR ACTIVITIES IN THESE TASKS FOR TODAY

| ACTIVITY | DESCRIPTION | SATISFACTION |
|----------|-------------|--------------|
| READING | | ☹ ☹ 😐 🙂 😄 |
| LISTENING | | ☹ ☹ 😐 🙂 😄 |
| WRITING | | ☹ ☹ 😐 🙂 😄 |
| SPEAKING | | ☹ ☹ 😐 🙂 😄 |
| STUDYING | | ☹ ☹ 😐 🙂 😄 |
| VOCABULARY | | ☹ ☹ 😐 🙂 😄 |

| LOG YOUR STUDY TIME | | | | | | | | | | | | TOTAL TIME |
|---------------------|--|--|--|--|--|--|--|--|--|--|--|------------|
| EACH BOX EQUALS 5 MINS. | | | | | | | | | | | | : |

| DAY & DATE | | STUDY STREAK # |
|---|---|---|
| LEARNING MOOD | ☹ ☹ 😐 🙂 😃 | # VERBS ACQUIRED |

## PAST STUDIES IN REVIEW

| VOCABULARY FROM YESTERDAY | GOALS FROM YESTERDAY |
|---|---|
| 1 | ☐ |
| 2 | ☐ |
| 3 | ☐ |

| VOCABULARY FROM 5 DAYS AGO | VOCABULARY FROM 10 DAYS AGO |
|---|---|
| 1 | 1 |
| 2 | 2 |
| 3 | 3 |

## PRIORITIES FOR TODAY

| VOCABULARY FOR TODAY | GOALS FOR TODAY |
|---|---|
| 1 | ☐ |
| 2 | ☐ |
| 3 | ☐ |

## DESCRIBE YOUR LEARNING EXPERIENCE FOR TODAY

## SPECIAL WORDS FOR TODAY

| DAILY WORD BUILDER | VERB OF THE DAY | COGNATE OF THE DAY |
|---|---|---|
| **Verdaderos Amigos** | **Beber** | **Acrobático** |
| n. m. pl. True friends. Real friends. | To Drink /g: Bebiendo / pp: Bebido | Adjective. From: Acrobatic (IC=ICO) |

## INTERESTING THINGS FROM TODAY

### FOUR SENTENCES THAT I READ, HEARD OR CREATED TODAY

**1**

**2**

**3**

**4**

## THINGS I HAVE QUESTIONS ABOUT

## DESCRIBE YOUR ACTIVITIES IN THESE TASKS FOR TODAY

| ACTIVITY | DESCRIPTION | SATISFACTION |
|---|---|---|
| READING | | ☹ ☹ 😐 🙂 😀 |
| LISTENING | | ☹ ☹ 😐 🙂 😀 |
| WRITING | | ☹ ☹ 😐 🙂 😀 |
| SPEAKING | | ☹ ☹ 😐 🙂 😀 |
| STUDYING | | ☹ ☹ 😐 🙂 😀 |
| VOCABULARY | | ☹ ☹ 😐 🙂 😀 |

| LOG YOUR STUDY TIME | | | | | | | | | | | | | | TOTAL TIME |
|---|---|---|---|---|---|---|---|---|---|---|---|---|---|---|
| EACH BOX EQUALS 5 MINS. | | | | | | | | | | | | | | : |

| DAY & DATE | | STUDY STREAK # |
|---|---|---|
| LEARNING MOOD ☹ ☹ 😐 🙂 😀 | | # VERBS ACQUIRED |

## PAST STUDIES IN REVIEW

| VOCABULARY FROM YESTERDAY | GOALS FROM YESTERDAY |
|---|---|
| 1 | ☐ |
| 2 | ☐ |
| 3 | ☐ |

| VOCABULARY FROM 5 DAYS AGO | VOCABULARY FROM 10 DAYS AGO |
|---|---|
| 1 | 1 |
| 2 | 2 |
| 3 | 3 |

## PRIORITIES FOR TODAY

| VOCABULARY FOR TODAY | GOALS FOR TODAY |
|---|---|
| 1 | ☐ |
| 2 | ☐ |
| 3 | ☐ |

## DESCRIBE YOUR LEARNING EXPERIENCE FOR TODAY

## SPECIAL WORDS FOR TODAY

| DAILY WORD BUILDER | VERB OF THE DAY | COGNATE OF THE DAY |
|---|---|---|
| **Verdadero Placer** | **Guardar** | **Exactamente** |
| n. m. Real pleasure. True pleasure. | To Guard, Take Care Of; To Keep, Hold On To /g: Guardando / pp: Guardado | Adverb. From: Exactly (LY=MENTE) |

## INTERESTING THINGS FROM TODAY
### FOUR SENTENCES THAT I READ, HEARD OR CREATED TODAY

**1**

**2**

**3**

**4**

## THINGS I HAVE QUESTIONS ABOUT

## DESCRIBE YOUR ACTIVITIES IN THESE TASKS FOR TODAY

| ACTIVITY | DESCRIPTION | SATISFACTION |
|----------|-------------|--------------|
| READING | | 😟😣😐🙂😀 |
| LISTENING | | 😟😣😐🙂😀 |
| WRITING | | 😟😣😐🙂😀 |
| SPEAKING | | 😟😣😐🙂😀 |
| STUDYING | | 😟😣😐🙂😀 |
| VOCABULARY | | 😟😣😐🙂😀 |

| LOG YOUR STUDY TIME | | | | | | | | | | | TOTAL TIME |
|---|---|---|---|---|---|---|---|---|---|---|---|
| EACH BOX EQUALS 5 MINS. | | | | | | | | | | | : |

| DAY & DATE | | STUDY STREAK # |
|---|---|---|
| LEARNING MOOD ☹ ☹ ☺ ☺ ☺ | | # VERBS ACQUIRED |

## PAST STUDIES IN REVIEW

| VOCABULARY FROM YESTERDAY | GOALS FROM YESTERDAY |
|---|---|
| 1 | ☐ |
| 2 | ☐ |
| 3 | ☐ |

| VOCABULARY FROM 5 DAYS AGO | VOCABULARY FROM 10 DAYS AGO |
|---|---|
| 1 | 1 |
| 2 | 2 |
| 3 | 3 |

## PRIORITIES FOR TODAY

| VOCABULARY FOR TODAY | GOALS FOR TODAY |
|---|---|
| 1 | ☐ |
| 2 | ☐ |
| 3 | ☐ |

## DESCRIBE YOUR LEARNING EXPERIENCE FOR TODAY

## SPECIAL WORDS FOR TODAY

| DAILY WORD BUILDER | VERB OF THE DAY | COGNATE OF THE DAY |
|---|---|---|
| **Verdadero Significado** | **Romper** | **Fotografía** |
| n. m. Real meaning. | To Break /g: Rompiendo / pp: Roto | Noun. From: Photography (Y=IA OR ÍA) |

## FOUR SENTENCES THAT I READ, HEARD OR CREATED TODAY

**1**

**2**

**3**

**4**

## THINGS I HAVE QUESTIONS ABOUT

## DESCRIBE YOUR ACTIVITIES IN THESE TASKS FOR TODAY

| ACTIVITY | DESCRIPTION | SATISFACTION |
|---|---|---|
| READING | | ☹ ☹ 😐 🙂 😄 |
| LISTENING | | ☹ ☹ 😐 🙂 😄 |
| WRITING | | ☹ ☹ 😐 🙂 😄 |
| SPEAKING | | ☹ ☹ 😐 🙂 😄 |
| STUDYING | | ☹ ☹ 😐 🙂 😄 |
| VOCABULARY | | ☹ ☹ 😐 🙂 😄 |

| LOG YOUR STUDY TIME | | | | | | | | | | | | | | TOTAL TIME |
|---|---|---|---|---|---|---|---|---|---|---|---|---|---|---|
| EACH BOX EQUALS 5 MINS. | | | | | | | | | | | | | | : |

| DAY & DATE | | STUDY STREAK # | |
|---|---|---|---|
| LEARNING MOOD | 😧 😦 😐 🙂 😃 | # VERBS ACQUIRED | |

## PAST STUDIES IN REVIEW

| VOCABULARY FROM YESTERDAY | GOALS FROM YESTERDAY |
|---|---|
| **1** | ☐ |
| **2** | ☐ |
| **3** | ☐ |

| VOCABULARY FROM 5 DAYS AGO | VOCABULARY FROM 10 DAYS AGO |
|---|---|
| **1** | **1** |
| **2** | **2** |
| **3** | **3** |

## PRIORITIES FOR TODAY

| VOCABULARY FOR TODAY | GOALS FOR TODAY |
|---|---|
| **1** | ☐ |
| **2** | ☐ |
| **3** | ☐ |

## DESCRIBE YOUR LEARNING EXPERIENCE FOR TODAY

---
---
---
---

## SPECIAL WORDS FOR TODAY

| DAILY WORD BUILDER | VERB OF THE DAY | COGNATE OF THE DAY |
|---|---|---|
| **Verdadera Magnitud** | **Aparecer** | **Complicación** |
| n. f. True size. | To Appear /g: Apareciendo / pp: Aparecido /Irr. | Noun. From: Complication (TION=CIÓN) |

## INTERESTING THINGS FROM TODAY

### FOUR SENTENCES THAT I READ, HEARD OR CREATED TODAY

**1**

**2**

**3**

**4**

## THINGS I HAVE QUESTIONS ABOUT

## DESCRIBE YOUR ACTIVITIES IN THESE TASKS FOR TODAY

| ACTIVITY | DESCRIPTION | SATISFACTION |
|---|---|---|
| READING | | 😞😟😐😊😃 |
| LISTENING | | 😞😟😐😊😃 |
| WRITING | | 😞😟😐😊😃 |
| SPEAKING | | 😞😟😐😊😃 |
| STUDYING | | 😞😟😐😊😃 |
| VOCABULARY | | 😞😟😐😊😃 |
| LOG YOUR STUDY TIME | | TOTAL TIME |
| EACH BOX EQUALS 5 MINS. | | : |

| DAY & DATE | | STUDY STREAK # | |
|---|---|---|---|
| LEARNING MOOD | ☹ ☹ 😐 🙂 😃 | # VERBS ACQUIRED | |

## PAST STUDIES IN REVIEW

| VOCABULARY FROM YESTERDAY | GOALS FROM YESTERDAY |
|---|---|
| 1 | ☐ |
| 2 | ☐ |
| 3 | ☐ |

| VOCABULARY FROM 5 DAYS AGO | VOCABULARY FROM 10 DAYS AGO |
|---|---|
| 1 | 1 |
| 2 | 2 |
| 3 | 3 |

## PRIORITIES FOR TODAY

| VOCABULARY FOR TODAY | GOALS FOR TODAY |
|---|---|
| 1 | ☐ |
| 2 | ☐ |
| 3 | ☐ |

## DESCRIBE YOUR LEARNING EXPERIENCE FOR TODAY

## SPECIAL WORDS FOR TODAY

| DAILY WORD BUILDER | VERB OF THE DAY | COGNATE OF THE DAY |
|---|---|---|
| **Verdaderos Derechos** | **Componer** | **Designar** |
| n. m. Real rights. | To Compose, Make Up, Put Together /g: Componiendo / pp: Compuesto /Irr. | Verb. From: Designate (ATE=AR) |

## INTERESTING THINGS FROM TODAY

### FOUR SENTENCES THAT I READ, HEARD OR CREATED TODAY

**1**

**2**

**3**

**4**

## THINGS I HAVE QUESTIONS ABOUT

## DESCRIBE YOUR ACTIVITIES IN THESE TASKS FOR TODAY

| ACTIVITY | DESCRIPTION | SATISFACTION |
|----------|-------------|--------------|
| READING | | ☹ ☹ 😐 ☺ ☺ |
| LISTENING | | ☹ ☹ 😐 ☺ ☺ |
| WRITING | | ☹ ☹ 😐 ☺ ☺ |
| SPEAKING | | ☹ ☹ 😐 ☺ ☺ |
| STUDYING | | ☹ ☹ 😐 ☺ ☺ |
| VOCABULARY | | ☹ ☹ 😐 ☺ ☺ |

| LOG YOUR STUDY TIME | | | | | | | | | | | | TOTAL TIME |
|---------------------|--|--|--|--|--|--|--|--|--|--|--|------------|
| EACH BOX EQUALS 5 MINS. | | | | | | | | | | | | : |

## THIS WEEK IN REVIEW

### VOCABULARY ACQUIRED

### BIGGEST ACHIEVEMENTS

- [ ]
- [ ]
- [ ]
- [ ]
- [ ]
- [ ]

### AREAS FOR IMPROVEMENT

1.
2.
3.
4.

## THINGS THAT I STILL HAVE QUESTIONS ABOUT

| | |
|---|---|
| | |
| | |
| | |

## FINAL MEASUREMENTS OF THIS WEEK

| TOTAL TIME THIS WEEK | TOTAL NEW VERBS | TOTAL NEW WORDS |
|---|---|---|
| | | |

## SELF-ASSESSMENT OF MY ACTIVITIES THIS WEEK

| ACTIVITIES | SPECIFIC ASSESSMENTS | SATISFACTION |
|---|---|---|
| READING | | 😞😟😐😊😄 |
| LISTENING | | 😞😟😐😊😄 |
| WRITING | | 😞😟😐😊😄 |
| SPEAKING | | 😞😟😐😊😄 |
| STUDYING | | 😞😟😐😊😄 |
| MOTIVATION | | 😞😟😐😊😄 |

| LOG YOUR STUDY TIME | | | | | | | | | | | TOTAL TIME |
|---|---|---|---|---|---|---|---|---|---|---|---|
| EACH BOX EQUALS 1 HOUR | | | | | | | | | | | : |

| DAY & DATE | | STUDY STREAK # |
|---|---|---|
| LEARNING MOOD | 😦 😞 😐 😊 😀 | # VERBS ACQUIRED |

## PAST STUDIES IN REVIEW

| VOCABULARY FROM YESTERDAY | GOALS FROM YESTERDAY |
|---|---|
| 1 | ☐ |
| 2 | ☐ |
| 3 | ☐ |

| VOCABULARY FROM 5 DAYS AGO | VOCABULARY FROM 10 DAYS AGO |
|---|---|
| 1 | 1 |
| 2 | 2 |
| 3 | 3 |

## PRIORITIES FOR TODAY

| VOCABULARY FOR TODAY | GOALS FOR TODAY |
|---|---|
| 1 | ☐ |
| 2 | ☐ |
| 3 | ☐ |

## DESCRIBE YOUR LEARNING EXPERIENCE FOR TODAY

_____

_____

_____

_____

## SPECIAL WORDS FOR TODAY

| DAILY WORD BUILDER | VERB OF THE DAY | COGNATE OF THE DAY |
|---|---|---|
| **Pies** | **Entender** | **Computar** |
| n. pl. m. Feet. | To Understand /g: Entendiendo / pp: Entendido /Irr. | Verb. From: Compute (E=AR OR IR) |

## INTERESTING THINGS FROM TODAY

### FOUR SENTENCES THAT I READ, HEARD OR CREATED TODAY

**1**

**2**

**3**

**4**

## THINGS I HAVE QUESTIONS ABOUT

## DESCRIBE YOUR ACTIVITIES IN THESE TASKS FOR TODAY

| ACTIVITY | DESCRIPTION | SATISFACTION |
|---|---|---|
| READING | | ☹ ☹ 😐 ☺ 😃 |
| LISTENING | | ☹ ☹ 😐 ☺ 😃 |
| WRITING | | ☹ ☹ 😐 ☺ 😃 |
| SPEAKING | | ☹ ☹ 😐 ☺ 😃 |
| STUDYING | | ☹ ☹ 😐 ☺ 😃 |
| VOCABULARY | | ☹ ☹ 😐 ☺ 😃 |

| LOG YOUR STUDY TIME | | | | | | | | | | | | | TOTAL TIME |
|---|---|---|---|---|---|---|---|---|---|---|---|---|---|
| EACH BOX EQUALS 5 MINS. | | | | | | | | | | | | | : |

| DAY & DATE | | STUDY STREAK # | |
|---|---|---|---|
| LEARNING MOOD | ☹ ☹ 😐 🙂 😀 | # VERBS ACQUIRED | |

## PAST STUDIES IN REVIEW

| VOCABULARY FROM YESTERDAY | GOALS FROM YESTERDAY |
|---|---|
| **1** | ☐ |
| **2** | ☐ |
| **3** | ☐ |

| VOCABULARY FROM 5 DAYS AGO | VOCABULARY FROM 10 DAYS AGO |
|---|---|
| **1** | **1** |
| **2** | **2** |
| **3** | **3** |

## PRIORITIES FOR TODAY

| VOCABULARY FOR TODAY | GOALS FOR TODAY |
|---|---|
| **1** | ☐ |
| **2** | ☐ |
| **3** | ☐ |

## DESCRIBE YOUR LEARNING EXPERIENCE FOR TODAY

## SPECIAL WORDS FOR TODAY

| DAILY WORD BUILDER | VERB OF THE DAY | COGNATE OF THE DAY |
|---|---|---|
| **Pies Descalzos** | **Salir** | **Conceptualizar** |
| n. m. Bare feet. | To Leave, Go Out /g: Saliendo / pp: Salido /Irr. | Verb. From: Conceptualize (E=AR OR IR) |

## INTERESTING THINGS FROM TODAY

### FOUR SENTENCES THAT I READ, HEARD OR CREATED TODAY

**1**

**2**

**3**

**4**

## THINGS I HAVE QUESTIONS ABOUT

## DESCRIBE YOUR ACTIVITIES IN THESE TASKS FOR TODAY

| ACTIVITY | DESCRIPTION | SATISFACTION |
|----------|-------------|--------------|
| READING | | 😡 😞 😐 🙂 😀 |
| LISTENING | | 😡 😞 😐 🙂 😀 |
| WRITING | | 😡 😞 😐 🙂 😀 |
| SPEAKING | | 😡 😞 😐 🙂 😀 |
| STUDYING | | 😡 😞 😐 🙂 😀 |
| VOCABULARY | | 😡 😞 😐 🙂 😀 |

| LOG YOUR STUDY TIME | | | | | | | | | | | | TOTAL TIME |
|---------------------|--|--|--|--|--|--|--|--|--|--|--|------------|
| EACH BOX EQUALS 5 MINS. | | | | | | | | | | | | : |

| DAY & DATE | | | | | | | STUDY STREAK # |
|---|---|---|---|---|---|---|---|
| LEARNING MOOD | ☹ | ☹ | ☺ | ☺ | ☺ | | # VERBS ACQUIRED |

## PAST STUDIES IN REVIEW

| VOCABULARY FROM YESTERDAY | GOALS FROM YESTERDAY |
|---|---|
| 1 | ☐ |
| 2 | ☐ |
| 3 | ☐ |

| VOCABULARY FROM 5 DAYS AGO | VOCABULARY FROM 10 DAYS AGO |
|---|---|
| 1 | 1 |
| 2 | 2 |
| 3 | 3 |

## PRIORITIES FOR TODAY

| VOCABULARY FOR TODAY | GOALS FOR TODAY |
|---|---|
| 1 | ☐ |
| 2 | ☐ |
| 3 | ☐ |

## DESCRIBE YOUR LEARNING EXPERIENCE FOR TODAY

## SPECIAL WORDS FOR TODAY

| DAILY WORD BUILDER | VERB OF THE DAY | COGNATE OF THE DAY |
|---|---|---|
| **Pies Cuadrados** | **Burlarse** | **Elegante** |
| n. m. pl. Square feet. | To Mock, Ridicule, Make Fun Of [Someone/Something] /g: Burlándose / pp: Burlado | Adjective. From: Elegant (NT=NTE) |

## INTERESTING THINGS FROM TODAY

### FOUR SENTENCES THAT I READ, HEARD OR CREATED TODAY

**1**

**2**

**3**

**4**

## THINGS I HAVE QUESTIONS ABOUT

## DESCRIBE YOUR ACTIVITIES IN THESE TASKS FOR TODAY

| ACTIVITY | DESCRIPTION | SATISFACTION |
|----------|-------------|--------------|
| READING | | ☹ ☹ 😐 🙂 😊 |
| LISTENING | | ☹ ☹ 😐 🙂 😊 |
| WRITING | | ☹ ☹ 😐 🙂 😊 |
| SPEAKING | | ☹ ☹ 😐 🙂 😊 |
| STUDYING | | ☹ ☹ 😐 🙂 😊 |
| VOCABULARY | | ☹ ☹ 😐 🙂 😊 |

| LOG YOUR STUDY TIME | | TOTAL TIME |
|---------------------|--|------------|
| EACH BOX EQUALS 5 MINS. | | : |

| DAY & DATE | | STUDY STREAK # |
|---|---|---|
| LEARNING MOOD | ☹ ☹ 😐 🙂 😃 | # VERBS ACQUIRED |

## PAST STUDIES IN REVIEW

| VOCABULARY FROM YESTERDAY | GOALS FROM YESTERDAY |
|---|---|
| 1 | ☐ |
| 2 | ☐ |
| 3 | ☐ |

| VOCABULARY FROM 5 DAYS AGO | VOCABULARY FROM 10 DAYS AGO |
|---|---|
| 1 | 1 |
| 2 | 2 |
| 3 | 3 |

## PRIORITIES FOR TODAY

| VOCABULARY FOR TODAY | GOALS FOR TODAY |
|---|---|
| 1 | ☐ |
| 2 | ☐ |
| 3 | ☐ |

## DESCRIBE YOUR LEARNING EXPERIENCE FOR TODAY

## SPECIAL WORDS FOR TODAY

| DAILY WORD BUILDER | VERB OF THE DAY | COGNATE OF THE DAY |
|---|---|---|
| **Juego de Pies** | **Gustar** | **Democracia** |
| n. m. Footwork. | To Please, Be Pleasing /g: Gustando / pp: Gustado | Noun. From: Democracy (Y=IA OR ÍA) |

## INTERESTING THINGS FROM TODAY

### FOUR SENTENCES THAT I READ, HEARD OR CREATED TODAY

**1**

**2**

**3**

**4**

## THINGS I HAVE QUESTIONS ABOUT

## DESCRIBE YOUR ACTIVITIES IN THESE TASKS FOR TODAY

| ACTIVITY | DESCRIPTION | SATISFACTION |
|---|---|---|
| READING | | 😟 😣 😐 🙂 😊 |
| LISTENING | | 😟 😣 😐 🙂 😊 |
| WRITING | | 😟 😣 😐 🙂 😊 |
| SPEAKING | | 😟 😣 😐 🙂 😊 |
| STUDYING | | 😟 😣 😐 🙂 😊 |
| VOCABULARY | | 😟 😣 😐 🙂 😊 |

| LOG YOUR STUDY TIME | | | | | | | | | | | | TOTAL TIME |
|---|---|---|---|---|---|---|---|---|---|---|---|---|
| EACH BOX EQUALS 5 MINS. | | | | | | | | | | | | : |

| DAY & DATE | | | STUDY STREAK # | |
|---|---|---|---|---|
| LEARNING MOOD | ☹ ☹ 😐 🙂 😃 | | # VERBS ACQUIRED | |

## PAST STUDIES IN REVIEW

| VOCABULARY FROM YESTERDAY | GOALS FROM YESTERDAY |
|---|---|
| 1 | ☐ |
| 2 | ☐ |
| 3 | ☐ |

| VOCABULARY FROM 5 DAYS AGO | VOCABULARY FROM 10 DAYS AGO |
|---|---|
| 1 | 1 |
| 2 | 2 |
| 3 | 3 |

## PRIORITIES FOR TODAY

| VOCABULARY FOR TODAY | GOALS FOR TODAY |
|---|---|
| 1 | ☐ |
| 2 | ☐ |
| 3 | ☐ |

## DESCRIBE YOUR LEARNING EXPERIENCE FOR TODAY

## SPECIAL WORDS FOR TODAY

| DAILY WORD BUILDER | VERB OF THE DAY | COGNATE OF THE DAY |
|---|---|---|
| **Bajo Los Pies** | **Saltar** | **Profesional** |
| adv. Underfoot. adv. Underfoot. | To Jump, Leap; To Jump Over, To Skip; To Omit /g: Saltando / pp: Saltado | Adjective. From: Professional (AL=AL) |

# INTERESTING THINGS FROM TODAY

## FOUR SENTENCES THAT I READ, HEARD OR CREATED TODAY

**1**

**2**

**3**

**4**

# THINGS I HAVE QUESTIONS ABOUT

# DESCRIBE YOUR ACTIVITIES IN THESE TASKS FOR TODAY

| ACTIVITY | DESCRIPTION | SATISFACTION |
|----------|-------------|--------------|
| READING | | ☹️😟😐🙂😃 |
| LISTENING | | ☹️😟😐🙂😃 |
| WRITING | | ☹️😟😐🙂😃 |
| SPEAKING | | ☹️😟😐🙂😃 |
| STUDYING | | ☹️😟😐🙂😃 |
| VOCABULARY | | ☹️😟😐🙂😃 |

| LOG YOUR STUDY TIME | | | | | | | | | | | | TOTAL TIME |
|---------------------|--|--|--|--|--|--|--|--|--|--|--|------------|
| EACH BOX EQUALS 5 MINS. | | | | | | | | | | | | : |

| LEARNING MOOD | ☹ 😟 😐 🙂 😃 | # VERBS ACQUIRED |

## PAST STUDIES IN REVIEW

| VOCABULARY FROM YESTERDAY | GOALS FROM YESTERDAY |
|---|---|
| **1** | ☐ |
| **2** | ☐ |
| **3** | ☐ |

| VOCABULARY FROM 5 DAYS AGO | VOCABULARY FROM 10 DAYS AGO |
|---|---|
| **1** | **1** |
| **2** | **2** |
| **3** | **3** |

## PRIORITIES FOR TODAY

| VOCABULARY FOR TODAY | GOALS FOR TODAY |
|---|---|
| **1** | ☐ |
| **2** | ☐ |
| **3** | ☐ |

## DESCRIBE YOUR LEARNING EXPERIENCE FOR TODAY

## SPECIAL WORDS FOR TODAY

| DAILY WORD BUILDER | VERB OF THE DAY | COGNATE OF THE DAY |
|---|---|---|
| **Arrastrar Los Pies** | **Aplicar** | **Información** |
| v. Shuffle. Dragging the heals. | To Apply /g: Aplicando / pp: Aplicado /Irr. | Noun. From: Information (TION=CIÓN) |

## INTERESTING THINGS FROM TODAY

### FOUR SENTENCES THAT I READ, HEARD OR CREATED TODAY

**1**

**2**

**3**

**4**

## THINGS I HAVE QUESTIONS ABOUT

## DESCRIBE YOUR ACTIVITIES IN THESE TASKS FOR TODAY

| ACTIVITY | DESCRIPTION | SATISFACTION |
|----------|-------------|--------------|
| READING | | ☹ ☹ 😐 ☺ ☺ |
| LISTENING | | ☹ ☹ 😐 ☺ ☺ |
| WRITING | | ☹ ☹ 😐 ☺ ☺ |
| SPEAKING | | ☹ ☹ 😐 ☺ ☺ |
| STUDYING | | ☹ ☹ 😐 ☺ ☺ |
| VOCABULARY | | ☹ ☹ 😐 ☺ ☺ |

| LOG YOUR STUDY TIME | | TOTAL TIME |
|---------------------|--|------------|
| EACH BOX EQUALS 5 MINS. | | : |

| DAY & DATE | | STUDY STREAK # | |
|---|---|---|---|
| LEARNING MOOD | ☹ ☹ 😐 🙂 😃 | # VERBS ACQUIRED | |

## PAST STUDIES IN REVIEW

| VOCABULARY FROM YESTERDAY | GOALS FROM YESTERDAY |
|---|---|
| 1 | ☐ |
| 2 | ☐ |
| 3 | ☐ |

| VOCABULARY FROM 5 DAYS AGO | VOCABULARY FROM 10 DAYS AGO |
|---|---|
| 1 | 1 |
| 2 | 2 |
| 3 | 3 |

## PRIORITIES FOR TODAY

| VOCABULARY FOR TODAY | GOALS FOR TODAY |
|---|---|
| 1 | ☐ |
| 2 | ☐ |
| 3 | ☐ |

## DESCRIBE YOUR LEARNING EXPERIENCE FOR TODAY

## SPECIAL WORDS FOR TODAY

| DAILY WORD BUILDER | VERB OF THE DAY | COGNATE OF THE DAY |
|---|---|---|
| **Pies Planos** | **Comunicar** | **La** |
| n. m. pl. Flat feet. | To Communicate, Transmit, Tell /g: Comunicando / pp: Comunicado /Irr. | Noun. From: Expedition (TION=CIÓN) |

## INTERESTING THINGS FROM TODAY

### FOUR SENTENCES THAT I READ, HEARD OR CREATED TODAY

**1**

**2**

**3**

**4**

## THINGS I HAVE QUESTIONS ABOUT

## DESCRIBE YOUR ACTIVITIES IN THESE TASKS FOR TODAY

| ACTIVITY | DESCRIPTION | SATISFACTION |
|---|---|---|
| READING | | ☹ ☹ 😐 🙂 😊 |
| LISTENING | | ☹ ☹ 😐 🙂 😊 |
| WRITING | | ☹ ☹ 😐 🙂 😊 |
| SPEAKING | | ☹ ☹ 😐 🙂 😊 |
| STUDYING | | ☹ ☹ 😐 🙂 😊 |
| VOCABULARY | | ☹ ☹ 😐 🙂 😊 |

| LOG YOUR STUDY TIME | | | | | | | | | | | | | TOTAL TIME |
|---|---|---|---|---|---|---|---|---|---|---|---|---|---|
| EACH BOX EQUALS 5 MINS. | | | | | | | | | | | | | : |

## THIS WEEK IN REVIEW

## VOCABULARY ACQUIRED

## BIGGEST ACHIEVEMENTS

☐

☐

☐

☐

☐

☐

## AREAS FOR IMPROVEMENT

1

2

3

4

## THINGS THAT I STILL HAVE QUESTIONS ABOUT

| | |
|---|---|
| | |
| | |
| | |

## FINAL MEASUREMENTS OF THIS WEEK

| TOTAL TIME THIS WEEK | TOTAL NEW VERBS | TOTAL NEW WORDS |
|---|---|---|
| | | |

## SELF-ASSESSMENT OF MY ACTIVITIES THIS WEEK

| ACTIVITIES | SPECIFIC ASSESSMENTS | SATISFACTION |
|---|---|---|
| READING | | ☹☹😐☺😄 |
| LISTENING | | ☹☹😐☺😄 |
| WRITING | | ☹☹😐☺😄 |
| SPEAKING | | ☹☹😐☺😄 |
| STUDYING | | ☹☹😐☺😄 |
| MOTIVATION | | ☹☹😐☺😄 |

| LOG YOUR STUDY TIME | | | | | | | | | | | | TOTAL TIME |
|---|---|---|---|---|---|---|---|---|---|---|---|---|
| EACH BOX EQUALS 1 HOUR | | | | | | | | | | | | : |

| DAY & DATE | | STUDY STREAK # |
|---|---|---|
| LEARNING MOOD  ☹ 😦 😐 😊 😃 | | # VERBS ACQUIRED |

## PAST STUDIES IN REVIEW

| VOCABULARY FROM YESTERDAY | GOALS FROM YESTERDAY |
|---|---|
| ❶ | ☐ |
| ❷ | ☐ |
| ❸ | ☐ |

| VOCABULARY FROM 5 DAYS AGO | VOCABULARY FROM 10 DAYS AGO |
|---|---|
| ❶ | ❶ |
| ❷ | ❷ |
| ❸ | ❸ |

## PRIORITIES FOR TODAY

| VOCABULARY FOR TODAY | GOALS FOR TODAY |
|---|---|
| ❶ | ☐ |
| ❷ | ☐ |
| ❸ | ☐ |

## DESCRIBE YOUR LEARNING EXPERIENCE FOR TODAY

## SPECIAL WORDS FOR TODAY

| DAILY WORD BUILDER | VERB OF THE DAY | COGNATE OF THE DAY |
|---|---|---|
| **Completo** | **Enviar** | **Hostil** |
| adj. m/f. Complete | To Send /g: Enviando / pp: Enviado /Irr. | Adjective. From: Hostile (ILE=IL) |

## INTERESTING THINGS FROM TODAY

### FOUR SENTENCES THAT I READ, HEARD OR CREATED TODAY

**1**

**2**

**3**

**4**

## THINGS I HAVE QUESTIONS ABOUT

## DESCRIBE YOUR ACTIVITIES IN THESE TASKS FOR TODAY

| ACTIVITY | DESCRIPTION | SATISFACTION |
|---|---|---|
| READING | | ☹ ☹ 😐 🙂 😃 |
| LISTENING | | ☹ ☹ 😐 🙂 😃 |
| WRITING | | ☹ ☹ 😐 🙂 😃 |
| SPEAKING | | ☹ ☹ 😐 🙂 😃 |
| STUDYING | | ☹ ☹ 😐 🙂 😃 |
| VOCABULARY | | ☹ ☹ 😐 🙂 😃 |

| LOG YOUR STUDY TIME | | | | | | | | | | | | | TOTAL TIME |
|---|---|---|---|---|---|---|---|---|---|---|---|---|---|
| EACH BOX EQUALS 5 MINS. | | | | | | | | | | | | | : |

| DAY & DATE | | STUDY STREAK # |
|---|---|---|
| LEARNING MOOD ☹ ☹ 😐 🙂 😀 | | # VERBS ACQUIRED |

## PAST STUDIES IN REVIEW

| VOCABULARY FROM YESTERDAY | GOALS FROM YESTERDAY |
|---|---|
| 1 | ☐ |
| 2 | ☐ |
| 3 | ☐ |

| VOCABULARY FROM 5 DAYS AGO | VOCABULARY FROM 10 DAYS AGO |
|---|---|
| 1 | 1 |
| 2 | 2 |
| 3 | 3 |

## PRIORITIES FOR TODAY

| VOCABULARY FOR TODAY | GOALS FOR TODAY |
|---|---|
| 1 | ☐ |
| 2 | ☐ |
| 3 | ☐ |

## DESCRIBE YOUR LEARNING EXPERIENCE FOR TODAY

## SPECIAL WORDS FOR TODAY

| DAILY WORD BUILDER | VERB OF THE DAY | COGNATE OF THE DAY |
|---|---|---|
| **Por Completo** | **Seguir** | **Agresión** |
| adv. Entirely. Thoroughly. | To Follow, Continue /g: Siguiendo / pp: Seguido /Irr. | Noun. From: Aggression (SION=SIÓN) |

# INTERESTING THINGS FROM TODAY

## FOUR SENTENCES THAT I READ, HEARD OR CREATED TODAY

**1**

**2**

**3**

**4**

# THINGS I HAVE QUESTIONS ABOUT

# DESCRIBE YOUR ACTIVITIES IN THESE TASKS FOR TODAY

| ACTIVITY | DESCRIPTION | SATISFACTION |
|---|---|---|
| READING | | ☹ ☹ 😐 🙂 😄 |
| LISTENING | | ☹ ☹ 😐 🙂 😄 |
| WRITING | | ☹ ☹ 😐 🙂 😄 |
| SPEAKING | | ☹ ☹ 😐 🙂 😄 |
| STUDYING | | ☹ ☹ 😐 🙂 😄 |
| VOCABULARY | | ☹ ☹ 😐 🙂 😄 |

| LOG YOUR STUDY TIME | | | | | | | | | | | | | TOTAL TIME |
|---|---|---|---|---|---|---|---|---|---|---|---|---|---|
| EACH BOX EQUALS 5 MINS. | | | | | | | | | | | | | : |

| DAY & DATE | | STUDY STREAK # | |
|---|---|---|---|
| LEARNING MOOD | ☹ ☹ 😐 🙂 😃 | # VERBS ACQUIRED | |

## PAST STUDIES IN REVIEW

| VOCABULARY FROM YESTERDAY | GOALS FROM YESTERDAY |
|---|---|
| 1 | ☐ |
| 2 | ☐ |
| 3 | ☐ |

| VOCABULARY FROM 5 DAYS AGO | VOCABULARY FROM 10 DAYS AGO |
|---|---|
| 1 | 1 |
| 2 | 2 |
| 3 | 3 |

## PRIORITIES FOR TODAY

| VOCABULARY FOR TODAY | GOALS FOR TODAY |
|---|---|
| 1 | ☐ |
| 2 | ☐ |
| 3 | ☐ |

## DESCRIBE YOUR LEARNING EXPERIENCE FOR TODAY

## SPECIAL WORDS FOR TODAY

| DAILY WORD BUILDER | VERB OF THE DAY | COGNATE OF THE DAY |
|---|---|---|
| **Tiempo Completo** | **Callarse** | **La** |
| n. m. Entire time. | To Keep Quiet, Be Quiet, Shut Up, Be Silent /g: Callándose / pp: Callado | Noun. From: Simplification (TION=CIÓN) |

## INTERESTING THINGS FROM TODAY

### FOUR SENTENCES THAT I READ, HEARD OR CREATED TODAY

**1**

**2**

**3**

**4**

## THINGS I HAVE QUESTIONS ABOUT

## DESCRIBE YOUR ACTIVITIES IN THESE TASKS FOR TODAY

| ACTIVITY | DESCRIPTION | SATISFACTION |
|---|---|---|
| READING | | 😖 😣 😐 🙂 😊 |
| LISTENING | | 😖 😣 😐 🙂 😊 |
| WRITING | | 😖 😣 😐 🙂 😊 |
| SPEAKING | | 😖 😣 😐 🙂 😊 |
| STUDYING | | 😖 😣 😐 🙂 😊 |
| VOCABULARY | | 😖 😣 😐 🙂 😊 |

| LOG YOUR STUDY TIME | | TOTAL TIME |
|---|---|---|
| EACH BOX EQUALS 5 MINS. | | : |

| DAY & DATE | | STUDY STREAK # | |
|---|---|---|---|
| LEARNING MOOD | ☹ ☹ 😐 🙂 😃 | # VERBS ACQUIRED | |

## PAST STUDIES IN REVIEW

| VOCABULARY FROM YESTERDAY | GOALS FROM YESTERDAY |
|---|---|
| 1 | ☐ |
| 2 | ☐ |
| 3 | ☐ |

| VOCABULARY FROM 5 DAYS AGO | VOCABULARY FROM 10 DAYS AGO |
|---|---|
| 1 | 1 |
| 2 | 2 |
| 3 | 3 |

## PRIORITIES FOR TODAY

| VOCABULARY FOR TODAY | GOALS FOR TODAY |
|---|---|
| 1 | ☐ |
| 2 | ☐ |
| 3 | ☐ |

## DESCRIBE YOUR LEARNING EXPERIENCE FOR TODAY

## SPECIAL WORDS FOR TODAY

| DAILY WORD BUILDER | VERB OF THE DAY | COGNATE OF THE DAY |
|---|---|---|
| **Más Completo** | **Hablar** | **Velocidad** |
| adj. More thorough. | To Speak /g: Hablando / pp: Hablado | Noun. From: Velocity (TY=IDAD) |

## INTERESTING THINGS FROM TODAY

### FOUR SENTENCES THAT I READ, HEARD OR CREATED TODAY

**1**

**2**

**3**

**4**

## THINGS I HAVE QUESTIONS ABOUT

## DESCRIBE YOUR ACTIVITIES IN THESE TASKS FOR TODAY

| ACTIVITY | DESCRIPTION | SATISFACTION |
|----------|-------------|--------------|
| READING | | 😞 😣 😐 🙂 😊 |
| LISTENING | | 😞 😣 😐 🙂 😊 |
| WRITING | | 😞 😣 😐 🙂 😊 |
| SPEAKING | | 😞 😣 😐 🙂 😊 |
| STUDYING | | 😞 😣 😐 🙂 😊 |
| VOCABULARY | | 😞 😣 😐 🙂 😊 |

| LOG YOUR STUDY TIME | | | | | | | | | | | | TOTAL TIME |
|---------------------|--|--|--|--|--|--|--|--|--|--|--|------------|
| EACH BOX EQUALS 5 MINS. | | | | | | | | | | | | : |

| DAY & DATE | | STUDY STREAK # |
|---|---|---|

| LEARNING MOOD |  | # VERBS ACQUIRED |
|---|---|---|

## PAST STUDIES IN REVIEW

| VOCABULARY FROM YESTERDAY | GOALS FROM YESTERDAY |
|---|---|
| 1 | ☐ |
| 2 | ☐ |
| 3 | ☐ |

| VOCABULARY FROM 5 DAYS AGO | VOCABULARY FROM 10 DAYS AGO |
|---|---|
| 1 | 1 |
| 2 | 2 |
| 3 | 3 |

## PRIORITIES FOR TODAY

| VOCABULARY FOR TODAY | GOALS FOR TODAY |
|---|---|
| 1 | ☐ |
| 2 | ☐ |
| 3 | ☐ |

## DESCRIBE YOUR LEARNING EXPERIENCE FOR TODAY

_____

_____

_____

_____

## SPECIAL WORDS FOR TODAY

| DAILY WORD BUILDER | VERB OF THE DAY | COGNATE OF THE DAY |
|---|---|---|
| **Oraciones Completas** | **Saludar** | **Diversión** |
| n. f. pl. Complete Sentences | To Greet, Salute, Hail, Welcome /g: Saludando / pp: Saludado | Noun. From: Diversion (SION=SIÓN) |

## INTERESTING THINGS FROM TODAY

### FOUR SENTENCES THAT I READ, HEARD OR CREATED TODAY

**1**

**2**

**3**

**4**

## THINGS I HAVE QUESTIONS ABOUT

## DESCRIBE YOUR ACTIVITIES IN THESE TASKS FOR TODAY

| ACTIVITY | DESCRIPTION | SATISFACTION |
|---|---|---|
| READING | | 😠 😟 😐 🙂 😀 |
| LISTENING | | 😠 😟 😐 🙂 😀 |
| WRITING | | 😠 😟 😐 🙂 😀 |
| SPEAKING | | 😠 😟 😐 🙂 😀 |
| STUDYING | | 😠 😟 😐 🙂 😀 |
| VOCABULARY | | 😠 😟 😐 🙂 😀 |

| LOG YOUR STUDY TIME | | | | | | | | | | | | TOTAL TIME |
|---|---|---|---|---|---|---|---|---|---|---|---|---|
| EACH BOX EQUALS 5 MINS. | | | | | | | | | | | | : |

| DAY & DATE | | STUDY STREAK # |
|---|---|---|
| LEARNING MOOD ☹ ☹ 😐 🙂 😀 | | # VERBS ACQUIRED |

## PAST STUDIES IN REVIEW

| VOCABULARY FROM YESTERDAY | GOALS FROM YESTERDAY |
|---|---|
| 1 | ☐ |
| 2 | ☐ |
| 3 | ☐ |

| VOCABULARY FROM 5 DAYS AGO | VOCABULARY FROM 10 DAYS AGO |
|---|---|
| 1 | 1 |
| 2 | 2 |
| 3 | 3 |

## PRIORITIES FOR TODAY

| VOCABULARY FOR TODAY | GOALS FOR TODAY |
|---|---|
| 1 | ☐ |
| 2 | ☐ |
| 3 | ☐ |

## DESCRIBE YOUR LEARNING EXPERIENCE FOR TODAY

## SPECIAL WORDS FOR TODAY

| DAILY WORD BUILDER | VERB OF THE DAY | COGNATE OF THE DAY |
|---|---|---|
| **Informe Completo** | **Apostar** | **Fluctuar** |
| n. m. Full report. | To Bet, Wager /g: Apostando / pp: Apostado /Irr. | Verb. From: Fluctuate (ATE=AR) |

## INTERESTING THINGS FROM TODAY

### FOUR SENTENCES THAT I READ, HEARD OR CREATED TODAY

**1**

**2**

**3**

**4**

## THINGS I HAVE QUESTIONS ABOUT

## DESCRIBE YOUR ACTIVITIES IN THESE TASKS FOR TODAY

| ACTIVITY | DESCRIPTION | SATISFACTION |
|---|---|---|
| READING | | 😖 😣 😐 🙂 😄 |
| LISTENING | | 😖 😣 😐 🙂 😄 |
| WRITING | | 😖 😣 😐 🙂 😄 |
| SPEAKING | | 😖 😣 😐 🙂 😄 |
| STUDYING | | 😖 😣 😐 🙂 😄 |
| VOCABULARY | | 😖 😣 😐 🙂 😄 |

| LOG YOUR STUDY TIME | | | | | | | | | | | TOTAL TIME |
|---|---|---|---|---|---|---|---|---|---|---|---|
| EACH BOX EQUALS 5 MINS. | | | | | | | | | | | : |

| DAY & DATE | | STUDY STREAK # |
|---|---|---|
| LEARNING MOOD ☹ ☹ 😐 🙂 😃 | | # VERBS ACQUIRED |

## PAST STUDIES IN REVIEW

| VOCABULARY FROM YESTERDAY | GOALS FROM YESTERDAY |
|---|---|
| 1 | ☐ |
| 2 | ☐ |
| 3 | ☐ |

| VOCABULARY FROM 5 DAYS AGO | VOCABULARY FROM 10 DAYS AGO |
|---|---|
| 1 | 1 |
| 2 | 2 |
| 3 | 3 |

## PRIORITIES FOR TODAY

| VOCABULARY FOR TODAY | GOALS FOR TODAY |
|---|---|
| 1 | ☐ |
| 2 | ☐ |
| 3 | ☐ |

## DESCRIBE YOUR LEARNING EXPERIENCE FOR TODAY

## SPECIAL WORDS FOR TODAY

| DAILY WORD BUILDER | VERB OF THE DAY | COGNATE OF THE DAY |
|---|---|---|
| **Jornada Completa** | **Comunicarse** | **Juvenil** |
| n. f. Full day. Whole day. | To Communicate, Correspond /g: Comunicándose / pp: Comunicado /Irr. | Noun. From: Juvenile (ILE=IL) |

## INTERESTING THINGS FROM TODAY

### FOUR SENTENCES THAT I READ, HEARD OR CREATED TODAY

**1**

**2**

**3**

**4**

## THINGS I HAVE QUESTIONS ABOUT

## DESCRIBE YOUR ACTIVITIES IN THESE TASKS FOR TODAY

| ACTIVITY | DESCRIPTION | SATISFACTION |
|---|---|---|
| READING | | ☹ ☹ 😐 🙂 😊 |
| LISTENING | | ☹ ☹ 😐 🙂 😊 |
| WRITING | | ☹ ☹ 😐 🙂 😊 |
| SPEAKING | | ☹ ☹ 😐 🙂 😊 |
| STUDYING | | ☹ ☹ 😐 🙂 😊 |
| VOCABULARY | | ☹ ☹ 😐 🙂 😊 |

| LOG YOUR STUDY TIME | | | | | | | | | | | | TOTAL TIME |
|---|---|---|---|---|---|---|---|---|---|---|---|---|
| EACH BOX EQUALS 5 MINS. | | | | | | | | | | | | : |

## THIS WEEK IN REVIEW

### VOCABULARY ACQUIRED

### BIGGEST ACHIEVEMENTS

☐         ☐

☐         ☐

☐         ☐

### AREAS FOR IMPROVEMENT

1

2

3

4

## THINGS THAT I STILL HAVE QUESTIONS ABOUT

| | |
|---|---|
| | |
| | |
| | |

## FINAL MEASUREMENTS OF THIS WEEK

| TOTAL TIME THIS WEEK | TOTAL NEW VERBS | TOTAL NEW WORDS |
|---|---|---|
| | | |

## SELF-ASSESSMENT OF MY ACTIVITIES THIS WEEK

| ACTIVITIES | SPECIFIC ASSESSMENTS | SATISFACTION |
|---|---|---|
| READING | | ☹ ☹ 😐 ☺ 😄 |
| LISTENING | | ☹ ☹ 😐 ☺ 😄 |
| WRITING | | ☹ ☹ 😐 ☺ 😄 |
| SPEAKING | | ☹ ☹ 😐 ☺ 😄 |
| STUDYING | | ☹ ☹ 😐 ☺ 😄 |
| MOTIVATION | | ☹ ☹ 😐 ☺ 😄 |

| LOG YOUR STUDY TIME | | | | | | | | | | | | | TOTAL TIME |
|---|---|---|---|---|---|---|---|---|---|---|---|---|---|
| EACH BOX EQUALS 1 HOUR | | | | | | | | | | | | | : |

| DAY & DATE | | STUDY STREAK # |
|---|---|---|
| LEARNING MOOD  ☹ ☹ 😐 🙂 😃 | | # VERBS ACQUIRED |

## PAST STUDIES IN REVIEW

| VOCABULARY FROM YESTERDAY | GOALS FROM YESTERDAY |
|---|---|
| 1 | ☐ |
| 2 | ☐ |
| 3 | ☐ |

| VOCABULARY FROM 5 DAYS AGO | VOCABULARY FROM 10 DAYS AGO |
|---|---|
| 1 | 1 |
| 2 | 2 |
| 3 | 3 |

## PRIORITIES FOR TODAY

| VOCABULARY FOR TODAY | GOALS FOR TODAY |
|---|---|
| 1 | ☐ |
| 2 | ☐ |
| 3 | ☐ |

## DESCRIBE YOUR LEARNING EXPERIENCE FOR TODAY

## SPECIAL WORDS FOR TODAY

| DAILY WORD BUILDER | VERB OF THE DAY | COGNATE OF THE DAY |
|---|---|---|
| **Ambos** | **Estar** | **Aversión** |
| Pron. m. Both. Ambas, f. | To Be /g: Estando / pp: Estado /Irr. | Noun. From: Aversion (SION=SIÓN) |

## INTERESTING THINGS FROM TODAY

### FOUR SENTENCES THAT I READ, HEARD OR CREATED TODAY

**1**

**2**

**3**

**4**

## THINGS I HAVE QUESTIONS ABOUT

## DESCRIBE YOUR ACTIVITIES IN THESE TASKS FOR TODAY

| ACTIVITY | DESCRIPTION | SATISFACTION |
|----------|-------------|--------------|
| READING | | 😞😟😐😊😄 |
| LISTENING | | 😞😟😐😊😄 |
| WRITING | | 😞😟😐😊😄 |
| SPEAKING | | 😞😟😐😊😄 |
| STUDYING | | 😞😟😐😊😄 |
| VOCABULARY | | 😞😟😐😊😄 |

| LOG YOUR STUDY TIME | | | | | | | | | | | | TOTAL TIME |
|---------------------|--|--|--|--|--|--|--|--|--|--|--|------------|
| EACH BOX EQUALS 5 MINS. | | | | | | | | | | | | : |

| DAY & DATE | | STUDY STREAK # |
|---|---|---|
| LEARNING MOOD | ☹ ☹ 😐 🙂 😀 | # VERBS ACQUIRED |

## PAST STUDIES IN REVIEW

| VOCABULARY FROM YESTERDAY | GOALS FROM YESTERDAY |
|---|---|
| 1 | ☐ |
| 2 | ☐ |
| 3 | ☐ |

| VOCABULARY FROM 5 DAYS AGO | VOCABULARY FROM 10 DAYS AGO |
|---|---|
| 1 | 1 |
| 2 | 2 |
| 3 | 3 |

## PRIORITIES FOR TODAY

| VOCABULARY FOR TODAY | GOALS FOR TODAY |
|---|---|
| 1 | ☐ |
| 2 | ☐ |
| 3 | ☐ |

## DESCRIBE YOUR LEARNING EXPERIENCE FOR TODAY

## SPECIAL WORDS FOR TODAY

| DAILY WORD BUILDER | VERB OF THE DAY | COGNATE OF THE DAY |
|---|---|---|
| **A Ambos Lados** | **Sentarse** | **Cónico** |
| adv. On Both Sides | To Sit Down, Seat Oneself /g: Sentándose / pp: Sentado /Irr. | Adjective. From: Conic (IC=ICO) |

## INTERESTING THINGS FROM TODAY

### FOUR SENTENCES THAT I READ, HEARD OR CREATED TODAY

**1**

**2**

**3**

**4**

## THINGS I HAVE QUESTIONS ABOUT

## DESCRIBE YOUR ACTIVITIES IN THESE TASKS FOR TODAY

| ACTIVITY | DESCRIPTION | SATISFACTION |
|---|---|---|
| READING | | ☹ 😣 😐 🙂 😃 |
| LISTENING | | ☹ 😣 😐 🙂 😃 |
| WRITING | | ☹ 😣 😐 🙂 😃 |
| SPEAKING | | ☹ 😣 😐 🙂 😃 |
| STUDYING | | ☹ 😣 😐 🙂 😃 |
| VOCABULARY | | ☹ 😣 😐 🙂 😃 |
| LOG YOUR STUDY TIME | | TOTAL TIME |
| EACH BOX EQUALS 5 MINS. | | : |

## PAST STUDIES IN REVIEW

| VOCABULARY FROM YESTERDAY | GOALS FROM YESTERDAY |
|---|---|
| 1 | ☐ |
| 2 | ☐ |
| 3 | ☐ |

| VOCABULARY FROM 5 DAYS AGO | VOCABULARY FROM 10 DAYS AGO |
|---|---|
| 1 | 1 |
| 2 | 2 |
| 3 | 3 |

## PRIORITIES FOR TODAY

| VOCABULARY FOR TODAY | GOALS FOR TODAY |
|---|---|
| 1 | ☐ |
| 2 | ☐ |
| 3 | ☐ |

## DESCRIBE YOUR LEARNING EXPERIENCE FOR TODAY

## SPECIAL WORDS FOR TODAY

| DAILY WORD BUILDER | VERB OF THE DAY | COGNATE OF THE DAY |
|---|---|---|
| **Ambos Sexos** | **Caminar** | **Confirmar** |
| n. m. pl. Both sexes | To Walk, Go /g: Caminando / pp: Caminado | Verb. From: Confirm (ADDING AR OR IR) |

## INTERESTING THINGS FROM TODAY

### FOUR SENTENCES THAT I READ, HEARD OR CREATED TODAY

**1**

**2**

**3**

**4**

## THINGS I HAVE QUESTIONS ABOUT

## DESCRIBE YOUR ACTIVITIES IN THESE TASKS FOR TODAY

| ACTIVITY | DESCRIPTION | SATISFACTION |
|---|---|---|
| READING | | ☹ ☹ 😐 ☺ 😄 |
| LISTENING | | ☹ ☹ 😐 ☺ 😄 |
| WRITING | | ☹ ☹ 😐 ☺ 😄 |
| SPEAKING | | ☹ ☹ 😐 ☺ 😄 |
| STUDYING | | ☹ ☹ 😐 ☺ 😄 |
| VOCABULARY | | ☹ ☹ 😐 ☺ 😄 |
| LOG YOUR STUDY TIME | | TOTAL TIME |
| EACH BOX EQUALS 5 MINS. | | : |

## PAST STUDIES IN REVIEW

| VOCABULARY FROM YESTERDAY | GOALS FROM YESTERDAY |
|---|---|
| **1** | ☐ |
| **2** | ☐ |
| **3** | ☐ |

| VOCABULARY FROM 5 DAYS AGO | VOCABULARY FROM 10 DAYS AGO |
|---|---|
| **1** | **1** |
| **2** | **2** |
| **3** | **3** |

## PRIORITIES FOR TODAY

| VOCABULARY FOR TODAY | GOALS FOR TODAY |
|---|---|
| **1** | ☐ |
| **2** | ☐ |
| **3** | ☐ |

## DESCRIBE YOUR LEARNING EXPERIENCE FOR TODAY

## SPECIAL WORDS FOR TODAY

| DAILY WORD BUILDER | VERB OF THE DAY | COGNATE OF THE DAY |
|---|---|---|
| **Ambos Casos** | **Incluir** | **Deformar** |
| n. m. Both Cases | To Include /g: Incluyendo / pp: Incluido | Verb. From: Deform (ADDING AR OR IR) |

## INTERESTING THINGS FROM TODAY
### FOUR SENTENCES THAT I READ, HEARD OR CREATED TODAY

**1**

**2**

**3**

**4**

## THINGS I HAVE QUESTIONS ABOUT

## DESCRIBE YOUR ACTIVITIES IN THESE TASKS FOR TODAY

| ACTIVITY | DESCRIPTION | SATISFACTION |
|----------|-------------|--------------|
| READING | | 😣😞😐🙂😄 |
| LISTENING | | 😣😞😐🙂😄 |
| WRITING | | 😣😞😐🙂😄 |
| SPEAKING | | 😣😞😐🙂😄 |
| STUDYING | | 😣😞😐🙂😄 |
| VOCABULARY | | 😣😞😐🙂😄 |
| LOG YOUR STUDY TIME | | TOTAL TIME |
| EACH BOX EQUALS 5 MINS. | | : |

| DAY & DATE | | STUDY STREAK # |
|---|---|---|
| LEARNING MOOD  ☹ ☹ 😐 🙂 😄 | | # VERBS ACQUIRED |

## PAST STUDIES IN REVIEW

| VOCABULARY FROM YESTERDAY | GOALS FROM YESTERDAY |
|---|---|
| 1 | ☐ |
| 2 | ☐ |
| 3 | ☐ |

| VOCABULARY FROM 5 DAYS AGO | VOCABULARY FROM 10 DAYS AGO |
|---|---|
| 1 | 1 |
| 2 | 2 |
| 3 | 3 |

## PRIORITIES FOR TODAY

| VOCABULARY FOR TODAY | GOALS FOR TODAY |
|---|---|
| 1 | ☐ |
| 2 | ☐ |
| 3 | ☐ |

## DESCRIBE YOUR LEARNING EXPERIENCE FOR TODAY

## SPECIAL WORDS FOR TODAY

| DAILY WORD BUILDER | VERB OF THE DAY | COGNATE OF THE DAY |
|---|---|---|
| **Ambos Sentidos** | **Subir** | **Admirar** |
| n. m. Both ways. | To Go Up, Rise, Move Up, Climb; To Lift Up, Raise Up /g: Subiendo / pp: Subido | Verb. From: Admire (E=AR OR IR) |

### FOUR SENTENCES THAT I READ, HEARD OR CREATED TODAY

**1**

**2**

**3**

**4**

## THINGS I HAVE QUESTIONS ABOUT

## DESCRIBE YOUR ACTIVITIES IN THESE TASKS FOR TODAY

| ACTIVITY | DESCRIPTION | SATISFACTION |
|---|---|---|
| READING | | ☹ ☹ 😐 🙂 😀 |
| LISTENING | | ☹ ☹ 😐 🙂 😀 |
| WRITING | | ☹ ☹ 😐 🙂 😀 |
| SPEAKING | | ☹ ☹ 😐 🙂 😀 |
| STUDYING | | ☹ ☹ 😐 🙂 😀 |
| VOCABULARY | | ☹ ☹ 😐 🙂 😀 |

| LOG YOUR STUDY TIME | | | | | | | | | | | | | TOTAL TIME |
|---|---|---|---|---|---|---|---|---|---|---|---|---|---|
| EACH BOX EQUALS 5 MINS. | | | | | | | | | | | | | : |

| DAY & DATE | | STUDY STREAK # |
|---|---|---|
| LEARNING MOOD ☹ 😠 😐 🙂 😀 | | # VERBS ACQUIRED |

## PAST STUDIES IN REVIEW

| VOCABULARY FROM YESTERDAY | GOALS FROM YESTERDAY |
|---|---|
| 1 | ☐ |
| 2 | ☐ |
| 3 | ☐ |

| VOCABULARY FROM 5 DAYS AGO | VOCABULARY FROM 10 DAYS AGO |
|---|---|
| 1 | 1 |
| 2 | 2 |
| 3 | 3 |

## PRIORITIES FOR TODAY

| VOCABULARY FOR TODAY | GOALS FOR TODAY |
|---|---|
| 1 | ☐ |
| 2 | ☐ |
| 3 | ☐ |

## DESCRIBE YOUR LEARNING EXPERIENCE FOR TODAY

## SPECIAL WORDS FOR TODAY

| DAILY WORD BUILDER | VERB OF THE DAY | COGNATE OF THE DAY |
|---|---|---|
| **Ambos Extremos** | **Apretar** | **Curioso** |
| n. m. Both ends. | To Be Too Tight; To Squeeze; To Tighten [Up]; /g: Apretando / pp: Apretado /Irr. | Adjective. From: Curious (OUS=OSO) |

## INTERESTING THINGS FROM TODAY

### FOUR SENTENCES THAT I READ, HEARD OR CREATED TODAY

**1**

**2**

**3**

**4**

## THINGS I HAVE QUESTIONS ABOUT

## DESCRIBE YOUR ACTIVITIES IN THESE TASKS FOR TODAY

| ACTIVITY | DESCRIPTION | SATISFACTION |
|---|---|---|
| READING | | ☹ ☹ 😐 🙂 😀 |
| LISTENING | | ☹ ☹ 😐 🙂 😀 |
| WRITING | | ☹ ☹ 😐 🙂 😀 |
| SPEAKING | | ☹ ☹ 😐 🙂 😀 |
| STUDYING | | ☹ ☹ 😐 🙂 😀 |
| VOCABULARY | | ☹ ☹ 😐 🙂 😀 |

| LOG YOUR STUDY TIME | | TOTAL TIME |
|---|---|---|
| EACH BOX EQUALS 5 MINS. | | : |

| DAY & DATE | | STUDY STREAK # |
|---|---|---|
| LEARNING MOOD | ☹ ☹ 😐 🙂 😃 | # VERBS ACQUIRED |

## PAST STUDIES IN REVIEW

| VOCABULARY FROM YESTERDAY | GOALS FROM YESTERDAY |
|---|---|
| 1 | ☐ |
| 2 | ☐ |
| 3 | ☐ |

| VOCABULARY FROM 5 DAYS AGO | VOCABULARY FROM 10 DAYS AGO |
|---|---|
| 1 | 1 |
| 2 | 2 |
| 3 | 3 |

## PRIORITIES FOR TODAY

| VOCABULARY FOR TODAY | GOALS FOR TODAY |
|---|---|
| 1 | ☐ |
| 2 | ☐ |
| 3 | ☐ |

## DESCRIBE YOUR LEARNING EXPERIENCE FOR TODAY

## SPECIAL WORDS FOR TODAY

| DAILY WORD BUILDER | VERB OF THE DAY | COGNATE OF THE DAY |
|---|---|---|
| **Ambas Opciones** | **Conducir** | **Cuestionable** |
| n. f. pl. Both options. | To Drive, Conduct /g: Conduciendo / pp: Conducido /Irr. | Adjective. From: Questionable (BLE=BLE) |

## INTERESTING THINGS FROM TODAY

### FOUR SENTENCES THAT I READ, HEARD OR CREATED TODAY

**1**

**2**

**3**

**4**

## THINGS I HAVE QUESTIONS ABOUT

## DESCRIBE YOUR ACTIVITIES IN THESE TASKS FOR TODAY

| ACTIVITY | DESCRIPTION | SATISFACTION |
|----------|-------------|--------------|
| READING | | ☹ ☹ ☹ ☺ ☺ |
| LISTENING | | ☹ ☹ ☹ ☺ ☺ |
| WRITING | | ☹ ☹ ☹ ☺ ☺ |
| SPEAKING | | ☹ ☹ ☹ ☺ ☺ |
| STUDYING | | ☹ ☹ ☹ ☺ ☺ |
| VOCABULARY | | ☹ ☹ ☹ ☺ ☺ |

| LOG YOUR STUDY TIME | | | | | | | | | | | | TOTAL TIME |
|---------------------|--|--|--|--|--|--|--|--|--|--|--|------------|
| EACH BOX EQUALS 5 MINS. | | | | | | | | | | | | : |

**WEEK NUMBER:**

## THIS WEEK IN REVIEW

### VOCABULARY ACQUIRED

### BIGGEST ACHIEVEMENTS

☐     ☐

☐     ☐

☐     ☐

### AREAS FOR IMPROVEMENT

1.
2.
3.
4.

## THINGS THAT I STILL HAVE QUESTIONS ABOUT

|  |  |
|---|---|
|  |  |
|  |  |
|  |  |

## FINAL MEASUREMENTS OF THIS WEEK

| TOTAL TIME THIS WEEK | TOTAL NEW VERBS | TOTAL NEW WORDS |
|---|---|---|
|  |  |  |

## SELF-ASSESSMENT OF MY ACTIVITIES THIS WEEK

| ACTIVITIES | SPECIFIC ASSESSMENTS | SATISFACTION |
|---|---|---|
| READING |  | ☹ ☹ 😐 🙂 😄 |
| LISTENING |  | ☹ ☹ 😐 🙂 😄 |
| WRITING |  | ☹ ☹ 😐 🙂 😄 |
| SPEAKING |  | ☹ ☹ 😐 🙂 😄 |
| STUDYING |  | ☹ ☹ 😐 🙂 😄 |
| MOTIVATION |  | ☹ ☹ 😐 🙂 😄 |

| LOG YOUR STUDY TIME |  | TOTAL TIME |
|---|---|---|
| EACH BOX EQUALS 1 HOUR |  | : |

| DAY & DATE | | STUDY STREAK # | |
|---|---|---|---|
| LEARNING MOOD | ☹ ☹ 😐 🙂 😀 | # VERBS ACQUIRED | |

## PAST STUDIES IN REVIEW

| VOCABULARY FROM YESTERDAY | GOALS FROM YESTERDAY |
|---|---|
| 1 | ☐ |
| 2 | ☐ |
| 3 | ☐ |

| VOCABULARY FROM 5 DAYS AGO | VOCABULARY FROM 10 DAYS AGO |
|---|---|
| 1 | 1 |
| 2 | 2 |
| 3 | 3 |

## PRIORITIES FOR TODAY

| VOCABULARY FOR TODAY | GOALS FOR TODAY |
|---|---|
| 1 | ☐ |
| 2 | ☐ |
| 3 | ☐ |

## DESCRIBE YOUR LEARNING EXPERIENCE FOR TODAY

## SPECIAL WORDS FOR TODAY

| DAILY WORD BUILDER | VERB OF THE DAY | COGNATE OF THE DAY |
|---|---|---|
| **Pieza** | **Hacer** | **Decorar** |
| n. f. Piece. Part. Item. | To Do, Make /g: Haciendo / pp: Hecho /Irr. | Verb. From: Decorate (ATE=AR) |

## INTERESTING THINGS FROM TODAY

### FOUR SENTENCES THAT I READ, HEARD OR CREATED TODAY

**1**

**2**

**3**

**4**

## THINGS I HAVE QUESTIONS ABOUT

## DESCRIBE YOUR ACTIVITIES IN THESE TASKS FOR TODAY

| ACTIVITY | DESCRIPTION | SATISFACTION |
|---|---|---|
| READING | | ☹ ☹ 😐 ☺ ☺ |
| LISTENING | | ☹ ☹ 😐 ☺ ☺ |
| WRITING | | ☹ ☹ 😐 ☺ ☺ |
| SPEAKING | | ☹ ☹ 😐 ☺ ☺ |
| STUDYING | | ☹ ☹ 😐 ☺ ☺ |
| VOCABULARY | | ☹ ☹ 😐 ☺ ☺ |

| LOG YOUR STUDY TIME | | | | | | | | | | | | | TOTAL TIME |
|---|---|---|---|---|---|---|---|---|---|---|---|---|---|
| EACH BOX EQUALS 5 MINS. | | | | | | | | | | | | | : |

| DAY & DATE | | | STUDY STREAK # | |
|---|---|---|---|---|
| LEARNING MOOD | ☹ ☹ 😐 🙂 😀 | | # VERBS ACQUIRED | |

## PAST STUDIES IN REVIEW

| VOCABULARY FROM YESTERDAY | GOALS FROM YESTERDAY |
|---|---|
| 1 | ☐ |
| 2 | ☐ |
| 3 | ☐ |

| VOCABULARY FROM 5 DAYS AGO | VOCABULARY FROM 10 DAYS AGO |
|---|---|
| 1 | 1 |
| 2 | 2 |
| 3 | 3 |

## PRIORITIES FOR TODAY

| VOCABULARY FOR TODAY | GOALS FOR TODAY |
|---|---|
| 1 | ☐ |
| 2 | ☐ |
| 3 | ☐ |

## DESCRIBE YOUR LEARNING EXPERIENCE FOR TODAY

## SPECIAL WORDS FOR TODAY

| DAILY WORD BUILDER | VERB OF THE DAY | COGNATE OF THE DAY |
|---|---|---|
| **Pieza Clave** | **Sentir** | **La** |
| n. f. Key element. Key piece. | To Feel, Regret /g: Sintiendo / pp: Sentido /Irr. | Verb. From: Cooperate (ATE=AR) |

## INTERESTING THINGS FROM TODAY

### FOUR SENTENCES THAT I READ, HEARD OR CREATED TODAY

**1**

**2**

**3**

**4**

## THINGS I HAVE QUESTIONS ABOUT

## DESCRIBE YOUR ACTIVITIES IN THESE TASKS FOR TODAY

| ACTIVITY | DESCRIPTION | SATISFACTION |
|---|---|---|
| READING | | 😣😦😐😊😃 |
| LISTENING | | 😣😦😐😊😃 |
| WRITING | | 😣😦😐😊😃 |
| SPEAKING | | 😣😦😐😊😃 |
| STUDYING | | 😣😦😐😊😃 |
| VOCABULARY | | 😣😦😐😊😃 |

| LOG YOUR STUDY TIME | | | | | | | | | | | | | TOTAL TIME |
|---|---|---|---|---|---|---|---|---|---|---|---|---|---|
| EACH BOX EQUALS 5 MINS. | | | | | | | | | | | | | : |

| DAY & DATE | | STUDY STREAK # |
|---|---|---|
| LEARNING MOOD  ☹ ☹ 😐 🙂 😃 | | # VERBS ACQUIRED |

## PAST STUDIES IN REVIEW

| VOCABULARY FROM YESTERDAY | GOALS FROM YESTERDAY |
|---|---|
| 1 | ☐ |
| 2 | ☐ |
| 3 | ☐ |

| VOCABULARY FROM 5 DAYS AGO | VOCABULARY FROM 10 DAYS AGO |
|---|---|
| 1 | 1 |
| 2 | 2 |
| 3 | 3 |

## PRIORITIES FOR TODAY

| VOCABULARY FOR TODAY | GOALS FOR TODAY |
|---|---|
| 1 | ☐ |
| 2 | ☐ |
| 3 | ☐ |

## DESCRIBE YOUR LEARNING EXPERIENCE FOR TODAY

## SPECIAL WORDS FOR TODAY

| DAILY WORD BUILDER | VERB OF THE DAY | COGNATE OF THE DAY |
|---|---|---|
| **Pieza Suelta** | **Cenar** | **Observar** |
| n. f. Single part. Spare part. Loose piece. | To Eat Dinner, Have Dinner; To Dine; To Have for Dinner /g: Cenando / pp: Cenado | Verb. From: Observe (E=AR OR IR) |

## INTERESTING THINGS FROM TODAY

### FOUR SENTENCES THAT I READ, HEARD OR CREATED TODAY

**1**

**2**

**3**

**4**

## THINGS I HAVE QUESTIONS ABOUT

## DESCRIBE YOUR ACTIVITIES IN THESE TASKS FOR TODAY

| ACTIVITY | DESCRIPTION | SATISFACTION |
|----------|-------------|--------------|
| READING | | ☹ ☹ 😐 🙂 😄 |
| LISTENING | | ☹ ☹ 😐 🙂 😄 |
| WRITING | | ☹ ☹ 😐 🙂 😄 |
| SPEAKING | | ☹ ☹ 😐 🙂 😄 |
| STUDYING | | ☹ ☹ 😐 🙂 😄 |
| VOCABULARY | | ☹ ☹ 😐 🙂 😄 |

| LOG YOUR STUDY TIME | | | | | | | | | | | | | TOTAL TIME |
|---------------------|--|--|--|--|--|--|--|--|--|--|--|--|------------|
| EACH BOX EQUALS 5 MINS. | | | | | | | | | | | | | : |

| DAY & DATE | | STUDY STREAK # |
|---|---|---|
| LEARNING MOOD  ☹ ☹ 😐 🙂 😀 | | # VERBS ACQUIRED |

## PAST STUDIES IN REVIEW

| VOCABULARY FROM YESTERDAY | GOALS FROM YESTERDAY |
|---|---|
| 1 | ☐ |
| 2 | ☐ |
| 3 | ☐ |

| VOCABULARY FROM 5 DAYS AGO | VOCABULARY FROM 10 DAYS AGO |
|---|---|
| 1 | 1 |
| 2 | 2 |
| 3 | 3 |

## PRIORITIES FOR TODAY

| VOCABULARY FOR TODAY | GOALS FOR TODAY |
|---|---|
| 1 | ☐ |
| 2 | ☐ |
| 3 | ☐ |

## DESCRIBE YOUR LEARNING EXPERIENCE FOR TODAY

## SPECIAL WORDS FOR TODAY

| DAILY WORD BUILDER | VERB OF THE DAY | COGNATE OF THE DAY |
|---|---|---|
| **Pieza de Arte** | **Intentar** | **Excepción** |
| n. f. Art piece | To Try, Attempt /g: Intentando / pp: Intentado | Noun. From: Exception (TION=CIÓN) |

## INTERESTING THINGS FROM TODAY

### FOUR SENTENCES THAT I READ, HEARD OR CREATED TODAY

**1**

**2**

**3**

**4**

## THINGS I HAVE QUESTIONS ABOUT

## DESCRIBE YOUR ACTIVITIES IN THESE TASKS FOR TODAY

| ACTIVITY | DESCRIPTION | SATISFACTION |
|---|---|---|
| READING | | ☹ ☹ ☺ ☺ ☺ |
| LISTENING | | ☹ ☹ ☺ ☺ ☺ |
| WRITING | | ☹ ☹ ☺ ☺ ☺ |
| SPEAKING | | ☹ ☹ ☺ ☺ ☺ |
| STUDYING | | ☹ ☹ ☺ ☺ ☺ |
| VOCABULARY | | ☹ ☹ ☺ ☺ ☺ |
| LOG YOUR STUDY TIME | | TOTAL TIME |
| EACH BOX EQUALS 5 MINS. | | : |

## PAST STUDIES IN REVIEW

| VOCABULARY FROM YESTERDAY | GOALS FROM YESTERDAY |
|---|---|
| 1 | ☐ |
| 2 | ☐ |
| 3 | ☐ |

| VOCABULARY FROM 5 DAYS AGO | VOCABULARY FROM 10 DAYS AGO |
|---|---|
| 1 | 1 |
| 2 | 2 |
| 3 | 3 |

## PRIORITIES FOR TODAY

| VOCABULARY FOR TODAY | GOALS FOR TODAY |
|---|---|
| 1 | ☐ |
| 2 | ☐ |
| 3 | ☐ |

## DESCRIBE YOUR LEARNING EXPERIENCE FOR TODAY

## SPECIAL WORDS FOR TODAY

| DAILY WORD BUILDER | VERB OF THE DAY | COGNATE OF THE DAY |
|---|---|---|
| **Pieza Fundamental** | **Tirar** | **Rectificar** |
| n. Fundamental. Fundamental part. Cruicial piece. | To Throw, Hurl; To Shoot, Fire; To Throw Away; To Pull [Out] /g: Tirando / pp: Tirado | Noun. From: Rectify (IFY=IFICAR) |

## INTERESTING THINGS FROM TODAY

### FOUR SENTENCES THAT I READ, HEARD OR CREATED TODAY

**1**

**2**

**3**

**4**

## THINGS I HAVE QUESTIONS ABOUT

## DESCRIBE YOUR ACTIVITIES IN THESE TASKS FOR TODAY

| ACTIVITY | DESCRIPTION | SATISFACTION |
|---|---|---|
| READING | | ☹ ☹ 😐 🙂 😃 |
| LISTENING | | ☹ ☹ 😐 🙂 😃 |
| WRITING | | ☹ ☹ 😐 🙂 😃 |
| SPEAKING | | ☹ ☹ 😐 🙂 😃 |
| STUDYING | | ☹ ☹ 😐 🙂 😃 |
| VOCABULARY | | ☹ ☹ 😐 🙂 😃 |

| LOG YOUR STUDY TIME | | | | | | | | | | | | | TOTAL TIME |
|---|---|---|---|---|---|---|---|---|---|---|---|---|---|
| EACH BOX EQUALS 5 MINS. | | | | | | | | | | | | | : |

| DAY & DATE | | | STUDY STREAK # |
|---|---|---|---|
| LEARNING MOOD | ☹ ☹ 😐 🙂 😀 | | # VERBS ACQUIRED |

## PAST STUDIES IN REVIEW

| VOCABULARY FROM YESTERDAY | GOALS FROM YESTERDAY |
|---|---|
| 1 | ☐ |
| 2 | ☐ |
| 3 | ☐ |

| VOCABULARY FROM 5 DAYS AGO | VOCABULARY FROM 10 DAYS AGO |
|---|---|
| 1 | 1 |
| 2 | 2 |
| 3 | 3 |

## PRIORITIES FOR TODAY

| VOCABULARY FOR TODAY | GOALS FOR TODAY |
|---|---|
| 1 | ☐ |
| 2 | ☐ |
| 3 | ☐ |

## DESCRIBE YOUR LEARNING EXPERIENCE FOR TODAY

## SPECIAL WORDS FOR TODAY

| DAILY WORD BUILDER | VERB OF THE DAY | COGNATE OF THE DAY |
|---|---|---|
| **Pieza Musical** | **Aprobar** | **Exclusión** |
| n. f. Piece of Music | To Pass /g: Aprobando / pp: Aprobado /Irr. | Noun. From: Exclusion (SION=SIÓN) |

## INTERESTING THINGS FROM TODAY

### FOUR SENTENCES THAT I READ, HEARD OR CREATED TODAY

**1**

**2**

**3**

**4**

## THINGS I HAVE QUESTIONS ABOUT

## DESCRIBE YOUR ACTIVITIES IN THESE TASKS FOR TODAY

| ACTIVITY | DESCRIPTION | SATISFACTION |
|----------|-------------|--------------|
| READING | | ☹ ☹ 😐 ☺ 😄 |
| LISTENING | | ☹ ☹ 😐 ☺ 😄 |
| WRITING | | ☹ ☹ 😐 ☺ 😄 |
| SPEAKING | | ☹ ☹ 😐 ☺ 😄 |
| STUDYING | | ☹ ☹ 😐 ☺ 😄 |
| VOCABULARY | | ☹ ☹ 😐 ☺ 😄 |

| LOG YOUR STUDY TIME | | | | | | | | | | | | | TOTAL TIME |
|---------------------|--|--|--|--|--|--|--|--|--|--|--|--|------------|
| EACH BOX EQUALS 5 MINS. | | | | | | | | | | | | | : |

| DAY & DATE | | STUDY STREAK # |
|---|---|---|
| LEARNING MOOD | ☹ ☹ 😐 🙂 😀 | # VERBS ACQUIRED |

## PAST STUDIES IN REVIEW

| VOCABULARY FROM YESTERDAY | GOALS FROM YESTERDAY |
|---|---|
| 1 | ☐ |
| 2 | ☐ |
| 3 | ☐ |

| VOCABULARY FROM 5 DAYS AGO | VOCABULARY FROM 10 DAYS AGO |
|---|---|
| 1 | 1 |
| 2 | 2 |
| 3 | 3 |

## PRIORITIES FOR TODAY

| VOCABULARY FOR TODAY | GOALS FOR TODAY |
|---|---|
| 1 | ☐ |
| 2 | ☐ |
| 3 | ☐ |

## DESCRIBE YOUR LEARNING EXPERIENCE FOR TODAY

_____

_____

_____

_____

## SPECIAL WORDS FOR TODAY

| DAILY WORD BUILDER | VERB OF THE DAY | COGNATE OF THE DAY |
|---|---|---|
| **Pieza de Recambio** | **Confesar** | **Abrasión** |
| n. f. Spart part. Replacement part. | To Confess /g: Confesando / pp: Confesado /Irr. | Noun. From: Abrasion (SION=SIÓN) |

## INTERESTING THINGS FROM TODAY

### FOUR SENTENCES THAT I READ, HEARD OR CREATED TODAY

**1**

**2**

**3**

**4**

## THINGS I HAVE QUESTIONS ABOUT

## DESCRIBE YOUR ACTIVITIES IN THESE TASKS FOR TODAY

| ACTIVITY | DESCRIPTION | SATISFACTION |
|---|---|---|
| READING | | ☹ ☹ 😐 🙂 😊 |
| LISTENING | | ☹ ☹ 😐 🙂 😊 |
| WRITING | | ☹ ☹ 😐 🙂 😊 |
| SPEAKING | | ☹ ☹ 😐 🙂 😊 |
| STUDYING | | ☹ ☹ 😐 🙂 😊 |
| VOCABULARY | | ☹ ☹ 😐 🙂 😊 |

| LOG YOUR STUDY TIME | | | | | | | | | | | | TOTAL TIME |
|---|---|---|---|---|---|---|---|---|---|---|---|---|
| EACH BOX EQUALS 5 MINS. | | | | | | | | | | | | : |

**WEEK NUMBER:**

## THIS WEEK IN REVIEW

### VOCABULARY ACQUIRED

### BIGGEST ACHIEVEMENTS

☐     ☐

☐     ☐

☐     ☐

### AREAS FOR IMPROVEMENT

1

2

3

4

## THINGS THAT I STILL HAVE QUESTIONS ABOUT

|  |  |
|--|--|
|  |  |
|  |  |
|  |  |

## FINAL MEASUREMENTS OF THIS WEEK

| TOTAL TIME THIS WEEK | TOTAL NEW VERBS | TOTAL NEW WORDS |
|---|---|---|
|  |  |  |

## SELF-ASSESSMENT OF MY ACTIVITIES THIS WEEK

| ACTIVITIES | SPECIFIC ASSESSMENTS | SATISFACTION |
|---|---|---|
| READING |  | ☹ ☹ 😐 🙂 😀 |
| LISTENING |  | ☹ ☹ 😐 🙂 😀 |
| WRITING |  | ☹ ☹ 😐 🙂 😀 |
| SPEAKING |  | ☹ ☹ 😐 🙂 😀 |
| STUDYING |  | ☹ ☹ 😐 🙂 😀 |
| MOTIVATION |  | ☹ ☹ 😐 🙂 😀 |

| LOG YOUR STUDY TIME | | | | | | | | | | | | TOTAL TIME |
|---|---|---|---|---|---|---|---|---|---|---|---|---|
| EACH BOX EQUALS 1 HOUR | | | | | | | | | | | | : |

# OUR RECOMMENDED ONLINE RESOURCES

**The Award for The Best Online Spanish Course**

Spanish With Paul (www.spanishwithpaul.com/join)

*Paul is the very best Spanish teacher on the internet. His course is clearly designed to take you to conversational fluency. With nine levels and hundreds of hours of videos, his coverage of Spanish is extremely thorough. His teaching style is unquestionably genius. In addtion to his language course, he has a 5,000 word vocabulary course that is the "must-have" vocabulary course for the serious student.*

**The Award for The Best Online Spanish Tutor**

Jude Vivas (www.holajude.com)

*Jude and her husband Luis offer rich, in-person tutoring via the internet. With hourly fees that are extremely affordable, they also offer group and Spanish-only courses. Jude is the only tutor that specializes in reinforcing lessons taught by Paul and can also create lessons based on your own goals.*

**The Award for The Best Online Spanish Translator**

DeepL (www.deepl.com/translator)

*Forget Google translate, DeepL is by far the most capable translator online.*

**The Award for the Best Facebook Spanish Language Learning Group**

Learning Spanish with Paul (www.facebook.com/LearningSpanishWithPaul)

*If you are studying Spanish with Paul, you need to join this Facebook group. This highly-active group will welcome you and work with you as you study Spanish. The author is one of the group's admins.*

**The Award for the Best Audio Pronunciations of Spanish Words**

Forvo (www.forvo.com)

*Forvo uses native speakers from around the Spanish-speaking world to demonstrate how to pronounce Spanish words.*

# NOTES

# NOTES

# NOTES

# NOTES

# NOTES

# NOTES

Printed in Great Britain
by Amazon